Crusade in the City

John Wanamaker

Crusade in the City:

Revivalism in Nineteenth-Century Philadelphia

Marion L. Bell

Lewisburg
Bucknell University Press
London: Associated University Presses

© 1977 by Associated University Presses, Inc.

Associated University Presses, Inc.
Cranbury, New Jersey 08512

Associated University Presses
Magdalen House
136–148 Tooley Street
London SE1 2TT, England

Library of Congress Cataloging in Publication Data

Bell, Marion L
 Crusade in the city.

 "The original version of this work was a doctoral dissertation at
Temple University."
 Bibliography: p.
 Includes index.
 1. Revivals—Pennsylvania—Philadelphia.
2. Philadelphia—Social life and customs. I. Title.
BV3775.P5B44 1977   269'.2'0974811   76-759
ISBN 0-8387-1929-5

For my husband, Jerome

Contents

Contents

Preface

My interest in revivalism is perhaps very much an outgrowth of America in the 1960s and 1970s. The development in this period of nonintellectual, nontheological religious expressions in the form of pentecostal and charismatic movements, stressing faith over reason and feeling over intellect, was at first a curiosity to one who was city bred and outside the Christian tradition. Then the inner dynamics of these movements took over, and I began to seek an understanding of revival movements of this sort not from the traditional theological view, but from the view of a historian of the city. I sought to understand the nature of revivalism within the urban ambience, what pressures and influences peculiar to the city shaped revivalism in America's large cities, and, conversely, how this revivalism affected America's industrializing cities. Revivalism remains to me, even after this long and detailed study of it, a lively and perennially interesting religious expression.

The original version of this work was a doctoral dissertation at Temple University. It was supervised by Dr. Allen F. Davis whose historical insights and great editorial skills helped me to clarify my task. Dr. Herbert Ershkowitz was especially generous with his time, interest, and encouragement, providing valuable perspectives and assistance. My grateful appreciation is also extended to

9

many other people. Dr. John B. Frantz of Pennsylvania State University was generous with his suggestions on material for the German Reformed Church aspect. Librarians were a source of much help, but my special thanks go to the research and reference personnel of the Presbyterian Historical Society in Philadelphia, who aided me during many pleasant as well as fruitful hours; Mr. John Randle, Assistant Librarian of the Young Mens Christian Association Historical Library in New York City; Mr. Maag of the St. George Methodist Church; Mr. Arthur Eglit of the First Baptist Church of Philadelphia; librarians at Swarthmore College and Haverford College Quaker Collections; Mr. Schock, Librarian of the Moody Bible Institute in Chicago; the Reverend Edmund Halsey, Curator of the Archives of the American Catholic Historical Society at the St. Charles Seminary in Overbrook, Pa., who was very helpful, as was the Reverend H. Daehler Hayes at the Old First Reformed Church of the United Church of Christ in Philadelphia (earlier called the German Reformed Church), who made available to me letters and manuscript material regarding Finney's stay at his church.

More personally, my deepest thanks to a very interested and understanding family, without whom this project would have been impossible.

Wallingford, Pennsylvania   Marion L. Bell

Introduction

It is a commonly accepted truth that America is a deeply religious country, a nation where religion occupies a unique and important position. Foreigners visiting the United States early recognized this phenomenon. In 1832 Mrs. Fanny Trollope remarked with some asperity that "a stranger, taking up his residence in any city in America must think the natives the most religious people on earth."[1] Her son, thirty years later, noted the same propensities: "The nation is religious in its tendencies. A man there is expected to belong to some church, and is not, I think, well looked on if he profess that he belongs to none."[2]

This interest in religion was contrary to the legal position of the church. For America, of course, had no established church, and this created a curious paradox. Philip Schaff, a conservative German churchman who lived and worked in America for ten years, returned to Germany to report to the theological faculty in Berlin that, although American religion seemed to be bedlam, with its riot of sects, unholy competition for members, and no vestige of authority, there was something taking place in America that Europeans failed to understand. In the voluntary system, he felt, lay the true promise of stability with religious commitment.[3]

America, of course, was not always so attached to religion. In colonial times, although New England was exceedingly theologically oriented, many areas of the South and the Middle Colonies were religiously indifferent. During the American Revolution the religious level of America dropped to an all-time low. Various factors had converged to divert Americans from their religious concerns. The prevalent attitude of the upper class and educated members of American society was of one shade or another of Enlightenment rationalism. In addition, there was an intense preoccupation with political affairs. Geographic mobility further diminished the power of religion on Americans. The fact remains that during the American Revolution fewer Americans were church members than at any time before or since. It is estimated that in 1776 only 5 percent of the population belonged to churches. While membership itself is a faulty gauge of belief, it is still a remarkably low figure. By 1960, for example, nearly 70 percent of Americans were church members, and the number has wavered thereabouts ever since.[4]

Most church historians attribute this dramatic growth to the waves of religious revivals that swept America periodically through the nineteenth century. The Great Revivals, sometimes called the Second Great Awakening, in the early decades of the century are called by Winthrop S. Hudson, a famous church historian, the "Protestant Counteroffensive."

To define my terms, I drew upon Hudson's definitions. Evangelism, he says, is "a theological emphasis upon the necessity for a conversion experience as the beginning point of a Christian life, while revivalism is a technique developed to induce that experience."[5] The central ingredient of the revival, the conversion, is a sudden, emotional, often cataclysmic experience whereby the individual has a change of heart and is remade as a person. The revivalist attempts to bring about this crisis and decision through a service or a series of services designed to bring men to an awareness of their sinfulness, to desire salvation, to experience conversion, and then, hopefully, to seek admission to a church.

There were three sorts of revivals in the Great Revivals of the nineteenth century. The Methodist camp meeting of the West was the scandal of the sedate East and of Europe, with its animal excitements, its night-long exhorting, its weeping, barking, and leaping.[6] The conservative New England revivals of Lyman Beecher and Nathaniel Taylor decried this emotional enthusiasm and were quietly harvesting souls in their own manner. It was the "New Measures" of Charles Grandison Finney, however, that came to be synonymous with the Great Revivals and that had the largest influence on American life. But in one form or another, religious revivalism was the central religious experience of countless Americans in the nineteenth century, and in order to understand the American mind and character, one must come to grips with the evangelical thrust of the revivals. Not only did they affect American churches, but they had an impact upon education, culture, and politics as well. They helped shape the character of American thought.

Revivalism as a facet of American social history has had competent chroniclers. William G. McLoughlin's *Modern Revivalism* is probably the most important book on the subject. In a broad yet deeply analytic treatment, McLoughlin deals with four broad major awakenings, attributing them, not to periods of economic or political crisis, nor to charismatic revivalists alone, but to a combination of four major circumstances, representing a reexamination and redefinition of the nation's social and intellectual values. But McLoughlin's analysis has no place for the Third Great Awakening of 1858, and often the data do not fit the anal-

They used to complain, oftentimes, that I was guilty of repetition in my preaching. I would take the same thought and turn it over and over, and illustrate it in various ways. I assured them that I thought it was necessary to do so, to make myself understood, and that I could not be persuaded to relinquish this practice by any of their arguments.[19]

His preaching, he concluded, was characterized thus: "It was a fire and a hammer breaking the rock." He had nothing but harsh denunciations of other sects like the Unitarians and the Universalists who attacked his revivals from one side, and denounced as well those who overemphasized man's passivity and depravity. Ministers who failed to cooperate with revivals wholeheartedly he condemned soundly as unconverted, cold, or worse.

It was his "New Measures," however, along with his style that met with the most abuse. In these he had compressed the full cycle of guilt, despair, hope, and assurance into a short period of time to bring about an intense religious experience. The most important element of the "New Measures" was the protracted meeting. Protracted meetings were the village counterpart of the camp meetings that played such a prominent role in the religion of the West. At first four days, then seven, later ten and twenty, they were periods during which the community was subjected to intense prayer and religious excitement. Often periods of fasting were included and served to heighten spiritual consciousness. The anxious seat, another of the "New Measures," was introduced in Rochester, New York, and was probably an adaptation from the Methodist "mourners bench" used in camp meetings early in the century.[20] Earlier, Finney had sometimes called upon those who were anxious after his high-powered sermons to stand up for a few moments in the congregation as an expression of their

desire for special prayer on their behalf. But soon he felt
this to be inadequate. He felt the need for something to
break down pride and cause full commitment. He started
using special seats set aside expressly for the purpose,

> where anxious may come and be addressed particularly,
> and be made subjects of prayer and sometimes conversed
> with individually.

Its purpose was twofold: getting the person to break the
chain of pride and feel a "sense of his condition," and as an
important tangible step toward conversion, the "public
manifestation of determination to be Christians."[21]

In addition to the anxious seat, "anxious meetings,"
sometimes lasting all night, were part of his "New Measures." They were held in the lecture room or the basement
of the church, or in private homes. Here the revivalist, local
ministers, and laymen spoke personally to the anxious,
trying to bring them to conversion. Another of his methods
that drew much fire was the practice of permitting women
to offer religious testimony publicly in meetings where men
were present. Many considered these "promiscuous meetings" improper and scandalous, but Finney considered it
not improper at all. Nor did he consider it improper to pray
for people by name, without their consent, which he frequently did, to the discomfiture and embarrassment of the
"sinner."

His great adversary was sin. "No sinner ever had an idea
that his sins were greater than they are. No sinner ever had
an adequate idea of how great a sinner he is."[22] Sensitive to
critics of his "New Measures," Finney explained that sometimes sinners became deranged through despair and anguish of mind. When this was the case, it was almost always
because those who dealt with them tried to encourage them
with false comfort. "They try to hold them up while God is
trying to break them down. And by and by, the sinner's

mind gets confused with his contrariety of influences, and he either goes deranged, or is driven to despair."[23] Therefore he cautioned against giving false comfort to sinners as a cruelty, and in this matter he had some gentle rebukes for the Reverend James Patterson in Philadelphia. While he and Patterson agreed on many matters, Patterson would tell sinners simply to turn toward Zion and they were saved. Finney quietly opposed this, as giving sinners a feeling of self-righteousness, instead of anxiety and sin. Finney wanted to heighten the torturous cycle of awareness of sin, submission, repentence, and salvation. Every moment they resisted they grew worse. If they were saved too easily, he warned Patterson, it was damaging to their souls. Patterson, says Finney, proved himself "remarkably teachable."[24]

Conservative New England revivalists like Beecher, Dwight, Nettleton, and Taylor blanched at Finney's approach. Disputes over his new methods and controversial style led to a conference at New Lebanon, New York, in July of 1827. It was a nine-day conference over alleged excesses of revivals, and brought together nine Eastern and nine Western ministers, Congregational and Presbyterian, to discuss the whole problem of revivals. The results were inconclusive, hence each side claimed victory. But as a consequence, participants realized that there was no radical difference of views.[25] By 1831 Beecher, who had earlier been hostile to Finney, signed the invitation for Finney to come to Boston for a series of revival meetings. Finney's brand of revivalism had triumphed; it came to be the normative pattern. With the internecine bickering settled by the New Lebanon conference, Finney was ready in 1828 to bring his evangelism into the important eastern city of Philadelphia.

2

Philadelphia—the Sacred and the Profane

The Philadelphia that Charles G. Finney sought to redeem was, in the 1820s, a city of great importance—the American metropolis of commerce, finance, literature, art, and science. While it was already losing economic supremacy to New York, it was still in 1820 larger than New York proper. In that year the population of the city, including Northern Liberties and Penn Township and the southern districts of Southwark, Moyamensing, and Passyunk, was 114,410.[1] It was the greatest manufacturing city in America, making carpets, soap, paint, glass, shot, and nearly all the type used in the United States. Travelers often noted its neatness and its well-paved streets. The orderly grid design imposed by William Penn at its founding was considered the model of city planning. Its homes were usually of red brick, interspersed here and there with wooden cottages, stables, and sheds. The brick homes, with their dark shutters and white marble steps, which were scrubbed daily, were much admired by visitors.[2] They were built on narrow lots and in rows, with an interior alley that often held rear houses or ysis. Nonetheless, the McLoughlin work is the best study of revivalism to date. A close second is Bernard Weisberger's *They Gathered at the River*. Weisberger concludes that revivalism had democratic implications, but a touch of conservatism at the core. After it was delivered of its reforms, he says, it was left barren, its inner vitality gone, and only the outer husk of form remained. William Sweet's work, *Revivalism in America*, has long been considered a classic. Sweet feels that revivalism has run its course, but while it is inadequate to deal with societal problems, its personal and individual emphasis is important if religion is to remain vital. More attention, however, has been given to rural revivalism than to its urban counterpart. Perry Miller's posthumous book, *The Life of the Mind in America*, however, found revivalism a dominant theme in America from 1800 to 1860, and dealt with the Awakening of 1858, a distinctively urban revival, in great detail. Timothy L. Smith in *Revivalism and Social Reform in Mid-Nineteenth Century America* examines revivalism between 1840 and 1865, and finds within it the seeds of the Social Gospel movement. Revivalism in Philadelphia received the attention of Russell E. Francis in his dissertation at the University of Pennsylvania entitled "Pentecost: 1858, A Study in Religious Revivalism." Lefferts A. Loetscher's article, "Presbyterianism and Revivalism in Philadelphia Since 1875," abstracted from his dissertation, treated Presbyterian revivalism in Philadelphia, starting with Dwight L. Moody. Both found significant revival activity in the city.[7]

No one, however, had done a case history of revivalism in a particular city within the context of industrialization and urbanization. No one had traced the changes in the institution over time. It is necessary to view revivalism in juxtaposition with patterns of urban growth and mobility. It is necessary to view it in the context of a changing society in order to understand how it changed, and whence came its support. These objects are best achieved through examining the institution as it developed in a particular city. This study indicates a need for similar studies in other cities in order to understand the penetration of revivalism into other urban centers.

Revivals and the City deals with evangelical revivalism in nineteenth-century Philadelphia. A local study always has to address itself to the question: Why study this city? Is it characteristic of other cities? Do the conclusions apply to other cities?

Perhaps the most cogent reason for selecting Philadelphia is that, as Allen F. Davis points out, Philadelphia has been curiously neglected by historians. Colonial Philadelphia has had interested scholars, but the later city has met with some neglect. Where there has been interest in the city, it is in the study of upper-class Philadelphia life.[8] The life of more modest Philadelphia has been inadequately studied. One important exception was an early one, *The Philadelphia Negro*, by William E. B. DuBois. Sam Bass Warner's *The Private City: Philadelphia in Three Periods of Its Growth* represents a much-needed response to the need for studies on Philadelphia. *The Peoples of Philadelphia: A History of Ethnic Groups and Lower-Class Life, 1790-1940*, edited by Allen F. Davis and Mark H. Haller, contains new research on various aspects of Philadelphia social history ranging from the eighteenth century through the 1920s.[9] The few studies of revivalism in Philadelphia have been characterized by tunnel-vision, that is, they have focused on only one aspect of revivalism, the 1858 manifestation or the Dwight Moody revivals, and they have been oriented to religious ideas rather than to social history.

Aside from the obvious need for more detailed study of the city of Philadelphia, there is yet another reason for selecting Philadelphia. It is my contention that conclusions derived here about Philadelphia will apply to other large cities, because Philadelphia in most important respects was like New York, Boston, Chicago, Baltimore, and so on. Most large cities in America shared a similar pattern of development. Most, for example were characterized in the eighteenth and early nineteenth century by social and economic heterogeneity and experienced face-to-face interpersonal relations. As the century wore on, with increased industrialization and immigration, there came a tendency for the wealthier to move to the outskirts, in ever-widening circles, while the poor tended to huddle in the centers of the city near industry. In city after city, this meant a loss of unity; it meant the end of the walking city of the eighteenth and early nineteenth century; it meant a breakdown of face-to-face relationships.[10] In all these large cities, the process of industrialization and immigration created dislocations and tensions.

There were differences, to be sure. Philadelphia was, after 1810, smaller than New York, but larger than all other cities, retaining its second place until 1890 when it was overtaken by Chicago. Philadelphia had a smaller proportion of foreign-born than other major cities, yet it was a city of immigrants, as were other cities.[11] It had a peculiar affinity to homes rather than tenements and apartments, which gave it a conservatism that property owning always implies. The Quaker ambience in Philadelphia, while intangible and often overestimated, perhaps made the city more staid and respectable. Blacks were somewhat more numerous in Philadelphia than in New York or Boston. Philadelphia, along with Chicago, was less scarred by slums, although in Philadelphia there were shanties and shacks for the poor hidden from view in back alleys behind the city's fine homes. The city's renowned "Father-Son-Holy Ghost" houses still exist, now restored and housing a sophisticated affluent population.[12] All large American cities, then, by 1870, shared common problems in transportation, water supply, lighting, communications, sewage disposal, police and fire services, and crime. There were differences in degree, but not in kind.

Sources for history of nonelites represent a particular problem. Ministers, of course, often leave diaries and letters. Congregations almost always have records, however sparse. The congregants, however, of nonelite churches usually live lives of relative obscurity. In addition, church statistics are notoriously untrustworthy. The American penchant for considering numbers a symbol of success gave American churches an impetus to seek large numbers of congregants as proof of success. Thus, all denominations have traditionally padded membership figures. Furthermore, frequent schisms and denominational breaks make religious statistics even trickier. Evangelists themselves are guilty of enormous overstatements. According to them, whole cities are aroused and all secular life comes to a stop as revivals fill people's consciousness. Newspapers and diaries show this to be obviously untrue, for they are filled with the multitude of events that fill most peoples' lives, and often barely mention the revivals, but it is easy to understand how the evangelists perceived this to be true. They are, as a class, imbued with a sense of their own destiny, of the sublime importance of their work. Furthermore, they are surrounded by admiring churchpeople, and are often misled as to the extent of the revival. They are simply not in touch with those elements in the city which are immune or hostile to their labors. Furthermore, as we shall see, many Christians are converted again and again at prayer meetings, a matter of some concern to the revivalist, who sought to reach the unconverted. Hence, even if revivalists kept statistics, which they did not, those statistics would often be unsound.

The current emphasis in history is upon quantitative data. Clearly, in certain historical research, the "numbers game" is invaluable, if used with critical and analytical aplomb. But numbers often pose as many questions as they answer. In many areas of social history, logical and impressionistic data are more meaningful than numbers. In evaluating the effect of religious phenomena upon the mind of participants, for example, one is dealing with matters that evade statistical analysis. Consequently, where statistics are useful, I have used them. But I have leaned more heavily upon traditional sources like newspapers, secular and religious journals, travelers' reports, letters, and diaries, which I feel to be more relevant to this study.

I have started with Charles G. Finney's revivals in Philadelphia in 1828. While Philadelphia had experienced revivalism earlier—Benjamin Franklin speaks of emptying his pockets to George Whitefield during the First Great Awakening—and while there had been periodic "outpourings" in various churches early in the 1800s, it is with Charles G. Finney that we find the clearest and most forthright expression of the new currents. He is the first American professional itinerant revivalist. Finney worked in Philadelphia in 1828 and 1829, so the 1820s provided me with a convenient starting point for the study. The Revivals of 1858, with noonday prayer meetings that swept American cities, will be examined next, for they provide an interesting transition between the earlier revivals and those of Dwight L. Moody which followed. I shall finish with the revivalism of Dwight L. Moody, who worked in Philadelphia at the Union Tabernacle meetings from November 1875 through January 1876.

The fifty-year span in Philadelphia reveals a broad, general configuration in revivalism as well as significant changes. Revivalism, we must conclude, was never the potent force in the city that it was in rural areas. Indeed, its claim to vastly enlarging church membership is not borne out by the evidence. Revivals caused temporary spurts, but church growth remained stable and must properly be attributed to other causes in American society. Indeed, revivalism was often a divisive force in church life. Promulgated as a way to fill churches emptied by the population patterns of the city, it was an attempt to counteract the growing trend to outlying areas.

Finney's emotional and guilt-laden revivals began as the religious expression of the poor, but his powerful personality was able to translate this religious phenomenon of the poor into the dominant mode of religious expression of the middle class. By the revivals of 1858 and even more so in 1875, revivals came to be accepted by mainstream Protestantism. By 1858, with boys flocking to the city from small towns and rural areas in order to "make good," revivals came to be a device for coping with the challenge of the city. Here was an institution that transmitted the rural evangelical message to people confused by their new urban milieu. It reaffirmed the traditional values and life-style that they identified as "American." Revivals became orderly, businesslike, an extension of the values of an industrializing society where success was the golden grail.

With Dwight L. Moody's Philadelphia campaign, the pattern was even more clearly defined. The anxiety-filled Finney revivals had mellowed to warm and cozy sentimentalism, and middle-class Protestants of all denominations thronged to them for an evening of pious diversion. Revivals became larger in size, more protracted in time, organized down to the smallest detail by businessmen in the community. As Bernard Weisberger so aptly put it, what had been conceived in ecstasy had been reduced to form. They used business methods and modern technology to further religious goals. These revivals incorporated the values of the popular culture and supported the shibboleths of the competitive enterprise system.

With Moody, the American business culture was fused with religion as never before. Revivals were aimed at preserving and maintaining the status quo. Bound to the business culture, they could not question it.

At the deepest level, Philadelphians sought through revivals to reaffirm their values amid a confusion of values, to validate their life style and their particular vision of America. It was a nostalgic backward glance at a simpler America of the past. Through revivalism, middle-class

Philadelphians sought to bring unity to an increasingly pluralistic society.

Early revivalism had been ambivalent. While it contained elements of reform, albeit of a highly individual nature, there was always a deeply conservative core. From the 1820s to the 1870s the gestalt of revivalism remained constant. Its world view, with its anti-intellectual stance, its apocalyptic vision of life, its sense of certitude and self-righteousness, hindered its adherents from dealing with the reality of American life. Unable to accept religious diversity, they were unable to accept the cultural pluralism that had developed in America. They grew increasingly out of step with the times. The revivalists who worked over Philadelphia between the 1820s and the 1870s were narrow, abstemious, anti-intellectual men, obsessed with personal guilt and personal salvation. They could not, within this framework, deal with the profusion of cultures and life styles that the city came to include. Furthermore, they could not deal in a positive manner with the excesses of American capitalism that were developing under their very eyes. The Philadelphia experience strongly suggests that mid-nineteenth-century revivalism, instead of providing the seeds of the Social Gospel movement, represents instead a simplistic conservatism, a nostalgic backward glance at an America that no longer existed. In fact, it is a straight line from Charles G. Finney to Dwight L. Moody.

Crusade in the City

1

A Fire and a Hammer

The emergence of an extraordinary man is always a curious fusion of a forceful, charismatic personality and a historic moment ready to receive him. He must possess certain qualities to dramatize his purpose, but he must, as well, serve the great social needs of his time. Charles Grandison Finney, the itinerant revivalist, is an example of this historic accident, this coming together of the personality and the moment in time. Finney understood and expressed the optimistic spirit and the dynamism of early nineteenth-century America. It was his adaptation of Protestant theology to the realities and needs of American life that made him the foremost evangelist of the nineteenth century. He left his mark upon a whole breed of men who followed him; he brought revivals, the style of religious life of the poor and uneducated, into the establishment churches of the middle class. In truth, he reshaped American Protestantism and left his indelible mark upon it.

Finney was a man not remarkable in physical appearance, but of a commanding presence and unusual self-confidence. He was impressively tall and slender, with a

receding chin and mouth, but his piercing, blue eyes attracted people's attention and kept it. A strong, well-
modulated voice, together with a dramatic use of his whole
body in his preaching, made him a memorable speaker.[1]

He was born in Warren, Connecticut, in 1792, the son of a
Revolutionary War veteran.[2] When he was two years of age,
the family moved to the "burned-over district" of western
New York, an area noted for its predisposition to enthusiastic religious movements.[3] He attended high school for a
time, but he never went to college. In his *Memoirs* he regretted that he never had a classical education. He picked up
some knowledge of Greek, Latin, and Hebrew, but never
enough to deal critically with English translations of the
Bible.[4] Finney was a young man with an intense mystical
streak and a strong asceticism. Throughout his life, he
experienced periods of despondency and depression. He
frequently prayed for hours and indulged often in days of
private fasting in which he had "visions in which a light
shone in my soul and almost prostrated me to the ground."[5]

In 1818 he started the study of law with Judge Benjamin
Wright in Adams, New York. It was at this time, however,
that he met the Presbyterian minister of Adams, the Reverend George Gale, and became interested in the church.
Although born a Congregationalist, he attended a Presbyterian Church like most Congregationalists who moved
west, for the Plan of Union in 1801 had determined that
Presbyterian polity was more suitable for that region. With
Gale's encouragement, he undertook the study of the Bible
and led the church choir. By 1821 he was in a state of
emotional crisis. He was still a clerk at the law office of
Judge Wright, but experiencing enormous feelings of guilt
and anxiety, fits of weeping, and inability to concentrate or
eat. His three-day ordeal culminating in conversion was the
turning-point of his life. Released from his burden of guilt
and anxiety, he decided to devote his life to religion. He was
then twenty-nine years of age. He resigned from his law

career, announcing to his legal mentor, "I have a retainer from the Lord Jesus Christ to plead His cause, and I cannot plead yours."[6]

Finney began missionary tours into northern New York state, experiencing gratifying success. In 1823 he was licensed to preach and six months later he was ordained. He was at the time without great knowledge of Presbyterian teachings. When asked by the licensing board if he subscribed to the Westminster Confession, the bulwark of orthodox Presbyterianism, Finney replied that he had not read it! It was perhaps his zeal and determination that impressed the board, and they ordained him. He had, in fact, already rejected the doctrine of original sin and man's inability to comply with the terms of the Gospel in favor of a more activist theology.

The spectacular revivals in the Mohawk Valley of New York, in Utica, Auburn, and Troy, elevated Finney from local to national fame in the years 1825 to 1827. This area had been bred in revivalism and religious enthusiasms of all sorts. For half a century adventurous youths, often younger sons of farmers seeking land, had been migrating to this region in western New York, bringing with them the religious enthusiasms of the earlier Great Awakening. In a sense, western New York provided the bridge between the Great Awakening of the colonial period and nineteenth-century revivalism. It was there that the ground was prepared for the new eruptions of the nineteenth century.[7] It was in these early successes in upstate New York that Finney defined his style, his methods, and this theology.

The Great Awakening of the 1730s and 1740s had been the first wave of religious enthusiasm in American history. It was an attempt to counter cold formality and institutionalism that had developed in the church. Under the ministry of Theodore J. Frelinghuysen, Gilbert and William Tennent, George Whitefield, and Jonathan Edwards, a blazing revival swept the colonies. Like all revivals, it emphasized emotionalism at the expense of reason, experience at the expense of ritual. It sought to respiritualize religious life and to arouse declining zeal. Edwards, the theologian of the Great Awakening, stressed conversion as the exclusive test of church membership in opposition to the Half-Way Covenant, which no longer required it. Paradoxically, although one of the greatest intellects in America, Edwards reinforced the religious attitude that elevated emotion over reason. But the eighteenth-century revivals were different from the Great Revivals of the nineteenth century in an important way. Jonathan Edwards, for example, saw revivals as a divine occurrence, as "outpourings of the Holy Spirit." This was consistent with orthodox Calvinism, for only God, not man, was capable of effecting salvation. Man was to wait hopefully but passively to be chosen as one of those saved.

By the time of the Great Revivals of the nineteenth century, an important theological and psychologoical shift had occurred. The passivity of the earlier view had become increasingly uncongenial to the American mind, and a new religious consensus had imperceptibly taken over Protestantism. According to this new, arminianized Calvinism, man could become a partner with God in his own salvation. His essential sinfulness could be overcome by a voluntary, conscious choice to accept Christ, and thereby he could achieve salvation. All men could be saved! Consequently, it was desirable, even necessary, to create the situation in which men would make that choice. This arminianism was best expressed by the Methodists, but it entered mainstream Protestantism through Charles G. Finney. Its implied activism was consistent with the political activism and participation that was concurrently being expressed by Jacksonian Democracy. The masses were seeking participation not only in the political and social life of the nation, but also in its religious life. This shift in emphasis transformed the revivalism of the eighteenth century into a powerful new weapon for Protestantism, and unleashed waves of evangelism that periodically swept over American society through the nineteenth century. It was Finney's historic task to resynthesize theological currents and make of revivalism an institution that became in his century almost universally accepted among American Protestants.

Finney openly scorned the Westminster Confession of Faith, the creedal basis of both the Presbyterian and Congregational churches since 1647, deploring its hierarchy and legalistic piety, its empty formalism. He decried specifically its pessimistic attitude to human nature and progress. Men are not subject to the arbitrary grace of God, insisted Finney, but have free will and the ability to make themselves morally ready for salvation. In Finney, the remaining determinism in the already diluted Calvinism of his day disappeared. He provided a simple way for men to express their pietistic impulses. It was an optimistic, activist philosophy. "Religion is something to do, not something to wait for."[8] He believed that a change of heart was the beginning and central experience of Christian life; that through repentence, by faith, one could achieve salvation. Not good works, or a moral life, but justification by faith is the essence of Finney's and all subsequent revivalists' beliefs. The individual and his salvation were the center of Finney's concern, and from salvation flowed all other good. His doctrine of millennialism was a common concept in antebellum America. In those halcyon days the world was seen to be getting better and better. Through the spread of Christianity, it was working toward a state of perfection, and eventually there would be a period of 1,000 years of universal peace and plenty, which would lay the foundation for the return of Christ and the ultimate establishment of God's kingdom on earth. Details were not unanimously agreed upon; there was another version of millennialism that predicted the coming of Christ followed by 1,000 years of universal peace and plenty. In one form or another, however, the doctrine of millennialism went hand-in-hand with the doctrine of progress in the first half of the nineteenth century. Millennialism both expressed and demanded an activist attitude toward society. "Whatever desires a person may have, if they are not carried out into actual choice and action, they are not virtuous," declared Finney.[9] "If they can see each opportunity where they can do more good, they must embrace it, whatever may be the sacrifice to themselves."[10] This was the heart and core of nineteenth-century evangelical activism, and Finney's converts embraced most of the great reform movements of his day, as well as a host of lesser ones. Little groups of young converts, "Finney's Holy Band," understood Finney's words as a call to action, and became involved in the myriad reform movements that laced and interlaced the land— temperance societies, tract and missionary societies, societies to reform prostitutes, societies to protect orphans and to improve conditions for the insane, and the reform that was soon to become the keystone of all reforms: abolitionism.

It was the moral reforms that were most meaningful to Finney's converts, for it was their firm conviction that first the individual must be reformed, and then the rest would flow from this naturally. But while Finney may have unleashed a flow of reformers, *his* concern was always individual sin, and his use of the term *doing good* has a subtle difference from the accepted usage today. The church, he said, should take hold of her young (meaning new) converts at the outset and "set them to work right." The converts must learn "how to pray, how to converse with people about their soul's salvation, how to attend anxious meetings and how to deal with inquiries, and how to SAVE SOULS."[11] According to Finney, sin could be of two types: sins of omission or sins of commission. The former included ingratitude to God, neglect of the Bible, unbelief, neglect of prayer, neglect of self-denial, want of feeling of piety, want of love for the souls of fellow-men, want of care for the heathen, neglect of family duties such as spiritual guidance, and neglect of social duties, which meant watching over one's brethren and being concerned over the state of their souls. "If you see them falling into the fire, you must speak up." Sins of commission included worldly mindedness, levity, pride, envy, censoriousness, slander, lying, cheating, hypocrisy in prayer. He attacked sins of fashionable display, luxury, novel-reading, theatergoing, dancing, card-playing, tightly laced corsets, drinking, coffee and tea drinking, and "that filthy poison, tobacco."[12]

While Finney was primarily interested in private sins, he undoubtedly considered slavery a sin. He had been against slavery from the days of his studies with George Gale, who was an ardent abolitionist. "Slavery is a sin which all Christians should oppose," he said unequivocally.[13] As a pastor, he refused membership to any who owned or trafficked in slaves. Yet there is proportionately little in his writings about anti-slavery, and his lack of strong support for the abolition movement drew criticism from Theodore Weld, who felt it necessary to defend Finney against the charges that he had not given the subject of abolitionism so much prominence in his preaching as he should have. "The truth is, Finney has always been in revivals of religion. It is his great business, aim, and absorbing passion . . . . Finney feels about revivals of religion as you and I do about anti-slavery . . . ."[14] When Theodore Weld tried to persuade the students of Oberlin to become abolitionist lecturers, Finney took the students aside and urged them not to do it, saying that the hope of the country, as well as the church and the slave, was in widespread revivals.[15] He wrote to Weld, with optimism and naiveté, that the whole slavery problem could be solved in two years if only "the publick mind can be engrossed with the subject of salvation and make abolition an appendage [of revivals] . . . ."[16] Clearly the role of Finney in antislavery reform has been overstated. His theological activism was translated by his abolitionist followers into an imperative for action, but Finney's primary concern was the individual and his salvation. All else was secondary.

It was Finney's style and methods, however, that met with the most abuse, and that caused such tremendous excitement. His style was central to his understanding of his mission. Through it, he attempted to maneuver individuals into making a conscious choice for Christ. Finney's revivals lacked the extravagant expressions of the frontier, where great outdoor gatherings lasted for several days, with noise, confusion, and uninhibited emotionalism. Still, they were characterized by much emotionalism, particularly in the early years. He writhed, groaned, gesticulated in the pulpit. The evils that are sometimes complained of by critics of revivals, he tells us, when they are real, are incidental and of small importance when compared with the amount of good produced.[17] He himself described the early revival meetings in New York State as scenes of emotional hysteria. Previously, he says, only ignorant Methodist and Baptist exhorters aroused such enthusiasm; now respectable Congregationalist and Presbyterian churchgoers fell into fits and writhed in agony. In addition to this powerful appeal to the emotions, his preaching style was unstudied and conversational. He decried the written sermons of seminary-trained ministers. Those sermons, he went on, degenerated into literary essays that were gratifying to literary tastes but were not spiritually edifying. They did not meet the wants of the soul. When men are in earnest, he explained, their language is plain and simple. Sentences are short and powerful; there is an appeal for action. This is why, he said, the ignorant Methodist preacher and the earnest Baptist preacher produce so much more effect than our most learned theologians and divines.[18] He borrowed illustrations from farmers and mechanics, and talked in a language they could understand. Repetition was important:

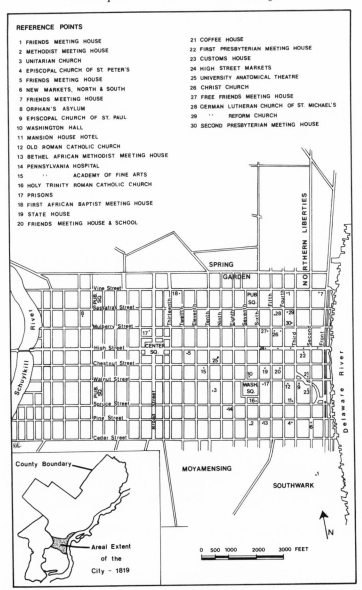

REFERENCE POINTS

1 FRIENDS MEETING HOUSE
2 METHODIST MEETING HOUSE
3 UNITARIAN CHURCH
4 EPISCOPAL CHURCH OF ST. PETER'S
5 FRIENDS MEETING HOUSE
6 NEW MARKETS, NORTH & SOUTH
7 FRIENDS MEETING HOUSE
8 ORPHAN'S ASYLUM
9 EPISCOPAL CHURCH OF ST. PAUL
10 WASHINGTON HALL
11 MANSION HOUSE HOTEL
12 OLD ROMAN CATHOLIC CHURCH
13 BETHEL AFRICAN METHODIST MEETING HOUSE
14 PENNSYLVANIA HOSPITAL
15 ''   ACADEMY OF FINE ARTS
16 HOLY TRINITY ROMAN CATHOLIC CHURCH
17 PRISONS
18 FIRST AFRICAN BAPTIST MEETING HOUSE
19 STATE HOUSE
20 FRIENDS MEETING HOUSE & SCHOOL

21 COFFEE HOUSE
22 FIRST PRESBYTERIAN MEETING HOUSE
23 CUSTOMS HOUSE
24 HIGH STREET MARKETS
25 UNIVERSITY ANATOMICAL THEATRE
26 CHRIST CHURCH
27 FREE FRIENDS MEETING HOUSE
28 GERMAN LUTHERAN CHURCH OF ST. MICHAEL'S
29 ''   REFORM CHURCH
30 SECOND PRESBYTERIAN MEETING HOUSE

Philadelphia, 1819

shacks for poorer people. While the center of population was moving away from the Delaware River, the city had not yet reached the social and economic segregation that would come later in the century. Social and economic heterogeneity was the hallmark of the age. Most areas of the new big city were a jumble of occupations, classes, shops, homes, immigrants, and native Americans. The carter kept his team in a stable behind his house, the shoemaker and his journeymen made shoes in the front room, proprietors of small stores lived with their families in the rear of the store or upstairs. A small factory, a foundry, or a machine shop took only a double lot.[3]

The rich lived in large airy mansions with broad halls running through them, and many had gardens and trees. The most fashionable area was Third and Spruce Streets and several blocks thereabout. Northern Liberties, while it held a few fine Quaker houses, was identified in most minds with butchers, drovers, and market people. While many blacks and poor whites lived in back alleys and side streets in all parts of the city, they were more numerous south of Cedar (later South) Street. Slavery had all but disappeared in Philadelphia: in 1811 there were only two slaves in the city and by 1820 only 211 in all of Pennsylvania.[4]

To the west, the city was built up essentially as far as Broad Street. Most of the east-west streets were built up and paved as far as Ninth or Tenth Street, with a scattering of houses as far as Broad Street. The north-south streets were paved, in whole or in part, as far as Eleventh Street. Outside of this compact area were open fields with occasional farms.

City leaders during the 1820s were becoming aware of New York's threat to Philadelphia's economic supremacy. New York was already exporting more than Philadelphia. It was favored by a salt-water port that could be kept open all year, unlike Philadelphia's, which froze up for several months in the winter, and by the completion of the Erie Canal in 1825, which provided a great boost to its economic life. Philadelphia felt it important to improve its connections with the interior and the West, and work was in progress on various canals. In 1825 the Schuylkill Canal opened, followed by the Union Canal, the Chesapeake and Delaware Canal, and the Lehigh Canal, all linking inland waterways to the major rivers of Philadelphia. While they were very useful in enriching Philadelphia's economic life, the city was never to recapture its economic supremacy from New York.[5]

The canal system was soon rendered useless by the development of the railroad. At first designed as an adjunct of the canal, by the 1830s the rail lines were built independently of the canals, creating new connections with rural areas. In addition to the railroad, better roads reduced the time between cities. Still, the trip from New York to Philadelphia took twelve hours over these roads in 1823. A regular stage replaced the private wagon and horseback. Passengers choked with dust over rutted roads in stages with no springs and no glass windows. Connections across the Delaware River to Camden were equally primitive.

Philadelphia and Camden had been connected by ferryboat since 1810, but for passengers only; horses and wagons were rowed across. A proposal in 1819 to construct a bridge across the Delaware aroused strenuous opposition, and it was not until 1926, over a century later, that the two cities were joined by a bridge. In 1825, an effort to light Philadelphia with gas likewise met with strong opposition. The plan was called "a folly, unsafe, unsure, a trouble, and a nuisance." It was considered, researched, and debated until 1835, when it was finally passed.

By the 1829s immigration was increasing, but immigrants, largely Irish and German, were generally scattered through the city. Social and economic heterogeneity was characteristic of the age, yet the beginnings of concentration were visible. There was a downtown, a few blocks of black people, occasional class and ethnic enclaves. German immigrants, for example, lived largely in the north side of town, but in large numbers in most of the wards of the city. Irish immigrants were scattered over the city, generally in backyard houses and alleys. If there was any concentration of poverty, it was ringing the city instead of at the core ringed by affluence. But in spite of these trends, the general pattern of social and economic heterogeneity persisted.[6]

There were still in the 1820s elements of a small-town life in Philadelphia. The country was not far removed from the city. Quail and woodchuck abounded around the city, and boys shot wild pigeons from rooftops. Schuylkill Point, later League Island, was covered with grass where cattle grazed. The Schuylkill abounded in fish, which were thought to be better than those caught in the Delaware; it is recorded that 439 were taken in one haul. It was no rare thing to see Indians in the streets of Philadelphia as late as 1825 or 1830. They often brought in crafts for sale, but they were already a demoralized people, often tipsy, and regarded as a great attraction. Streets had Conestoga Wagons in from Pittsburgh, laden with country produce. There was a lively street life—chimney sweeps in numbers, usually black boys, calling their trade musically; a town crier, while he had lost many functions to the newspaper, still rang his bell calling the hour and announcing lost children, cows, horses, or other property. In the summer Philadelphians bathed and swam in the Delaware and Schuylkill Rivers. The same rivers provided ice-skating in winter. When the ice was strong enough, horses dragged sledges and wagons laden with goods across the river, and to points up or down river as well.

A noteworthy feature of the city was the markets on High Street. They extended for more than a mile, were held every day but Sunday, and were a lively scene with lavish displays of poultry, vegetables, fruit, and butter brought in churns, all displayed in white napery on benches and stalls. The fishwives sold their husbands' daily catch at the river end of the street. Frequently a prize cow would be paraded down the street, gaily decorated, with announcements that meat from this fine animal would be on sale the day after it was slaughtered. Visitors noted the variety, abundance, and neatness of the proceedings, also the immaculate white aprons of the butchers and other tradespeople. There were other markets as well, though none so large. The Head-house Market served those who found High Street too far; markets at Northern Liberties and Southwark were popular with residents of those areas, for prices were cheaper.[7] Water was pumped into town from the newly built (1819) waterworks, and was carried by servants from public pumps in the streets or private pumps in the back yard. Little by little, it was being introduced into houses, but it was always cold, for there were no warming arrangements.

The police department had a paid but lax constabulary. These men had no duties in daylight, when people were expected to police themselves with the aid of the mayor and a few constables on call. At night each watchman had his beat, which he walked with a stick and a rattle. When this rattle was heard, householders were expected to stick their heads out the window, and they would often come to the aid of the watchman. Fire companies were the terror of the community. Earlier all citizens, including prominent men, had participated in them, but by the 1820s, the prominent were no longer involved in the voluntary fire department, and the young men volunteers were mostly hoodlum types who made fire companies less than respectable. Young volunteers often put in false alarms for the fun of a run or a fracas with a rival company, for they were equally eager for a fire or a fight. There was no redress, although much bitter condemnation was heard. The fire companies were considered a necessary evil.[8]

Face-to-face relationships were being sacrificed to bigness; clubs and associations proliferated to replace earlier forms of community life. Philadelphia was entering a period of change in size, in organization, and in human relationships.[9] There must have been many who mourned the passing of the city they knew.

Unquestionably, Philadelphia was a cultural and intellectual leader. There were in 1823 eleven daily newspapers to New York's seven. There were learned institutions of all kinds: the Franklin Institute, the American Philosophical Society, the Academy of Natural Sciences, the University of Pennsylvania, and Jefferson Medical College. The Philadelphia Library, established in 1825, containing the 4,000 volumes of James Logan's collection, was one of America's most important. The city had two theaters and several musical societies. Yet the cultural life of any great city is partaken of by only a small elite. The average citizen is involved with more mundane matters of life, and it was the tavern he frequented for lounging, transacting business, or gaming, rather than the learned institution.[10] This is the reality that has been obscured by the more elite histories of Philadelphia.

Visitors to the city complained that it was dull, monotonous, uninteresting. Charles Dickens considered the city handsome, but "distractingly regular," and more provincial than Boston or New York.[11] The city needed more hotels, many complained, the few there being dirty, noisy, dark, and inconvenient. Mrs. Trollope noted the contrast with European cities:

> In the evenings the streets are entirely dark except where a stray lamp marks a hotel or the like. In the evening no shops are open but the apothecary. No steps are heard, no sound of music, no carriages on the streets—by 10 o'clock in the evening, all is silence.[12]

The decade of the 1820s had seen some symbolic events in the city. In 1826 the Liberty Bell had tolled for Adams and Jefferson, two of the last three signers of the Declaration of Independence, signifying that the revolutionary generation had just about disappeared. In addition, Lafayette, the last surviving general of the Revolution, returned to American in 1824 upon invitation of Congress. It was fifty years after the Declaration of Independence, forty years since independence had been recognized. Arriving in New York in August of 1824, he was expected in Philadelphia at the end of September. Independence Hall had been purchased by the city in 1818 when the state legislature was considering demolition to sell the land for building lots. It had been in squalor but was now cleaned for the occasion. Troops were constantly arriving from interim points to participate in the celebration. On the twenty-seventh, the three-mile-long procession entered the city, complete with riflemen and calvary companies, taking more than an hour to pass a given point. People had bought tickets for seats on hundreds of scaffolds that had been built. Crowds filled the streets, ships in the harbor fired salutes, and it was a glorious, week-long celebration that warmed the old general's heart.[13] Even the less thoughtful were aware that with the passing away of the Revolutionary War generation, an era had ended.

This was Philadelphia in the early decades of the nineteenth century. But what was the condition of religious life in the city? How intensive was it and how diversified was the life of the spirit in Philadelphia? Were there predispositions favorable to revivalism? One can only speculate on many of these questions, for there are no sophisticated demographic studies of this period. One can, however, make some rather simple observations about the city's religious milieu.

The end of the Revolutionary Era produced a major institutional change, one that was uniquely American, namely, disestablishment. American churches would from then onward be voluntary churches. The First Amendment, that "Congress shall make no law respecting the establishment of religion, or prohibiting the free exercise thereof" was but the institutionalization of what had been developing in the previous 175 years. America stumbled into disestablishment, it has been said, not by virtue but by accident. There were so many religious groups in America that no one of them could press its advantage, for if it was a majority in one region, it might well be a minority in another. Denominations understood themselves to be, from the legal point of view, voluntary associations of private citizens. Indeed, most of them had sought and fully welcomed the establishment of the principle of full religious liberty. While Protestantism as a whole found it hard in the nineteenth century to relinquish its preferred position, denominations had no such difficulty.[14]

With disestablishment, denominations realized that an active program of spreading the Gospel would be needed to build and sustain membership. In addition, the churches had been disrupted by the war—pastors had marched off with the troops, congregations had been scattered, meetinghouses had been requisitioned as barracks. Furthermore, the religious philosophy of deism had spread, principally among intellectuals. After the excesses of the French Revolution, deism was viewed by established churches as a threat to organized religion. While in America deism never developed the hostile anticlerical stance of European deism, still Thomas Paine's frontal attacks smarted. Unitarianism, the philosophy of deism institutionalized, came to represent for mainstream Protestantism the threat of "freethinking" and "infidelity." Another problem, the flow of population westward, created the fear that unless civilizing and Christianizing influences from the East were brought to bear, the West would lapse into barbarism. A positive thrust was needed to counter the dangers of apathy, freethinking, and dispersion.

Colonial experience had shown the church leaders that "spiritual" or "evangelical" religion was the answer to their problems. But the Revolution had left the churches in various states of disarray. They had all suffered, of course, but some had fared better than others. The greatest casualty of the Revolution, of course, was the Anglican Church. It was stripped overnight of privileges, prestige, and support. Its ranks were depleted by loyalist defection to England and Canada, and by Methodist defection. With the appointment of an American bishop and the break with the English church, the new Protestant Episcopal church faced no very promising future. The major role of organizing an American church was played by William White and William Smith, both of Philadelphia. White was a Rector of Christ Church and chaplain to the Continental Congress. As a result of the work of these two men, the Protestant Episcopal liturgy was revised and arrangements made for consecration of bishops.[15]

Philadelphia's Episcopalians represented the highest social class in the city. In 1828 there were six Episcopal churches in Philadelphia, including Old Christ Church and St. Peter and St. Paul's.[16] Both churches were already too far downtown for families settled west of Eighth Street, and new churches had to be established to meet their needs. Moreover, the Episcopal church contained a low church or Evangelical party as well as a high-church party. It was, of course, this group of Episcopalians who looked favorably upon the active thrust of the revivals, upon prayer meetings and emotional preaching. High and low parties were evenly divided in numbers in Philadelphia, and Bishop William White, while a high churchman, was conciliatory to the low-church elements and refused to discipline any breach in high-church practice.[17] Consequently, while Episcopalians were few in number and elite in class, they contained elements favorable to an evangelical thrust.

The Quakers had suffered heavily during the Revolution, for their refusal to take a position was interpreted, often correctly, as loyalism. They emerged from the revolutionary era in a weakened position. While they still had many influential members in Philadelphia, they were no

longer the dominating force in the city. In 1812 they had
erected the Twelfth and Market Street meetinghouse; in
1814 they built and occupied a large, new building in
Northern Liberties, an area with a large Quaker settlement.
By the 1820s Quakers had five meetinghouses, including
one for Free Quakers. While they no longer dominated
Philadelphia life, the Quakers had still imprinted a certain
quality on the city—that of quiet moderation, of restraint.
Observers noticed that " . . .they are observant of prop-
rieties. The Philadelphians are no traffickers in extremes of
any sort."[18] Yet, for all this decorum, there were trends
among Quakers characteristic of other Protestant denominations. By 1827-28, evangelical trends within Quakerism
had caused a rift that culminated in the Hicksite separation.
Orthodox Quakers, who had strong evangelical tendencies,
were strongest in the city, while Hicksites clustered in the
rural areas. Urban Quakers were kindly disposed toward
revival tendencies.

While tradition had it that Quakers had the dominant
place in Philadelphia, the city was by now undeniably Presbyterian. Presbyterians had in fact become the important
religious presence in Philadelphia.[19] In 1828 the city had
twelve Presbyterian churches, including the independent
Reformed Church of the Reverend Samuel B. Wylie. The
more affluent and educated people tended to belong to the
Episcopal and Presbyterian churches, with the lower classes
and the uneducated worshiping in Baptist and Methodist
churches.[20] Presbyterians enjoyed the prestige of being
strongly identified with the winning side of the Revolution.
Like the churches of other denominations, Presbyterian
churches moved with the population westward toward
Broad Street, to the north of Northern Liberties, and toward southern districts in Southwark and Moyamensing.
The First Presbyterian Church on the south side of Market
Street, for example, was by 1821 entirely surrounded by

stores, and in that year the congregation built a new building at Seventh and Locust Streets on Washington Square. Other churches had spread in like manner: the First Presbyterian Church of Northern Liberties was started in 1814 as an offshoot of the Second Presbyterian Church at Third and Arch Streets; the First Presbyterian Church of Kensington at Fourth and Girard was organized in 1814. The early decades of the century witnessed a resurgence of the old split in Presbyterianism; "Old Light" and "New Light" Presbyterians of the Great Awakening reemerged as "Old School" Presbyterians, who resisted revivalism in favor of traditional Presbyterian doctrine, and "New School" Presbyterians, who tended toward the new measures. Philadelphia, like the entire North, was strongly "New School," and contained important ministers who looked kindly to revivals.

Methodism, an outgrowth of the Church of England, had seized the winning of independence as an opportunity to form themselves into a separate church. Philadelphia Methodists in 1828 had six churches, for Methodism had been slow to grow in Philadelphia. This denomination, with its emotional approach, its Arminian theology, and its hostility to educated clergy, had, of course, originated the "circuit rider," an itinerant minister responsible for a large geographical area, who had been dominant in camp meetings of the West. Consequently the presence of Methodists in Philadelphia, however small or poor, provided a positive element in the reception revivalism was to receive.

Although some of the 7,331 black people remained in mixed churches, by 1828 there were ten exclusively black churches in the city. They included nearly all denominations, yet the majority of blacks were Methodist in affiliation. The most popular of these churches was the African Methodist Episcopal Bethel Church, originated under the leadership of Richard Allen. Black religion had from its inception in America been heavily revivalistic and the new religious trends in the early nineteenth century endorsed earlier trends in the black church.

There were only five Baptist churches, for although they had arrived early, they had not been active in Philadelphia, nor in Pennsylvania. In 1829 the entire state of Pennsylvania contained only about 7,000 Baptists. Philadelphia Baptists performed their ritual immersions in the Schuylkill River at the foot of Spruce Street.[21] Along with the Methodists, Baptists represented the less well-educated and poorer churchgoers of the city. They shared the class predisposition to emotional, highly spiritual religion. Lutherans counted but three churches, but were proud of their "Old Swedes," which by the 1820s no longer used Swedish but English, and whose congregation was merely of Swedish descent. Colonial Lutheranism, led by Heinrich (Henry) M. Muhlenberg, was heavily involved in the revivals of the Great Awakening and many Lutherans had participated in the extravagances of the camp meetings. Among urban Lutherans, there was considerable resistance to revivals. In general, it was the English-speaking denominations, labeled "American Lutherans," who tended toward these measures. There were two German Reformed churches in Philadelphia. The most important of them was the large church of the Rev. Samuel Helffenstein on Race Street. The German Reformed churches clung to the traditional Heidelberg Catechism, which emphasized historic continuity and education, but with the introduction of English into German Reformed services in Philadelphia in 1819, the revival influence entered the church for the first time.

Smaller churches included two small Dutch Reformed churches and one Universalist church. The one Unitarian church, however, was important beyond its size. Unitarianism, a theological offspring of New England Congregationalism, was in fact the intellectual child of the Enlightenment. By 1825 when the American Unitarian Association was formed, there were 120 Unitarian congregations in the United States. Philadelphia's single congregation was not so active as its Boston counterpart, yet it numbered among its members many of the wealthiest, best educated, and most influential civic leaders in the city. Led by the Reverend William Henry Furness, it was a small but influential segment of the Philadelphia religious community.

Four Roman Catholic churches managed the religious needs of the city's Catholics. This church, of course, did not become a real presence in the city until the Irish immigration of the 1840s. Philadelphia's tiny Jewish community of some 450 people in the 1820s had but one synagogue, Mikveh Israel. The larger German immigration was yet to come. Many of the early Sephardic Jews, as the Jews originating in Spain and Portugal were called, and the early German Jews, had achieved wealth, education, and influence in the city. The congregation, though small, received the loyal support of an elite membership, although it contained middle-class and poor Jews as well.

Philadelphia in the 1820s contained, then, a broad spectrum of religious life. This, however, was but part of the city's milieu. Many remained unchurched. It has been estimated that by 1835 only one out of every eight Americans was a church member.[22] It was, after all, a political age, not a religious one. Getting ahead, the old American shibboleth, was the supreme concern in an expanding, optimistic society. Still, ministers had influence and power. Often these reached out and irritated the larger community. A law of 1798 allowed churches to stretch chains across the streets during the hours of service. While this perturbed many citizens, for doctors were unable to reach their patients and firemen could not reach burning buildings, the law was not repealed until 1831.[23]

Philadelphia was a major city in 1828, a bastion of Eastern culture. It was important, if revivals were to be truly successful, for them to be powerful in cities as well as in the countryside. Consequently, Philadelphia became the focal point for the labors of Charles Finney and the scene of a protracted effort on his part to bring his "New Measures" to city dwellers.

3
They See the Light

Finney brought his revivals to Philadelphia in the autumn of 1827. He worked regularly in two churches and occupied the pulpit in others by invitation. His revivals in Philadelphia are of extreme interest, for never have his emotionally charged revivals been examined within the context of a city. The Philadelphia experience reveals that Finney's revivalism in Philadelphia was not so successful as his rural revivals. Finney caused great dissension and near-collapse of one church, and a delayed schism in another. In both there was a sharp rise in church membership during and immediately after his revivals; in neither was this rise maintained. While his theology and style held the most appeal to the uneducated and poor, Finney brought revivals to the attention of the respectable and comfortable middle classes, and even occasionally to the well-to-do in the city. With Finney, the sporadic revivals in Philadelphia churches were swept up in a vast movement that was overtaking American Protestantism.

Church leaders were becoming aware that in the cities lay the future of religion. Unless revivals could succeed there, religion would be doomed to have very little impact

49

upon American society. Albert Barnes voiced the prevailing sentiments in a sermon "Revivals of Religion in Cities and Small Towns." Barnes was for 37 years the minister of the First Presbyterian Church of Philadelphia on Washington Square. Admittedly, he said, revivals have occurred more frequently in the country than in large cities. But the influence of the city is so great that a revival there could have great effect on the country as well. There were obstacles, to be sure, to revivalism in the city, obstacles from above and from below. The vast portion of the city's population was the lower stratum of society, "ignorant, degraded, sensual, idle, worthless, and these cannot be reached by church institutions. These beggars patrolling our streets, whose story is, in general, but a veil to their faults," said Barnes, "don't enter churches and it is these people who must be elevated."[1]

Not only the poor obstructed revivals, but the rich as well. "For this class, distant climes pour in their luxuries, the theaters open their doors; splendid mansis [sic] rise . . . these people are ignorant of the Gospel and hostile to revivals."[2] In the city, there was vast wealth concentrated in the hands of comparatively few, and this wealth was drawn away from its legitimate goal to other pursuits. "The effect of true religion is to lead men to consecrate their property honestly and wholly to God, nor can there be any true religion where this is not done." Urban wealth is abused, said Barnes; vast sums are spent for houses, apparel, political purposes, schools, colleges, and vices like the theater. Middle-class Christians should consecrate their money to the churches. Revivals would teach them the true value of property and the true intent of the Giver in bestowing it on them: "to consecrate the wealth in cities to churches."[3]

America had long cherished a rural ideal. By tradition, virtue and purity were products of the bucolic life, while the city nourished sin and degradation.[4] The cities were perceived as cesspools of iniquity. According to the Reverend Barnes, "every great metropolis of the world bears a striking resemblance to Sodom . . . ."[5]

> If there is any peculiar guilt on earth, it will be found there . . . . If there is any crime peculiarly dark, deep, offensive, loathsome in the sight of heaven, it will be found in such places. If Satan has any strong holds which he fortifies with peculiar care, and guards with peculiar vigilance, they are the large cities of the world. In all ages they have constituted, as they do now, the principal obstructions to the spread of religion.[6]

Barnes understood that part of the problem was in the lack of social controls in the city. In the country village, he pointed out, the infidel usually stood alone. He was known and his character was understood. In the city, however, he could make as many converts as he pleased, for there, in the dense and crowded population, people were as strangers to each other, and there were not strong ties binding men. He understood, too, that revivalism generally fared well in areas where people felt a sense of community and close interpersonal relationships. In cities he perceived a "melancholy coldness" that was inhibiting to revivals. Yet, in spite of these difficulties, only revivals could meet the challenge to religion in cities.

Charles Finney, fresh from his successes in upstate New York, had been warned about the dangers of the city. As friends advised him shortly after he came to Philadelphia,

> Modern cities are dangerous places to souls, not so much from the example of the world, or from opposition, but from flattery and polite attrition. You need double the grace, my dear Brother, in Philadelphia or New York.[7]

The city had been experiencing occasional revivals in individual churches in the 1820s and even earlier. News of the Great Revivals in the West were filtering into the city through individuals and through religious periodicals, which avidly reported such revival activity. Such revivals as occurred in the city were congregational, sponsored by local ministers, and for the benefit of the congregation involved. The spring of 1816 had seen a revival in the Fifth Presbyterian Church under the Reverend Thomas Skinner that had resulted in additions to the Northern Liberties Church and to other churches in the city.[8] In 1822 there were revivals in the First Presbyterian Church of Kensington, and in 1823 in the First Presbyterian Church of Philadelphia. The Reverend James Patterson's First Presbyterian Church of Northern Liberties had experienced a revival in 1816, another in 1821, and another in 1822.[9] The Reverend Jacob Gruber of St. George's Methodist Church was bringing revival methods to his church, as were some Baptist ministers.[10] Presbyterianism, however, felt the most direct and immediate impact of revivalism. Orthodox Presbyterians were clinging staunchly to the old Calvinism of the seventeenth-century Westminster Confession of Faith, and most Presbyterian churchmen abhorred revivalism. Ashbel Green, pastor of the Second Presbyterian Church in Philadelphia for twenty-five years and editor of the *Christian Advocate* (earlier called the *Presbyterian Magazine*), voiced the caution that many felt. In an editorial in 1823 he expressed strong evangelistic sentiments:

> Every real Christian regards the salvation of souls as infinitely the most important and interesting concern of our world. To this, all other concerns are subordinate and should be subservient. It is of more importance to save a soul than to found an empire.[11]

Yet, his attitude toward revivalism was cautious. In December 1827 he reprinted Finney's sermon "Can Two Walk Together Except They Be Agreed?"[12] In this sermon, Finney defended revivals against his critics. Many ministers and Christians visiting revivals, he said, often raised objections to the means used; they were annoyed by the warmth of the meetings. In raising these objections, they were taking sides with sinners, declared Finney. The case might occur "where the church and people may awake while the shepherd sleeps and will not awake. This will inevitably alienate their affections from him, and destroy their confidence in him . . . they may find themselves unable to walk together, because they are not agreed . . . . let the church shake off their sleepy minister; they are better without him, than with him."[13] Although Ashbel Green reprinted the sermon, he found much in it to criticize. He knew very little of the author of the sermon, said Green, except what he had seen published, and had no wish to impeach his integrity. "But if he be ever so honest, or if he is even pious, his errors and delusions may, on that very account be not the less, but abundantly the more injurious." He cautioned against "ostentation and noise, calling men hard names, an overbearing, provoking manner, censuring the unconverted as stupid, cold, dead; against groaning, speaking out, falling down . . . ." There are sound conversions, he said, connected with careful nurturing of children, and revivals in churches where the Gospel had been long and faithfully preached. But these take place gradually, silently, without any great convulsion. It was the itinerant preachers, "often zealous, . . . usually ignorant of doctrines and principles of religion," whom he rebuked. "These extravagances are the reproach of revivals. They open the mouths of scoffers and discourage many pious people."[14]

Traditional or orthodox Presbyterianism, then, resisted the new currents. But there were those in Philadelphia who welcomed them. There were zealous ministers who had been involved with revivals of a congregational nature for some time. The Reverend James Patterson, pastor of the First Presbyterian Church of Northern Liberties, was one of them. He was a New School man, and his temperament suited his role. The Reverend Patterson was tall and prophetlike, with piercing eyes, dark hair, and long features. He was filled with glowing zeal and intensity. A thundering voice and denunciatory style impressed his congregants with the terror of God. A colleague decided:

> His general aspect in the pulpit was stern and severe. His mission was to sinners. His great office rebuke and warning. His main motive the terrors of the Almighty .... His denunciations of guilt were scathing; his predictions of coming wrath graphic and overwhelming.[15]

Patterson's intensity was contagious. It was not unusual for the entire congregation to be melted into tears when he gave a sermon, and he himself often wept as well. He often spoke with such force that he grew ill. On March 13, 1820, after seventeen consecutive meetings, he wrote, he was thoroughly exhausted.[16] He disdained refinements of thought or elegance of phrase, but used timely illustrations and transparently clear language. His sermons were sometimes marked by crudeness and bad taste, and his rough and uncouth manner alienated the wealthy, the tasteful, and the refined, but he was well loved by the ordinary people in his congregation. Indeed, in eulogy, he was called "the preacher of the masses."[17]

He had been born on a farm in Bucks County, Pennsylvania, in 1779, where he grew up intending to be a farmer himself. Physical problems, however, disqualified him from that work. Illness and a crisis during his sixteenth year led to the distress of mind he speaks of in his diary, and he spent hours reading the Bible. After two years of "despair, gloom, and fear," he was able to achieve a conversion and peace of mind. After his conversion, he was graduated from Jefferson College in Canonburg, Pennsylvania, studied theology at Princeton Theological Seminary, and was licensed to preach. In 1814, at thirty-five years of age, he came to Northern Liberties, and was unanimously elected pastor of the First Presbyterian Church of Northern Liberties, at Buttonwood Street below Sixth, where he was to remain for twenty-three years. This congregation had originated in a separation from the influential Second Presbyterian Church at Third and Arch Street. The Second Presbyterian was a church of long involvement in revivals, having sprung from the ministry of George Whitefield in the Great Awakening. Its first pastor had been the Rev. Gilbert Tennent, son of the famous revivalist William Tennent. In 1777 the Second Presbyterian Church of Philadelphia began missionary activities in the area known as Northern Liberties. The new church was organized in 1813 and on January 11, 1814, James Patterson was installed as its first minister.[18]

Northern Libertes was a growing part of the city — the new suburbs. Most families of wealth and position lived in the old part of the city, while the Northern Liberties section contained the poorer and less educated. There were many German immigrants in the area and some Quakers, and a few wealthier families, but the more affluent generally preferred churches that reflected their tastes. There were fifty-two people in Patterson's first congregation, "3/4 of them women, 9/10 of them poor, all untrained, undisciplined."[19] In describing the congregation, Patterson said, "Ignorance and vice, its most invariable concomitant, abounded; the sanctuary and institutions of religion were neglected by very many of its inhabitants."[20] The building was neat and spacious, but the number attending not very encouraging. Patterson instituted a new order of things. He built up interest by using placards and advertisements to attract people to his church.[21] He supplemented revival excitements through home visits. Shortly after he assumed pastorship, he established prayer meetings, in which members of the church would take part and were led to exhortation and extemporaneous speaking. This lay preaching caused considerable criticism among Presbyterians of other churches. He was sustained in the innovation, however, by several leading Philadelphia Presbyterian ministers, among them the prestigious Reverend James P. Wilson and the important Reverend Thomas H. Skinner, but the main body of the clergy and many of the laity were against him. In 1815 he established the Union Sabbath-School Association of the Northern Liberties, one of the first of its kind in Philadelphia, and others followed. More than one hundred children were enrolled, mainly from poor families.[22] He was concerned with the problem of young men of modest means who wanted to enter the ministry, and tried to form a society to help them, but was unsuccessful, although he often housed theology students with his own family. From 1816 through five consecutive summers, he held services on the commons in open fields.[23] There was a seven-month revival in 1816, another in 1821, yet another in 1822. The 1816 revival was preceded by prayer meetings for the purpose of "supplicating the reviving influences of the Spirit of God" for nearly ninety consecutive nights.[24]

Many of the congregation disapproved of the revivals, but Patterson was not to be deterred. There were some who were attracted to these meetings by curiosity; they came to witness the weeping and the groaning. The new converts, however, were largely "young persons between thirteen and twenty years of age. Only four of the seventy admitted were above thirty years of age."[25] Patterson believed the young to be particularly susceptible to revival efforts:

> The morning of life is a period peculiarly proper for the cultivation of piety. Then the heart is tender, and more susceptible of divine impressions, than when it has been hardened by a long continuance in sin. At this period the mind is comparatively free from prejudice, and good habits are more easily formed; and when formed, they are more permanent.[26]

There were sermons especially directed at youth and often special services for young people.[27] Patterson advertised them by handbills and in newspapers. A special service for young men in 1831 was crowded with young men in the lower part of the church, and the galleries crowded with young women. "After the sermon, those who were disposed to follow the church were asked to withdraw to the session room for conversation and about four hundred men did so."[28]

The more conservative churchgoers were troubled by the excesses of feeling and action that Patterson brought to the church.

> I think Mr. P. would have done more good had he husbanded his strength instead of pouring it all forth. It is possible to overwork the revival spirit with too much enthusiasm and the result will be fatal to the progress of the work. Mr. P. has an excellent spirit, he is always at his post . . . but his means of accomplishing are not good. His preaching is desultory and scathing.[29]

Although the Reverend Patterson was concerned with the young, it was the poor of his district who he felt most needed religion. He was astonished by their "lack of knowledge of one's soul, Christ, and all religious matters." They were poor, he felt, because of this ignorance and impiety. Religion was the answer to their problems, not charity. Consequently he vigorously opposed the poor tax. In a letter to city officials on January 8, 1833, he asserted that the city and its districts was saddled with the enormous poor tax of $150,000 per year, a grand sum of three million dollars between 1803 and 1824, because of riotous living on the part of its poor — open profanation of the Sabbath and drunkenness.

> Sabbath breaking and drunkenness are kindred vices. These Sunday pleasure excursions to the country in steamboats and railroad cars, are always attended with drinking spirits, less or more, and are usually the first step of a citizen in the ruin of himself, and not in-

frequently end by leaving himself and family an expense on the community. A poor tax on this country is almost another name for a tax to support drunkards and their distressed families.[30]

He proposed legislation to prevent work on Sunday, punishable by fine and imprisonment, and laws to prohibit Sabbath drinking. Patterson even connected deaths from the cholera epidemic with profanation of the Sabbath. He devised a chart showing that for six consecutive weeks in Philadelphia, deaths on Monday far exceeded those on Sunday, and concluded that it was "a direct voice from heaven proclaim[ing] more loudly the great disadvantage of profaning the Sabbath."[31]

The minister of the Northern Liberties Church was openly opposed to slavery, viewing it as a moral issue.

As sure as the sun shines, SLAVERY must come to an end; and all its abettors, if they persist in it, *will be destroyed* ... America *must suffer*; if something is not done and that *speedily too*, to release from the most *cruel bondage*, more than A MILLION AND A HALF OF IMMORTAL BEINGS, whom she holds in chains, and that both soul and body, that they cannot serve God .... With the increasing growth of Christianity among us, it is impossible that slavery can exist. Christianity and slavery cannot be identified .... Slavery ... is ... the greatest practical evil that ever afflicted the human race.[32]

His solution, however, was a moderate one. He embraced the American Colonization Society, whose plan was to send all willing free blacks and as many of the slaves as masters would free to Africa.[33] While Patterson's views on slavery were openly stated, the overwhelming message of his sermons dealt not with slavery, but with individual sin and redemption. Among the dozens of his sermons that remain, only a tiny portion of them involve slavery. Similarly, antislavery occupies very little of his diary. Clearly Patterson, like Finney, was primarily interested in saving souls; any other interest was peripheral. His racial views, even those on slavery, were essentially conservative.

It is not at all clear that ministers who sought congregational revivals were all of Patterson's type. There were others who were cultivated and literate men. The Reverend Stephen Tyng of the evangelical wing of the Episcopal Church was a forceful man who favored congregational revivals, yet he was dignified and cultured. The Rev. Thomas H. Skinner, a New School Presbyterian, also bore marks of refinement and literary style. It was perhaps a matter of temperament that caused some ministers to be drawn to a more spiritual and emotional understanding of their mission. These ministers, however, all chose to keep revivalism within the congregational framework. Patterson himself was drawn to the life of an itinerant revivalist after his contact with Finney. During the autumn of 1828, he was intensely agitated about the problem. He wanted to resign his pastoral situation to devote himself to traveling and preaching. An old friend even offered him $1,000 per year to do so, but family responsibilities, he said, caused him to remain at his post.[34]

On April 20, 1824, James Patterson first wrote to Finney, who was then in Troy, New York, inviting him to come to Philadelphia for a revival. "I think this region is ripe for revivals and all that is wanting is a proper person to sound the alarm."[35] He never got an answer to his invitation, and almost a year later, he wrote Finney again, urging him to come. Finney should go to the great cities in order to do good on a larger scale, insisted Patterson, for cities have an amazing influence on the community at large. He emphasized the importance of Philadelphia as the center of Presbyterianism in the United States. Presbyterians were constantly mingling with other citizens, therefore they were very influential. With the right kind of management, Patterson concluded, revivals would succeed in the city as they had in the country.[36] Finney's anxieties about bringing his revivals to the city must have been assuaged by Patterson's pleas and by other invitations from Philadelphia admirers as well.[37] He acceded to the entreaties and agreed to bring his revivals to Philadelphia. At first he came twice a week from Wilmington, Delaware, where he was working with the Reverend James Gilbert. It was a hard routine: he traveled by steamboat, preaching in Philadelphia in the evening, and returning the next day to preach at Wilmington, alternating evening services between Wilmington and Philadelphia. It was a distance of only forty miles, but a difficult trip in 1828. After some months, he was convinced that Philadelphia was ready for revivals. He was probably also tired of the long and wearisome journeys. In any case, he decided to give his whole time to Philadelphia. It was then sometime around January 17, 1828.[38]

Relations between Patterson and Finney were cordial. The itinerant revivalist spoke admiringly of the minister of the church in Northern Liberties: "He would preach with the tears rolling down his cheeks, and with an earnestness and pathos that were striking."[39] Patterson's congregation was well prepared for Finney by a long acquaintance with their minister's methods. "He had a praying people," affirmed Finney.

The revivals were an immediate success. The church was packed every night to hear Finney's powerful sermons. The huge, staring eyes and the gesticulating arms, the denunciations of guilt and depravity sent shivers down spines. An emotional fever spread through the audience night after night. It was an exciting time for the congregation in Northern Liberties.

Despite their basic agreement on revival techniques, the two ministers differed on certain details. One of them was the proper tactic to be used with sinners. Finney worried that Patterson was too soft with sinners, that he created a mood of self-righteousness instead of heightening feelings of guilt and sinfulness. He convinced Patterson not to soothe and meliorate the sinner's anxieties, for this was doing penitents a disservice. One must bring inexorable pressure on them to submit, repent, and be saved. Patterson saw the error of his ways and acquiesced to Finney's approach.

The itinerant revivalist and his admirers had expected great criticism from the Presbyterian establishment of the city, but, to their astonishment, they found surprisingly little opposition. Nearly all the Presbyterian churches received Finney in their pulpits. Among the churches opened to Finney were the two most important Presbyterian churches in the city: the First Presbyterian Church and the Fifth Presbyterian Church. Dr. James P. Wilson, pastor of the First Presbyterian Church, was a leader of the moderates, and one of the most influential ministers of the denomination. He was an educated man, a graduate of the University of Pennsylvania, who had been admitted to the bar, and was in 1828 ending his long association with First Presbyterian. This learned minister, an unimpassioned and deliberate speaker himself, had opened his pulpit to Finney before he retired in May 1828. Finney's friends considered it a great coup for Finney to have been invited to speak at Dr. Wilson's church and to be so well-received by the more influential congregation. He was received as well in the pulpit of Dr. Thomas H. Skinner, another important Philadelphia Presbyterian. Skinner had been co-pastor with Dr. Janeway of the Second Presbyterian Church in Philadelphia, of which the Northern Liberties church was an offshoot. When in 1816 he espoused New School views differing from those of Dr. Janeway, an Old School man, Skinner quietly withdrew with a number of his parish to become pastor of the Fifth Presbyterian Church on Locust Street. Skinner was a prominent New

Schooler; his style, though it bore marks of culture and polish, was natural and easy, and his ministry witnessed numerous and powerful revivals.[40]

Finney exulted in the success of his revivals, telling friends that they "took powerful hold" in Philadelphia. In spite of this, he concluded after being in the city for a few months that the churches in Philadelphia were in a dreadful state. He spoke of Philadelphia as "this Anti-Revival City . . . which is in almost solid darkness . . . and in her putrid embrace she holds all the country north and south, locked up in loathsome horrid death." Still, in spite of the coldness of the city, he reported that between forty and fifty had already been examined for membership in Patterson's church, and numbers had been received into other churches, or were still unexamined. "We want ten times as much help as we have. Hundreds are willing to be visited, and anxious to be, whom we cannot go and see . . . . The young men in this region don't know how to visit, and most of the ministers would adopt the soothing system."[41]

In the summer of 1828, Finney left for a short time to visit his wife's parents in Oneida county, receiving while there expressions of gratitude from Patterson's congregation.[42]

When he returned to Philadelphia, he went to the German Reformed Church on Race Street. This church was the mother of nearly all Reformed churches in Philadelphia. Theologically, churches that followed the Calvinist tradition were styled "Reformed," and America was heavily populated with those in Reformed or Calvinist churches. In this sense, the Congregationalists might be called English Reformed, the Presbyterian Scotch Reformed. Baptists were Calvinist in origin as well. The Calvinist orientation, then, was shared by many American denominations. Among the German immigrants in the early nineteenth century, nearly all were Protestants, evenly divided between Lutheran and Reformed.

The Philadelphia Germans stemmed from a 1727 immigration of four hundred who made their way to Philadelphia under the ministry of George Michael Weiss, from the Palatinate in Germany.[43] The German immigrants stayed in groups, rather than spreading out as did the Scotch-Irish. Theologically, the German Reformed Church held to the Heidelberg Catechism, which emphasized the historical continuity of the church and stressed education based upon regular pastoral training of youth. Therefore, they generally resisted revivalism and held to their traditional beliefs. The retention of the German language helped insulate them from the disruptive influence of American society.[44] In heavily German regions such as Allentown, Bethlehem, and the Easton area, where the use of the German language was retained, "New Measures" were vigorously opposed in an effort at retaining the traditional ways of their church. Thus, the language barrier had kept the influence of English-speaking revivalists to a minimum.[45] But as time went on, the use of the German language became a problem with American born and bred congregants. They pressed for the use of English in services. It was the churches that admitted English into their services that were then susceptible to the revivalism that was to be the source of difficulty.

The minister of the German Reformed Church in Philadelphia was the Reverend Samuel Helffenstein. Helffenstein was born in Germantown, outside of Philadelphia, in 1775, the son of a German Reformed pastor. He was a delicate youth with an emotional nature and a gift for speaking.[46] At twenty-four, he was called to the German Reformed Church in Philadelphia with a salary and a free house as parsonage. For some years all went well with the Reverend Helffenstein, who ministered to his congregation exclusively in the German language. But on April 2, 1804, a vote to have occasional preaching in the English language marked the beginning of serious trouble. The vote was a tie, but due to procedural difficulties, it was declared illegal. There was, however, increasing pressure for English, and in 1805 the Synod recommended that the English language be used for every third Sabbath for the benefit of those who did not understand German. At this time, Dr. Helffenstein voted negatively. There was another tie and all amicable arrangements failed. Many who favored the English language withdrew. They were usually younger people, increasingly inclined toward the vernacular of the country in which they lived. In 1816 there was trouble anew, and this time Dr. Helffenstein was in favor of the use of the English language in services. He was dismissed by the Board, which was favorable to German.[47] Helffenstein brought this problem directly to the congregation and explained what the board had done. There were strong expressions of sympathy for the pastor, but next Sabbath the Board had closed the doors of the church to him, and Helffenstein was forced to meet his congregation in the school house. The matter was taken to court and a writ of mandamus commanded the Corporation to open the church and give the pastor possession of the pulpit. When he entered the next Sabbath, the leader of the Corporation arose and led his party out of the church. This was in 1817. The withdrawal apparently cleared the congregation of opposition to the use of English, for in 1819 it was unanimously resolved to alternate German and English in services.[48] Members and pastor increasingly felt that no church in the city could cut itself off from new membership by using two languages in services, and finally, in 1828, the use of German was dropped. It was not without strains that churches were brought into the American mainstream.[49]

The Rev. Helffenstein's church was one of the first German Reformed churches to make the language transition. The use of English for church services opened the church to new methods and currents that were affecting other denominations. A letter was dispatched to Finney from the congregation of the church, with the consent of its pastor to preach in the church. The proposal had drawn sharp opposition from obdurate members of the congregation, but it had been pushed through. Finney was invited to come for a period of six months, to preach on Sunday afternoons and evenings and on Thursday evenings as well. Finney's reputation had preceded him. The congregation was eager to hear from the man about whom so much had been said.[50]

With Finney, the German Reformed Church on Race Street felt the impact of the Great Revival. In his Memoirs, Finney described the church as the largest house of worship in the city; he claimed that it seated 3,000 people when the house was packed and the aisles filled, but it is unlikely that the church seated more than a thousand, with possibly standing room for a hundred or so in the aisles. Nonetheless, he preached there regularly from August 27, 1828, through January 5, 1829.[51] Week after week the church rang with his tirades against sin and his thundering invective. His work caused a severe crisis in the church, for having experienced Finney's "New Measures," the congregation grew increasingly dissatisfied with the Rev. Helffenstein. They wanted the full houses and excitement that a popular preacher brought. They hungered to sustain the high excitement of Finney's revivals.

> Some of the most eficient [*sic*] men say that a change must take place speedily or the church will dwindle away to nothing, their object then is to get clear of Mr. H., introduce a popular preacher and alter their charter.... They want a popular preacher so that their house may be once more filled. Matters coming to a crisis.[52]

Letters to Finney at the time express the deep longing for the warm and spirited preaching Finney had given them. A letter to Finney in New York in 1830 described the state of religion in Philadelphia:

This is a cold dead place. I cannot forbear weeping over the desolation of Zion. How different from days that are past! No spirit of prayer, no ardent desire for the conversion of sinners.[53]

The congregation wanted to make the church a center for revival operations, with Finney in charge. Helffenstein would have to go. He still had some support, but it was among those with little influence. The majority of the Vestry and of the congregation opposed him.[54] The old man, veteran of some 30 years with the congregation, was asked to leave. He resisted, suggesting instead that he accept half his salary, or $500 instead of $1,000 annually, and accept an assistant to divide up the preaching chores.[55] His offer was refused and a struggle ensued, both sides seeking legal counsel. Helffenstein appealed to the sympathy of the members of the congregation: his activity was lessening, he was an "old and faithful teacher [whose energy had] diminished in the long and unwearied services of those who threaten to displace [him]." His contract could be broken only by mutual consent, and he opposed the example of forcing out the "aged and inform to want and suffering and the honest and faithful to disgrace and abuse."[56] Some in the church defended him against the action of the Corporation of the Church. They considered it "unchristian and unjust for a church after availing itself of the services of a minister during the active period of his life to discard him when he approaches old age in disregard of a contract which he was solicited to form, and which he has done nothing to violate. He has been faithful in his duties for more than thirty years, and should not be thus discarded."[57] In spite of this defense, the pastoral relationship between Dr. Helffenstein and his church was dissolved in the spring of 1830. Reluctant to leave his pastorate of thirty years, he finally agreed to resign on the condition that he get the current year's salary, could preach two more Sundays, and could live rent free in the house that adjoined the church until November 12, 1831, at which time he would pay rent or leave.[58] Helffenstein continued to hold services for a time in a room at the corner of Fourth and Vine Streets with a few members favorable to him, and he finally settled in Montgomery County, where he died in 1866 at ninety-one years of age.[59]

Thus rid of their minister, by the end of the summer a letter went to Finney in New York: the church was ready and they desired Finney to come.[60] Almost a year was to elapse before Finney finally declined. He regretted that, although he felt deep interest in the welfare of the congregation, he could not help them at present. He promised, however, to try to get them an appropriate minister. "I am persuaded that you need a man of no ordinary stamp and that a common man would not succeed there," he advised.[61] It is certain from the correspondence that Finney was well aware of the dissension he had caused in the German Reformed Church at Philadelphia, yet he disclaimed knowledge of it. In his *Memoirs*, he said: "I never had labored anywhere where I was received more cordially, and where Christians, and especially converts, appeared better than they did there. There was no jar or schism among them that I ever knew of, and I never heard of any disastrous influence resulting from that revival."[62] Nevertheless, the church fell into disarray, as the membership statistics below indicate. After two years without a minister, matters were brought back to normalcy by the Reverend William T. Sprole, who led the congregation until 1837, and later by the Reverend Joseph F. Berg, a warm and dedicated revivalist minister who assumed the pastorate. Subsequent years brought frequent revivals and protracted meetings that drew vast crowds. The church building was once again filled with both members and the curious, and both church and pastor enjoyed prominence.[63] By 1840 revivalism was receiving much attention from Philadelphia German Reformed congregations. It received official endorsement from *The Messenger*, the leading periodical of the church. But opposition was forming.[64] From its theological citadel at Mercersburg, Pennsylvania, the German Reformed Church resisted the intrusion. This opposition was symbolized and expressed by the Reverend John W. Nevin, Professor of Theology at the Seminary, in his tract of 1843, *The Anxious Bench*.[65] This tract sharply criticized the "New Measures" for their "man-centered theology" and their excessive emotionalism that obstructed true religion, and urged a return to the German Reformed heritage, symbolized by the use of the Heidelberg Catechism. Nevin and his colleague at Mercersburg, the Reverend Phillip Schaff, the German theologian who had been brought to that institution, were responsible for bringing the church back to its traditional doctrine, and for forcing out the new measures.

Clearly Finney's revivalism was destructive of the harmony of the German Reformed Church. His injunctions to get rid of "sleepy ministers" had a direct influence on the congregation's treatment of the Reverend Helffenstein. Among Presbyterians, the impact of Finney's brand of revivalism was delayed but equally divisive. The Presbyterians had been feeling the force of revivalism for some time. The church was becoming seriously divided into "New School Presbyterians," who favored revivalism and shared the new activism of the revivalists, and the "Old School Presbyterians," who resisted revivalism in favor of traditional Presbyterian doctrine as represented by the Westminster Confession: original sin, the unregeneracy of man, and God's sovereignty over salvation. These differences were complicated by the antislavery issue, for many of the New School men were avid antislavery activists. It was a sectional difference as well, for the New School Presbyterians were stronger in the North while the Old School dominated the South. Serious differences were developing, then, in the church. The coming to Philadelphia of the controversial Reverend Albert Barnes brought the conflict into the open.

Albert Barnes was a New School man who had been born of a Methodist family in Rome, New York, in 1798. He had planned a career in medicine, but at the age of twenty-one, while a senior at Hamilton College, he had been converted in a revival at the college and decided to enter the ministry.[66] Barnes attended Princeton Theological Seminary and was licensed to preach in 1823. His first ministry at Morristown, New Jersey, was the scene of a powerful revival and it was here that he delivered the sermon "The Way of Salvation" that brought him to the attention of the First Presbyterian Church of Philadelphia. His call to that church in 1830 started a series of events that eventually split the church.

Almost immediately upon arrival, Barnes was charged with doctrinal error on the basis of statements in his sermon "The Way of Salvation." He had in this sermon been critical of the Westminster doctrine, with particular emphasis on the doctrine of original sin. Both moderates and Old School men combined to accuse Barnes of denying that men were guilty of Adam's sin. He subverted scriptural teachings of God's sovereignty and man's depravity, they declared. He claimed that the unregenerate had the ability to contribute to their own salvation.[67] This view, of course, was the theological foundation of revivalism. The charges against Barnes were sustained by both the Presbytery and the Synod of Philadelphia, and in 1831 the case reached the General Assembly, the highest court for ultimate decisions in Presbyterianism. Warfare broke out in full force between Old and New School factions for the first time. Ashbel Green, editor of the *Christian Advocate*, reported that "there occurred such disorder and confusion as we have never witnessed in the General Assembly and which we devoutly pray we may never see again."[68] Throughout the Assembly, the New School majority prevailed, and Barnes was acquited with only an admonition. After the Assembly, other "heretics" were brought to trial by Green and the conservative forces. Barnes, in 1835, was brought to a second trial, this time over "Notes on the Epistle to the Romans," another sermon. He was charged with repeating earlier errors, but after heated debate he was again sustained. Barnes held frequent revivals at the First Presbyterian Church, and over the years his church admitted hundreds of new converts.[69] In 1841 he preached the series of sermons "Revivals of Religion in Cities and Large Towns," which were widely reprinted and distributed. Like many other New School men, Albert Barnes was forceful in denouncing slavery. He worked in his own channels, however, never attending an antislavery convention nor joining an antislavery society. But for most of his thirty-seven years at the First Presbyterian Church of Philadelphia, he crusaded against slavery, as well as intemperance and other social evils.[70]

The Barnes case illustrates in microcosm the problem of the Presbyterian Church in America in the antebellum era. By 1837 inner tensions had split the Presbyterians into the Old School and the New School, each claiming to be the General Assembly of the Presbyterian Church of the United States of America. Whether revivalism alone without the antislavery issue would have caused such deep cleavage in the church is problematical. Clearly revivalism and antislavery were deeply interrelated. Nevertheless, revivalism was a major factor and Finney's work in Philadelphia made revivalism in that city a much stronger force than it had been theretofore. Out of the Barnes controversy and undoubtedly similar controversies in Presbyterian congregations all over the country, came the realization that the Presbyterian church was facing insuperable differences that it was unable to reconcile and the church was split in two.

Just as revivals brought bitter controversy to the Presbyterians in Philadelphia, they brought dissension and litigation to Philadelphia Baptists as well. The period from 1816 to 1835 has been called by Baptists "The Period of

Contention."[71] Essentially, except for the doctrine of baptism, Baptists were in agreement with other orthodox congregations on matters of doctrine, government, and worship. They had been divided by the First Great Awakening into "Old Lights" and "New Lights," and in the Second Great Awakening they were similarly divided. The "General Baptists" were Arminian in theology, accepting salvation for all men; the "Particular Baptists" felt that only the elect would be saved. Hence the latter opposed missionary societies, Bible societies, temperence agitation, and Sunday schools, all of which they regarded as man-made efforts to evangelize, and as unscriptural and contrary to their emphasis on predestination. Conversion was entirely an act of God; emotionalism was to be avoided.[72]

The Particular Baptists were strongest in the South, but they also predominated in Philadelphia as well, where they were in positions of leadership.[73] It was the Philadelphia General Baptists, however, who were enthusiastic followers of Charles Finney in Philadelphia and, despite the fact that Finney was a Presbyterian, Philadelphia's General Baptists often participated in his meetings.[74] Certain of Finney's theological views were congenial to Baptists. They had never placed education foremost in requirements for their ministers, insisting that personal piety was more important. Thus Philadelphia General Baptists were joining the new theological consensus, and their divergence from the old views caused sharp clashes.

The trouble in Philadelphia began before Finney came. Henry Holcombe, the minister of the important First Baptist Church of Philadelphia had published in 1823 the second edition of a book called *Primitive Theology*, some chapters of which had been preached as sermons. In it he had shaken the belief of many in the orthodox Calvinism of the day, and had asserted that faith was attainable by human means. This was promptly labeled a heresy by the Association; it was charged that Holcombe had become a "Swedenborgian, a Unitarian, an Arminian, and was becoming a Universalist."[75] Holcombe was a man of deep piety, but of a quick temper and arbitrary conduct. The controversy that followed had the majority of the First Baptist Church on Holcombe's side and the Deacons and their adherents on the other. Both parties attempted reconciliation, but their efforts failed. In May 1824, in the midst of the dispute, Dr. Holcombe died and he was succeeded by Dr. William T. Brantly, but the controversy continued. The Deacons were suspended and their adherents excluded. This group, seventy in number, applied for membership to the Philadelphia Baptist Association as the First Baptist Church, under the claim that they carried the traditional doctrines and the majority had departed from the faith; they "had erred and abandoned the grounds on which the church was original constituted . . . ."[76] This minority, who clung to orthodox Calvinism and refused to submit to the will of the majority, was reported to be "more influential, whether from age, office, or wealth."[77] The other 430 members also claimed legitimacy, and the church was torn into bitter segments. The 70 excluded members were granted a charter from the Philadelphia Baptist Association. This was protested by the other 430 members. The case was brought to court and in 1829 the court granted the charter to the minority on the technicality that while the church had existed since 1698, it had never been incorporated. The church remained split until 1835, when it was reunited.[78]

Whether resistance to revivalism among Philadelphia Baptists was responsible for the slow growth of that denomination is unclear. A Philadelphia Baptist editor reported in 1829 that Pennsylvania, one of the largest states in the union, contained only about 7,000 Baptists, attributing the weakness of this denomination to a "lukewarm attitude" on the part of Baptists in the area.[79] Presbyterians and Methodists were more successful in the middle states, and it was not until the 1850s that the Baptists entered their period of rapid growth in Pennsylvania. As years went on,

Holcombe's heresy became an accepted part of church theology and revivalism grew to have an increasingly important role in Philadelphia Baptist circles. Statistics reveal the chaos wrought by Finney in the German Reformed Church. As a result of Finney's labors in that church and the dismissal of the Reverend Helffenstein, the church in 1829 and for two years afterward failed to report membership statistics. When statistics were resumed in 1832, the church was down to fifty-one members.[80] In the Presbyterian Church, Finney's work caused an immediate sharp rise in numbers added to the Northern Liberties church in 1828 and 1829, and, less clearly, to the Presbytery of Philadelphia.[81] The years after the revivals show resumption of the slow steady rise that might be expected. The table indicates also that there must have been considerable attrition, as well as increases in membership. In 1829, for example, 105 members added to the 1,026 listed would give far more than 1,039 members listed in 1830, unless we assume some attrition that might be due to deaths, moving away from a church, changing denominational affiliation, or dropping church membership altogether. Given the geographic mobility of the time, moving away from the church must have been a significant cause of the attrition, and revivals were seen as useful in combating this horizontal mobility. As families moved in the traditional zonal pattern, new members were constantly being sought to keep the churches filled. A resolution of May 28, 1828, in the General Assembly of the Presbyterian Church reported a great number of churches vacant due to the number of people moving to the western part of the city, and suggested increased evangelism among the "heathen" as a cure.[82] The rising number of Presbyterian churches in Philadelphia, from forty in 1825 to fifty in 1832, must have been due to this trend.

The evidence available suggests that revivals were of only short-term value to churches in increasing membership. The long-term upward trend is perhaps more significant.

TABLE 3.1

Number of Communicants:
The German Reformed Church, Philadelphia

Year	Number of Communicants
1824	no report
1825	293
1826	no report
1827	285
1828	295
1829	no report
1830	no report
1831	no report
1832	
June	51
Sept.	104
Dec.	117
1833	183
1834	
March	190
June	207
Sept.	223
Dec.	228
1835	
March	232
June	240
Sept.	247
Dec.	252

Source: Statistics from 1824-1831, from the Minutes of the Synod of the German Reformed Church, in the Historical Society of the Reformed Church, Franklin and Marshall College, Lancaster, Pa.

NOTE: From 1832-1835, statistics were not sent to the Synod, but were available through the "Records of Communion Services and New Members Confirmed and Received into the German Reformed Church from 1832-1876," OFRC, Philadelphia.

TABLE 3.2
Number of Communicants:
First Presbyterian Church of Northern Liberties
and Philadelphia Presbytery

First Presbyterian Church of Northern Liberties			Philadelphia Presbytery		
Year	Total	Added Last Year	Total	No. of Churches	Added Last Year
1825	900		5806	40	
1826	900	18	6077	45	
1827	900		6189	46	471
1828	1000	100	6743	42	479
1829	1026	105	6763	44	462
1830	1039	47	7186	42	522
1831	1039		8102	46	521
1832	1100	119	8305	50	1160
1833	1100	66	9119		

Source: From the Minutes of the General Assembly of the Presbyterian Church, Presbyterian Historical Society, Philadelphia, Pa.

Even considering the attrition, it reflected two conditions. The first was an absolute rise in population. The second, which was dependent upon the first, was a change in quality of life as a result of an enlarged population. Relationships became more impersonal, and there was a trend toward anonymity in the city. Consequently people felt a need to establish social location, to relate themselves to the community at large through membership in a smaller group that effectively reflected their ideals, values, and life styles. Churches are the traditional American mode of achieving this end. The slow, steady rise in church membership was probably due to the need for social location, rather than to revivals. Twentieth-century data validate this hypothesis. Since 1900, while revivalism in major evangelical denominations has declined, church membership in the United States has, on the whole, increased.[83] Clearly, while revivals brought excitement to churches, they offered no sustained benefits.

Revival enthusiasts attempted in 1829 to build a revival church, but failed to find sufficient support and the plan was abandoned. The small group of Finney's admirers had found a piece of land between Market and Arch Streets, and between Fifth and Sixth, and planned to purchase the lot and ask for subscriptions to build the church. Until it was built, they expected that the Musical Fund Society's hall or some other convenient place could be used as a meeting place.[84] They urged Finney to come and preach in the church when it was completed. But by the end of February discouragement set in, for interest flagged and Finney, occupied in his work in Reading, did not respond to their pleas.[85] Consequently, Finney's followers in Philadelphia failed in their attempts to build a revival church. "I am afraid it cannot be done," a disappointed follower wrote to Finney; "if talking would have built a church we should have had one long before you left this place but that kind of faith has been found inadequate and the matter rests where it was when you left this city."[86]

Friends of revivals established, however, a committee to promote revivals. "The Association for the Promotion of Revivals" existed for ten months, meeting every Tuesday evening for business and prayer alternately. Finney was elected a member of the association, and a copy of the constitution was sent along to him. Little could be done, however, to keep revivals at the levels they had reached while Finney was in the city. While, in New York, Finney's followers built the Broadway Tabernacle for revivals, Philadelphia was unable to sustain enough interest to accomplish the same thing.

Finney's appeal was largely to the less-educated, lower classes. Patterson's church was, by his own analysis, mostly poor, untrained, and undisciplined. Finney himself reported his success with uneducated lumbermen, factory workers, people of modest means. He would occasionally mention conversions of upper-class followers: a lawyer, a businessman, a richly dressed young woman, people who had never before been reached by revivals. But these were at this time exceptions. His great success in Philadelphia was among the lowly, the untrained, the uneducated.

The most important impact of Finney upon Philadelphia, however, and upon American religion, was the development of a new kind of preacher, the itinerant revivalist. This traveling evangelist, with no fixed post, sought to increase membership and piety among established congregations. In the development of the itinerant revivalist, Finney's style and theology were to become the prototype for dozens of men and women of nearly all denominations who were to follow.

4

Crisis at Noon

The revivals of the Second Great Awakening appealed most, as we have seen, to the lower classes and the uneducated. It was among that segment of the population that Finney's apocalyptic style and his message of salvation met with the greatest approval. But beyond class structure, it was the young people who were dominant in the turbulent revivals of the period and who were represented to an unusually significant degree among new converts. The evidence reveals that adolescents provided the bulk of the sudden conversions that were the central experience of the revival. For a whole group of young people, the conversion was a rite of passage into maturity.

The interest of the young had important social and intellectual implications. The revival movement was fueled by the energy and zeal of these young people and became an important social movement. Conversely, the young converts were shaped as individuals by the mentality of the revival, and the life of the mind in America was thereby subtly affected.

Let us examine adolescence as it is understood today. This period of life has long been of interest to the psychologist and the educator. New interdisciplinary studies, however, have whetted the interest of the historian in this time of life. The volatile youth culture of the 1960s confirmed the interest of social scientists and historians in efforts to understand adolescence in the context of that time, as well as in historical perspective. Much of the groundwork upon which later study was based was laid by the eminent psychiatrist Erik H. Erikson.[1] Erikson divided life into stages, each with its developmental tasks and its characteristic crisis. He freed historians from the mind-set of the Freudians, who tended to subordinate later stages of life to that of childhood. His "identity crisis" became the touchstone to reality for a generation of young people. More importantly for historians, he showed in his innovative works on Luther and Gandhi the mutual interpenetration of the individual and society: that the social process molds the individual, but is in turn remolded by him, in a complex social dialectic.[2]

The interest of historians and psychohistorians then, is not adolescence in itself, but adolescence in its relationship with society and particularly with social change. The term itself requires some definition, and this is no easy task. To attempt it is to try to place within chronological limits a phenomenon that is developmental rather than chronological. Nevertheless, adolescence, the period between childhood and adulthood, when the individual becomes physically an adult and assumes a life's work and a formed personality, may be said to extend at its broadest limits from 11 or 12 to 25 or thereabouts, although most commonly it is understood as the time between ages 13 and 20. It is best understood symptomatically rather than chronologically however, since it is the accomplishment of developmental tasks that enables the individual to enter maturity. Kenneth Kenniston attempts to draw out of adolescence a distinct phase between adolescence and adulthood (roughly from 18 to 30), which he feels is now emerging as a distinct time of life.[3] Examination reveals that it is the latter stage of adolescence, which he has cut off from the earlier stage. As he puts it, the adolescent is struggling to define who he is; youth begins to sense who he is.[4] Most social scientists, however, use the terms *youth* and *adolescence* interchangeably, and I shall do the same.[5]

In one sense, youth or adolescence constitutes a universal phenomenon. It is first of all a biological phenomenon and as such it is more or less similar in all societies. But it is always defined in cultural terms, hence the different aspects and manifestations in individual cultures and over time. John and Virginia Demos have suggested that adolescence did not exist before the end of the nineteenth century; that it was a "discovery," so to speak, of G. Stanley Hall, who made adolescence the focus of psychological study at the turn of the century.[6] According to the Demoses, adolescence arose with urbanization and industrialization, when the previous continuity between generations broke down and new options in career and life style opened to the young person. It is undeniable that the youth culture of today did not exist before industrialization and urbanization, but to conclude that adolescence did not exist is dangerously solipsistic. It may not have had twentieth-century characteristics, but it existed physiologically, sexually, and behaviorally, and many people recognized its unique qualities. The transition from childhood to adulthood is never in any society completely continuous. According to sociological theory, when there are relatively sharp discontinuities between childhood and maturity, a ritualized set of behavior emerges to ensure that the transition be clearly marked. When such rites are weak, a youth culture is likely to develop, not explicitly anti-adult, but nonadult, allowing the youth a waiting period before entering the adult world. While adolescence as a youth culture did not exist early in the nineteenth century, the psychophysiological elements surely did, as did discontinuity in sufficient degree to warrant the conclusion that adolescence or youth did indeed exist at that time.

Early in the nineteenth century, evangelicals recognized that adolescence, or youth, as they called it, was the ideal time to induce religious conversion; there was something in the nature of youth that rendered it especially suited to conversion. An article in *The Magazine of the German Reformed Church* in 1829, by an unnamed author who signed himself "Juvenis," divided life into four stages: childhood, youth, manhood, and old age. Each age, it said, had salient features. "Quickness of perception, promptness in judging, ardency and susceptibility of feeling and affection, sanguineness of hope, impatience of desire and vivacity of imagination seem to be among the most prominent intellectual features of the young mind."[7] Churches must reach out to these young people, concluded the article, in order that they express these characteristics in church life, rather than in secular vocations and enterprises. Albert Barnes, in his sermon on revivals in cities, noted that the city was particularly dangerous to youth. "There are passions in youth that may easily be enkindled, there are alluring arts that may readily be made to decay them . . . every vice looks to the young for patronage."[8] Clearly, the time of life between childhood and maturity was seen as a period with unique characteristics and vulnerabilities.

There are no hard statistics on the numbers of young people involved in the Second Great Awakening of the early decades of the nineteenth century, but only a mass of impressionistic data. Out of memoirs, accounts of foreign visitors, and religious periodicals, emerges the picture of an extraordinary involvement of adolescents in these revivals. Charles G. Finney made frequent mention of the conversion of young people. He told of an eighteen-year-old girl who experienced tragedy in her personal life when her fiancé, to whom she had postponed marriage until she became a Christian, was accidentally killed. She took to following Finney home at the close of every meeting, " . . . a look of wildness in her face that indicated a state of mind that was unendurable."[9] Finney was able to convert the young lady in his characteristic fashion: by bringing her to a peak of emotional anxiety and guilt, and then a cataclysmic conversion that brought with it salvation. Finney's anxious bench, his charismatic exhortation, his warmly emotional meetings often lasting late into the night and for several days, were peculiarly suited to the traumas of adolescence. One does not need psychiatric training to perceive that the young woman above was troubled by matters other than theological. James Patterson, the revivalist minister of the First Presbyterian Church of Northern Liberties, reported in 1818 the conversion of an apprentice, a boy of 14, who was involved in disputes with his master over his habit of staying up at night to read the Bible and pray, and over his reluctance to work on the Sabbath. The master threatened and punished the boy, saying that such reading filled his mind with nonsense.[10]

Finney reported great success in converting young lumbermen who came down the river with their rafts to Philadelphia in the spring, after a long winter of isolation. It had been a long and lonely winter, and in the spring of 1829 when the Delaware was high, the lumbermen floated down from the unsettled region at the headwaters of the river. Many of these young men had been living alone or with three or four other men, in a region alienated from the institutions of society—from church, from family, from school. They were an uneducated and uncouth lot, many of them little more than children. They went to Finney's revivals in Philadelphia, were converted, and when they returned upriver, they took revivalism with them. A letter to Finney in Auburn, New York, in 1831 told him that an extensive revival had occurred in the lumber region without benefit of clergy.[11]

Patterson told of the 1816 revivals in his church, when conversions were "for the most part young persons between 13 and 20 years of age." Only 4 of the 70 converted were above 30 years of age, and only 1 of these 4 had arrived at 60 years of age.[12] Patterson felt that young people were particularly susceptible to revivals and often held special services for young men and women.

Foreign visitors describing camp meeting revealed similar situations. Francis Lieber, in describing a camp meeting in Westchester, about 23 miles from Philadelphia, noted chiefly young women participating in the meeting.[13] Frances Trollope, describing a revival meeting in Cincinnati, noted the same preponderance of youth, largely young girls.[14] Religious periodicals of the time abound with the influence of revivals on young people in urban as well as rural revival meetings. *The Messenger* reported in April 1830, "We have been favored the past season with a pleasing revival of religion, and have admitted 70 to the church, mostly young people . . . ."[15] A year earlier, the same magazine contained a letter from Jonathan Helffenstein, telling about revivals in Frederick, Maryland, in which "upwards of 80 profess having passed from death unto life . . . . The young are in general the subjects."[16] In a letter to a lady in New York, the Reverend Alfred Ely, pastor of the Congregational Church at Monson, Massachusetts, wrote, "We have been favored the past season with a pleasing revival of religion, and have admitted seventy to the church, mostly young people . . . ."[17] In April 1831 reports of revivals at Yale College were "the object of intense interest because of the talent and learning of these young men."[18]

Those who wrote the rash of revival handbooks that came out of the 1830s and 1840s recognized that youth was peculiarly susceptible. The Reverend James Porter noted that the subjects of conversion were "chiefly the young, usually the children of religious parents, and 2/3 females."[19] Even children were occasionally spoken of as subjects of revivals. Fish's *Handbook of Revivals* contains a whole chapter devoted to children, called "Child Piety and Profession." He felt that children were unusually plastic and malleable, and saw no scriptural foundation for hesitancy at converting children.[20] But most revivalists sought not children, but the young who fall under the adolescent category.

Edwin D. Starbuck, a student of William James at Harvard, attempted in 1904 to bring the phenomenon of conversion under scientific analysis.[21] He made a statistical study of persons of various Protestant denominations and found that conversion did not occur with the same frequency in all periods of life. Using Presbyterians, Methodists, Baptists, Quakers, and Episcopalians, he found that the conversion experience belonged almost exclusively to the years between 12 and 25. The event generally came earlier in females, most frequently at 13 and 16 years of age, while males most frequently experienced conversion at the age of 17.[22] He concluded that conversion was an adolescent phenomenon.

The question remains: how can we explain the obvious appeal of religious revivals to young people? Starbuck was part of an era that sought to bring the mysteries of religion under the scrutiny of science. William James's classic *Varieties of Religious Experience* was another of these attempts to examine religion scientifically. Starbuck, James, and a host of other men sought to mitigate the hostility that had developed between religion and science at the end of the nineteenth century.[23] Thus the social scientists of the late nineteenth and early twentieth century saw revivals in purely positivist terms: they were not the product of rational thought, hence of emotionalism and hysteria, psychically induced, perhaps even pathological.

The evangelical explanation of conversion, on the other hand, is that although it may be brought on by human means, conversion is a mystical process. In the drama of guilt and repentance, acceptance of Christ, and salvation, was the hand of the Divine. Conversion was seen purely in theological terms. Both analyses must be rejected, I think, in favor of an analysis that takes into account the nature of adolescence and the crisis of consciousness that that period of life involves.

The distinct characteristic of youth have long been noted. Many have described the penchant for emotional enthusiasm, sudden changes of mood, strong idealism, and a tendency to follow extremes. Kenneth Kenniston describes the period this way:

> Adolescence involves a drastic reversal of behavior, accompanied by major psychological changes and conflicts. The pre-adolescent pattern of outgoing activity is changed, often in a few months, to a new style of seclusiveness, a feeling of social awkwardness and moral inferiority coupled with intense intellectual concerns, and, at times, with extreme religiosity. The outgoing pre-adolescent becomes almost overnight the shy, awkward and tormented early adolescent.[24]

It is a two-pronged crisis. First, there is the newly developing sexuality. The adolescent has problems in dealing with sexual desires, masturbation, and sexual fantasies that come with the rapid physiological changes. These feelings arouse in most adolescents a sense of anxiety, often of guilt and shame. To a youth raised in a strict evangelical home, such feelings could be particularly troubling. There is a deeply felt need for release from this sense of guilt, for a feeling of God's forgiveness of sin. Starbuck found this feeling among his samples: most adolescents said they were brought to conversion, not from love of God or Christ, but from fear of death and of hell.[25] There are some who see the sexual aspect of conversion as the primary cause. George Godwin, in *The Great Revivalists*, felt that conversion was a sexually induced phenomenon.[26] But burgeoning sexuality is only one aspect of the crisis of adolescence. Kenniston saw the double task of adolescence as "to resolve the awakening sexuality and the new social demands into a newly integrated personality." It was a process seldom untroubled. As early as 1904, Starbuck was describing what we call today the "identity crisis" of adolescence:

> As the child moves from the smaller limited world of existence into the larger world, he is dimly conscious of its existence and its demands. There is often a clash between individual will and the social will.... Youth is in a state of mental congestion. Adolescence is one of the most critical periods of development.... The germinating personality is poised between an infinite variety of possibilities.

At the end of this troubled period, said Starbuck, a reorganization, a reconstruction of religious experience, a stabilization take place. The young person has worked out his beliefs. Adolescence is the period when a new personality is formed, "the birth of selfhood, the awakening of a self-conscious personality," and this, he says, is one of the central facts that bring harmony and unity into the multiplicity of adolescent phenomena.[27]

In 1958 Erik Erikson viewed the major crisis of adolescence in much the same way as Starbuck, and labeled it "the identity crisis."

> it occurs in that period of the life cycle when each youth must forge for himself some central perspective and direction, some working unity, out of the effective remnants of his childhood and the hopes of his anticipated adulthood; he must detect some meaningful resemblance between what he has come to see in himself

and what his sharpened awareness tells him others judge and expect him to be . . . . In some young people, in some classes, at some periods in history, this crisis will be minimal; in other people, classes and periods, the crisis will be clearly marked off as a critical period, a kind of "second birth," apt to be aggravated either by widespread neuroticisms or by pervasive ideological unrest. Some young individuals will succumb to this crisis in all manner of neurotic, psychotic, or delinquent behavior; others will resolve it through participation in ideological movements passionately concerned with religion or politics, nature or art. Still others, although suffering and deviating dangerously through what appears to be a prolonged adolescence, eventually come to contribute an original bit to an emerging style of life.[28]

The period of adolescence then, should be viewed as one of the crises of life, and the conversion experience as a particular expression of this crisis. It is an example of the way in which a specific cultural group (evangelical Christianity) has ritualized the problems of adolescence and made them manageable for its young people. Richard Rubenstein, Jewish theologian and psychoanalyst, points out that Jews have their Bar Mitzvah, the Lutherans and Catholics their confirmation, both of which occur during the adolescent period. Primitive tribes have their puberty rites during the adolescent period. All of these rituals may appear ethically or rationally meaningless, but all rituals serve to dramatize our feelings concerning enormously important areas of life. They help the individual pass through the crises of life, "to alleviate the conflicts inherent in the worst moments and heighten the joys of the best." Rituals enable people to cope, both consciously and unconsciously, with the crises of life, and to work out their emotions and fears in a socially acceptable way.[29]

Let us examine one sudden conversion in the light of this analysis. Most conversion accounts suffer from "single vision." They are theologically oriented and include no information outside of the personal anguish of the moment. Consequently, they are of no use in trying to understand the life context of that conversion. The experience needs to be viewed within the matrix of the individual's life.

The experience of Tom Watson, Southern populist leader of the nineteenth and early twentieth century, is of extreme interest in illuminating the relationship between the life-crisis and the conversion.

Born in Georgia in 1856, Tom grew up in a society dislocated by the Civil War. His father, unable to maintain a plantation without the labor upon which the system rested, was forced to sell the family home and land. It was a declining and desolate situation and Tom was raised in poverty and piety. He was, however, a bright boy, with literary and musical interests unusual for his age. The pastor of the Baptist church took an interest in him and urged him to apply to Mercer University, a small Baptist College, arranging for deferred tuition payment. At age 16, Tom entered as a freshman.

Upon graduation, however, poverty remained. He tramped the streets of Augusta vainly seeking employment. He was forced to sell his books at auction. "Youth is bidding me goodbye forever...."[30] The future seemed "robed in gloom" and "attended by shadows." He lay on the banks of the Savannah River, writing gloomy poetry. Finally came an opportunity to read law with a local judge. The boy passed the bar examination and received a license to practice law at 19. Starting practice, he was unable to make enough money to survive. "I couldn't stand the crisis," he reported in his Journal.[31] He was forced to sell his horse and take a position teaching in a small private school.

Time hung heavy, and he filled it with writing poetry and making love to village girls. The Baptist community was shocked. "It didn't require much wisdom to see that profligacy was ruining me." Every attempt to improve his situation was doomed to failure. When the school closed in June, he tried for a lecturing post with the state Temperance Society. The office was abolished. October 1876 found him utterly destitute and working as a plow hand for old Jimmie Thompson.

> At night, my fiddle waked the silence among the pines . . . . I got morose, moody and sulky as a mad bull. I used to lay [sic] down under the pines and try to imagine where the dickens I was drifting to, and what awful change had come over the spirit of my dream that I was getting so near the bottom.[32]

In the midst of this nadir of despair, an old teacher agreed to advance him some money until he got started as a lawyer. He started practice again, determined to succeed. He threw himself into an orgy of work, studying law far into the night, often not getting to bed at all. He dressed plainly, ate a cold supper in his office, handled the few cases that came his way. When a revival came along, he embraced it with impulsive emotion. Tom Watson was a fervent convert.

> The evangelist got hold of me in such a way that I not only cried and "took on" myself, but I picked out the hardest old case in the congregation, pried him loose from his seat, dragged him down the aisle and landed him on the mourner's bench.[33]

He was then 20 or 21 years of age, a youth living a spartan regime, abnegating luxuries and sex, engaged in a desperate attempt to establish himself in a profession. His conversion must be viewed within the context of a difficult struggle for identity. It has components of sexual guilt and feelings of anxiety about the direction in which to go. The revival, occurring when it did, provided a mechanism for handling the feelings he was experiencing, the crisis he was undergoing. It represented for him a rite in the passage to maturity. Through the revival, the evangelical machinery, designedly or not, emphasizes, abridges, and regulates the crisis of adolescence. For the young person who viewed the world from the evangelical point of view, conversion became the socially acceptable manner of dealing with adolescent turmoil. The influence of group expectation was important. Starbuck showed that "the force of the popular mind, with affirmation and repetition and contagion played a large part."[34] Conversion, however, is but one of the alternatives of adolescence. To a young person from a different religious tradition, the adolescent trauma might seek another kind of expression, perhaps in secular or ideological terms. Conversion serves the evangelical community and the individual in a specific way, as rituals have served the individual and the group from time immemorial. It is paradoxical that the evangelical churches, which had long emphasized individual religious experience and denigrated ritualism, elevated conversion into a ritual out of a basic human need. This analysis does not eliminate the theological component of conversion, for part of the individual's identity crisis is, indeed, existential, and involves deep questions about the nature of existence, of God, of life itself. But to view conversion as simply a theological phenomenon is to misunderstand the complexity of the human personality.

The significance of the involvement of young people in revivals is twofold. The ability of the revival to serve as a rite of passage into maturity meant that large numbers of young people swelled the revival movement, making it a visible social movement and lending their support to the various reforms that were the outgrowth of the revivals. But it also meant that significant numbers of young people were shaped at a vulnerable time in their life by the mind-set of revivals—by the drama of sin and salvation. Their habits of mind were shaped by the revivals and these habits persisted into adulthood. Through the revivals they knew that theirs was the only authentic religious experience; that through faith instead of good works one was saved from eternal damnation. Anti-intellectualism and individualistic pietism permeated thousands of young people involved in revivals and helped create the mind of America. These young people were inclined to be less intellectual and less flexible than most, more moralistic and more inclined to see life in terms of absolutes. They were less able to comprehend the complexity of the world. Adolescent conversion was a significant experience for thousands of Americans, and its implications cannot be ignored in understanding the life of the mind in America.

The importance of women in revivals is equally significant. Church life has long been an accepted area for the engagement of women's energies. Foreign observers who noted the preponderance of women in churches, sometimes wondered what men did with themselves on Sunday while the women were at church. Not only were women a visible majority in the churches, but they dominated revivals and prayer meetings, urging their husbands, fathers, and sons toward conversion.[35] In addition, women workers were unusually active in tract and mission societies as well.

Many accounts suggest that women were especially vulnerable to conversion attempts. The Reverend Porter commented that the subjects of conversion were 2/3 female; Frances Trollope noticed a preponderance of youth, and largely young women; Francis Lieber noted the same, as was mentioned earlier.[36]

Lieber suggested that the reason for this phenomenon was that females had "weak nerves." It is more likely that the reason was frozen in the social realities of the nineteenth century. Women lived in a bifurcated world in nineteenth-century America; on one hand society expressed respect and admiration for their sterling qualities, and on the other, almost totally denied them civic, legal, religious, and economic freedom.[37] In almost every sphere outside the home, women were severely restricted. They were legally dead—unable to control their own earnings, sign legal papers, or hold property in their own right. They were effectively excluded, not only from the franchise, but from political matters in general. Politics was considered an improper sphere for women's participation. When leading abolitionists met in Philadelphia in 1833 to found the American Anti-Slavery Society, they permitted a few women to attend and to speak from the floor, but not to join or sign the "Declaration of Sentiments and Purposes."[38] When the Grimké sisters addressed mixed audiences on behalf of antislavery, great controversy broke out: "We appreciate the unostentatious prayers of women in advancing the cause of religion at home and abroad, in Sabbath-schools, in leading religious inquiries to the pastors for instruction . . . . But when she assumes the place and time of man as a public reformer . . . her character becomes unnatural."[39] When extraordinary women like the Grimké sisters, Lucy Stone, or Lucretia Mott spoke out, it was at enormous expense in terms of notoriety, and brought jeers and open hostility to them.

Women worked in industrial occupations during the early nineteenth century, often in the home, making cloth, shoes, and garments. With the invention of the spinning jenny, however, home work shrank and opportunities for factor work diminished for women. Many employments were then closed to them by custom and habit. Despite frequent pronunciations about the delicacy of women and the need to protect them, in 1833 women earned only one fourth of men's wages, and three quarters of Philadelphia's working women did not receive as much for an entire week's work of 13 to 14 hours per day as journeymen received in some branches for a single day of 10 hours.[40]

Most churches in Philadelphia required women to keep silent in church on the grounds that it was unseemly for women to speak in public. This stricture was based upon biblical injunction, but it was not universally practiced. Alone among the larger religious denominations, the Quakers permitted women to participate in church affairs, allowing them to speak in meeting and ordaining them ministers. Since the ministry was "the gift of God," the Quakers felt that "neither in reason nor in nature can there be found sufficient grounds for excluding them from the ministry."[41] In addition to stationary ministers, two well-known Quaker revivalists were women: Eliza P. Gurney and Sarah Smiley.[42] In general, the stronger the ritual and tradition in the church, the more restricted it was for women. Churches with an institutionalized access to the clergy, like seminary requirements, effectively eliminated women as preachers.

Thus women's sphere in early-nineteenth-century America was a large dose of home and children, religious training of children (but only in the home), and perhaps some charitable activity together with other women. They might, in addition, indulge their interest in the arts, or reading, or some other such passive pastime. But for the woman of an evangelical bent, there were even fewer outlets for her energies outside the home. "It is the paradox of a 'religion of the heart' that it should be notorious for the inhibition of all spontaneity."[43] Evangelical women were prohibited from intellectual pursuits or artistic endeavors open to other women because evangelical Protestantism was unable to distinguish between intellectual or creative activity and degenerate vice. Their beliefs precluded worldly-mindedness, levity, theatergoing, novel-reading, card-playing, dancing, drinking (even coffee or tea), and smoking tobacco, and even tight corset-wearing was prohibited![44] The "New Measures" of Charles Finney, however, suddenly enabled these women to participate in religious affairs. They could openly offer testimony at mixed meetings. In addition, times of revivals offered a splendid opportunity for socializing in a socially acceptable manner. There was not only Sunday church to attend but, in times of revivals, nightly meetings filled with warm, spiritual love, at which all would sing hymns, pray, exhort, eat and drink, then sing, pray and exhort again, long into the night. It was an outlet not to be underestimated for women so deeply confined in every other way. In addition to all the social political, economic, legal, and religious restrictions noted above, there were sexual ones as well. An early-nineteenth-century woman was not expected by men to have a sexual nature, nor did she understand her own sexuality. It is not unrealistic to suppose that her frustrations could be vented satisfactorily in the religious sphere in the area of revivals, where warm and spontaneous displays of feeling could be expressed openly without criticism. The descriptions of women in revival prayer meetings and in camp meetings exude a curiously erotic aura. Mrs. Trollope described beautiful young females writhing, with features distorted and limbs trembling, falling to their knees. They were the object of mystic caresses. "More than once I saw a young neck encircled by a reverent arm. Violent hysterics and convulsions seized many of them." She described prayer meetings in which women were caressed and encouraged when they confessed sin.[45] The sexual component of conversions has been often noted, but inadequately studied.

The preponderance of women in revivals must be viewed, I think, not only in theological terms, or in terms of a rite of passage into maturity, but also as a reaction against the severe, yet subtle and often unspoken limitations that women had learned to live with at enormous cost to their well-being. Revivals provided for many thousands of women an acceptable outlet that worked to sublimate their deepest longings. At every level, nineteenth-century evangelical Christianity offered to women an enlarged sphere of activity—as converts at revival meetings, as participants in church services, and as itinerant ministers.

5
From Ecstasy to Form

While revivalism was causing harsh feelings to explode into schisms and court litigation, it was at the same time developing into a recognized institution in church life. What had begun in the frenzy of emotional enthusiasm on the frontier was, in the city, becoming increasingly formalized and standardized. The revival became ritualized through handbooks and through the development of dozens of reform societies. The reforms promulgated, varied though they were, were not the pragmatic changes of practical reformers, but the pietistic, moralistic reforms of the religiously convinced, irritatingly sure of their truth. True to their original impulse in the revivals of the Second Great Awakening, they were reforms that were aimed at individual redemption. They were never able to deal with the social dimension of human problems. Reformers of the period were notoriously indifferent to the feelings and beliefs of others, and when milder inducements did not work, they would resort to coercive measures. Reform of the period was imbued with a tunnel vision regarding man and society that was the residue of its source.

Many churchmen recognized that periods of revivals were ways to keep churches filled in the face of the centrifugal forces of the city. They sought to utilize the techniques of the revivals to bring new membership to congregations diminishing through the growth pattern of the city. Population was pushing out from the old inner city, often away from places of work to new residences in areas where there were more space and newer homes.[1] At first the push was to fill up the areas near Broad Street; later, population would cross the river into the new suburbs of West Philadelphia. To the north, the same thing was happening as people moved away from the populated areas into the extreme end of Northern Liberties and beyond. It became inconvenient to return to churches in the old neighborhood. Consequently, people either dropped their church affiliation or joined together to form a small new church. Many apparently took the former path and the need became apparent to perceptive churchmen to meet this challenge and revitalize the weakening institution. They also understood the need for new members to keep the inner-city churches viable. Revivals were the most likely way to do this, they felt, and guides for conducting such revivals were needed. The revival handbook came to be the primary instrument in the standardization of revivals.

Through the decades of the 1830s through the 1850s, a vast literature developed that provided instruction for any who desired to conduct a revival. These books and pamphlets were widely circulated among ministers and church people, and came to be the reference tools for generations of revivalists. The early 1830s saw several pamphlets. One called *Letters on Revivals* by E. Porter appeared in 1832. Porter believed in the importance of "continued, powerful, general revivals."[2] He gave practical advice to those who conduct a revival. Even earlier an evangelical Episcopalian, A. V. Griswold, had written *Discourses on the Most*

Important Doctrines and Duties of the Christian Religion, aimed at the same purpose.[3]

The most influential of the revival handbooks was Charles G. Finney's *Lectures on Revivals of Religion*. It was read and used by dozens of itinerant revivalists who traveled the land in his wake.[4] First published in 1835, the book began as a series of articles in the *New York Evangelist* aimed at rescuing that periodical from loss of subscribers because of the reforming zeal of its ardent antislavery editor, Joshua Leavitt. Finney, returning from a cruise for his health, was asked by Leavitt to write a series of articles on revivals. Since Finney's forte was the spoken word, he agreed instead to preach a series of Friday night lectures to members of his Chatham Street Chapel. The lectures were transcribed by Leavitt from notes and memory and then were printed in the *Evangelist*. When demand for back issues became heavy, the lectures were collected into a book. The volume sold for one dollar and was the most popular and widely read of all revival literature. Twelve thousand copies were sold in the first three months after publication. There were several reprints of 2,000 each and well over a hundred thousand copies printed in England during Finney's lifetime. The book was translated into French, German, and Welsh, and in 1868 Finney edited a revised *Lectures on Revivals*, leaving it essentially unchanged.[5]

The book provided a complete guide to organizing and conducting a revival, giving practical advice culled from Finney's great experience. He advocated preaching in a conversational style to reach people at their level, discussed the appropriate use of gestures, staunchly defended his "New Measures." The whole procedure, said Finney, must be aimed at bringing the sinner to the highest possible level of anxiety before the release of conversion.[6] *Lectures on Revivals of Religion* contained as well the activist philosophy that made such a significant imprint on antebellum society. Here was the call to action that was so important an aspect of early-nineteenth-century evangelism. Religion was something to do, not something to wait for. One must make choices and take action. Finney's book was clearly the most important instruction book on revivals of the nineteenth century.

A year later the Rev. Thomas H. Skinner, a Philadelphia Presbyterian of the New School persuasion brought out a new book, *Thoughts on Evangelizing the World*, which was widely read in Philadelphia.[7] Co-pastor with Dr. Janeway in the Second Presbyterian Church of Philadelphia, Dr. Skinner by 1816 had begun to have differences with his colleague. Skinner's New School views clashed with Dr. Janeway's Old School tendencies. In that year Skinner with seventy of his parishioners withdrew and formed the Fifth Presbyterian Church of Philadelphia. Dr. Skinner led his church into numerous and powerful revivals.[8] *Thoughts on Evangelizing the World* defended zeal in spreading the Gospel, although Skinner advised zeal with discretion. But lukewarmness was a greater danger: "It is an active age and much as we should lament the extravagances of a few in the church, the apathy of the many is a thousand-fold more to be deplored."[9] In later years, Skinner was to withdraw his support from revivals, but in the 1830s and 1840s he was an ardent advocate of revivalism.[10]

In 1849 the Rev. James Porter, a minister in Cabotville, Massachusetts, published *Revivals of Religion: Their Theory, Means, Obstructions, Uses, and Importance*.[11] Porter leaned heavily on Finney, quoting his *Lectures on Revivals of Religion* with great frequency.[12] This handbook reiterated Finney's instructions on revivals. Like Finney, Porter attacked cold formality in religion and defended emotional enthusiasm as a necessary attribute of revivals. He advocated a great deal of storytelling on the part of the revivalist, with illustrations drawn from common life. Any diversion hindered revivals, said Porter, be it war, pestilence, or a contention in the church. "For this reason, we have been constrained to regret the return of the season for lyceums and other lectures and exhibitions. Such attractions are the signal of retreat from the house of God."[13] Porter emphasized an activist spirit. Young converts must be set to work converting others. "An idle Christian, is a paradox."[14] Through the revival handbooks, then, the "New Measures" became standard revival procedure. By the 1850s a vast literature of pamphlets and books on the subject showed that revivals had indeed become a part of the repertory of American church life.

As the revival handbook provided the instructions for generations of evangelists, the voluntary societies that grew out of the revivals provided the instruments for achieving their goals. A network of interdenominational voluntary societies proliferated in the decades before the Civil War, energized by the millennial view and the activist philosophy inherent in revivalism. These societies were part of the religious structure and yet apart from it. They provided an ancillary service in an area where many denominations could forget doctrinal differences and cooperate with each other. Thus the religious impulse was channeled into dozens of organizations, often interlocking in membership, leadership, and objectives. There were three basic types of societies: those devoted to issues of public or private morality, such as temperance and antislavery; societies charitable in goal, such as those to care for orphans, school the needy, reclaim wayward women; finally, those devoted to specific religious needs, such as maintaining the Sabbath, distributing tracts, and converting sinners, lapsed Christians, and Jews. Even the first two categories, however, were aimed at reclaiming men's souls, for to champion the inherent rights of the slave or the orphan was of no avail unless he was saved and entered the Christian life. Thus an army of evangelicals, armed with buoyant optimism, addressed itself to reforming man in preparation for God's reign on earth. It was an enterprise worthy of the dream.

In Philadelphia the societies developed in the same interdenominational pattern as elsewhere. The American Sunday School Union in Philadelphia was organized in 1824.[15] The Pennsylvania Bible Society was organized in 1808 and incorporated two years later on January 10, 1810, as the Bible Society of Philadelphia, attempting to place a Bible in every Pennsylvania home in three years. On January 10, 1828, a society of young men was instituted for the purpose of supplying every family in the city that had none with a copy of the Holy Bible. Some two months later, by the 28th of February, they reported that 2,412 Bibles had been distributed, and the work was accomplished.[16] The PhiladelphiaTract Society began in 1815 when an organization composed largely of Presbyterians worked for a few years, and in 1824 it became an auxiliary of the American Tract Society.

The tract was a short, usually dogmatic, persuasively written leaflet that was distributed as widely as possible. Costs were met by donations from members of the society as well as other interested parties, and commission agents were sent out to distribute the tracts. Tracts became the conventional means for extending religion by way of the printed word. Members of the society who were involved in distributing them visited prisons, saloons, police stations, firemen's and seamen's boarding houses. They were often insulted and jeered at, but they were not dissuaded. They also visited families of Jews and Roman Catholics in an effort to convert them. The Orphans Society, organized March 20, 1814, by ladies connected with the Second Presbyterian Church, sought to provide sustenance, both physical and spiritual, to Philadelphia orphans. The Philadelphia Soup Society was operating in 1818 at 20 Springett's Alley, providing soup daily for the poor. The Seamen's Society, established first in New York in 1816, was followed by a Philadelphia branch in 1819. It was led by Joseph Eastburn, an evangelical noted for his labors for the insane in jails and almshouses, but who soon concentrated his energies in the Mariners Church of Philadelphia.[17] Missionary work among the Jews was a part of the reforms pursued by evangelical Christians. The Society for Meliorating the Condition of the Jews was established in New York in 1820 and found its way to Philadelphia in 1823.[18] While evangelists were not the only participants in this myriad of organizations, the societies were heavily supported by evangelical ministers and church people and received their most consistent financing from them. In these organizations the converts of the great revivals found an outlet for their abundant energies.[19]

Revivals and temperance went hand in hand, giving the temperance movement its peculiar intensity. Most revivalists favored not moderation in drinking, but total abstinence, and the temperance movement soon began moving toward that goal in dealing with the problem of alcohol. Americans had long been a hard-drinking people, and many Americans were concerned with the effect of this habit. In addition to the real problem of drinking, temperance became the symbol for a life style that was becoming increasingly threatened by changes in American society. But abstinence was not the established custom even among the early sects. While Wesley had decreed abstinence among Methodists, they had often been lax, and until 1810 or thereabouts, liquor was served at ministerial ordinations and meetings of the congregation. Presbyterians, rarely as restrictive as Methodists, had done the same. Quakers had early taken a stand against the widespread custom of drinking. The Episcopalians were divided along the lines of evangelical and high church people, while Lutherans, Unitarians, and Universalists provided no leadership to temperance reform. The increasing sentiment for total abstinence paralleled the burst of revivalism in the early nineteenth century. In spite of the fact that it lacked biblical example, the Bible and Christ himself being examples to the contrary, abstinence was pressed as the goal of temperance reformers. Such an approach was consistent with the mind-set of revivalism. Life was seen in sets of alternatives: one was destined for either heaven or hell, one was either saved or damned, one either drank or abstained. There was no place in the framework of the evangelical mind for a middle ground. Almost without exception, revival preachers and itinerant revivalists favored abstinence. Charles G. Finney insisted upon total abstinence. Jacob Knapp, the Baptist revivalist, attacked liquor interests and drinking with a vengeance.

In Philadelphia the Reverend Albert Barnes provides a good example of the evangelical attitude toward drinking. He drank neither hard liquor nor wine. "I early embraced, in the most rigid form, personally and with great respect to my preaching, the great principle of the temperance reformation—that of entire abstinence from all intoxicating beverages," he reported.[20] He felt drinking to be the prime cause of pauperism. The community, he felt, was forced to support

> ninety-nine out of every hundred of whom are made paupers by the direct or indirect influence of intoxication; to pay the expenses of building prisons, and conducting the business of the courts, and supporting convicts for burglary, arson, brawls and manslaughter, nine cases out of every ten of which are produced by intemperance.[21]

Since he felt intemperance to be the cause of nearly all the evils of society, he preached often and vociferously on temperance. He was active in the Pennsylvania Temperance Society and was one of the first to favor prohibitory legislation.

In addition to Barnes, Philadelphia's leading revivalist minister, James Patterson, spoke frequently on intemperance, and when the old Northern Liberties Temperance Society split over the question of drinking wine, Patterson was among those who formed the Union Total Abstinence Society of Northern Liberties.[22] The Reverend Stephen H. Tyng, leader of the evangelical branch of the Episcopalians and an ardent revivalist, was extremely active in temperance work. There was a complex network of relationships among these reformers and their organizations. Many were involved in multiple causes, and many organizations shared the work of sister organizations. Tract societies were used for temperance messages. The Reverend George Boyd was active both in temperance and the American Society to Meliorate the Condition of the Jews, the primary organization aimed at converting Jews. The Reverend John Chambers, who held one of the first prayer meetings in Philadelphia, was active in temperance work.[23] The Reverend Charles Hoover of the First Presbyterian Church of Southwark also combined revivalism with temperance work. Indeed, meetings of the American Temperance Society began with a prayer and the entire proceedings had a decidedly religious flavor. Heavily evangelical in flavor, this society soon veered toward total abstinence.[24]

Temperance reformers, bred in revivalistic zeal, had few scruples about resorting to coercive measures. Arthur Tappan, New York philanthropist who was active in the abolition movement, was a warm believer in revivalism, often attending prayer meetings nightly. He insisted that his clerks attend such meetings twice a week and regular services twice on Sunday. On Monday morning they had to report which church they attended, the name of the clergyman, and the texts used.[25] If mild inducements failed, coercive measures were used. Arthur and his brother Lewis organized Christian spy cells to watch tavern keepers and other dispensers of pleasure, and report the infractions of long-ignored city ordinances to city authorities.[26]

It was abolitionism, however, that soon became the keystone of the vast cluster of reforms and dominated all other reforms until the Civil War. In Philadelphia evangelical abolitionism developed alongside the earlier Quaker abolitionism. The first abolition society in Philadelphia dates back to 1775. It was called "The Society for the Relief of Free Negroes Unlawfully Held in Bondage," and it met at the Sun Tavern on 2nd Street. Many, probably most, were Friends. It was reorganized in 1784 with Benjamin Franklin as president and Benjamin Rush as secretary.[27] Quakers, from the early days of George Fox, were interested in antislavery reform, and Philadelphia Quakers expressed this attitude early and clearly. But in the nineteenth century a new stream of influence was added to Philadelphia abolitionism—the evangelists of the revivals. The American Anti-Slavery Society was formed in Philadelphia on December 4, 1833. Arthur Tappan was elected president and 12 of the 56 representatives were evangelical ministers and the rest evangelical members.[28] Five months later the Philadelphia Anti-Slavery Society was organized, composed almost entirely of Friends.[29] Philadelphia abolitionism, then, contained the diverse currents of Quaker abolitionism and evangelical reform.

Charles Finney had been opposed to slavery since he was a young man, possibly from his connection with his theological mentor, George Gale, who was a strong opponent of slavery. In 1834 Finney excluded slaveholders from communion at his Chatham Street Chapel.[30] His followers became avid antislavery men, although in later years Finney moderated his antislavery views in favor of revivalism, urging his students to place abolitionism secondary to revivalism.[31] James Patterson, the revivalist minister of the First Presbyterian Church of Northern

Liberties, was an open opponent of slavery, as was Albert Barnes, the Presbyterian New Schooler. In Philadelphia the evangelical reformers enlarged the earlier Quaker abolitionism, giving it a new strength and intensity.

Evangelical reform in all its variety was shaped and nourished by the millennial vision of a world peopled by Christians, making ready for Christ's reign on earth. All was possible if men were converted and lived a Christian life. There were no insoluble problems, no structural inequalities, no political evils that honesty, piety, and temperate living could not solve. The individual was the heart and core of evangelical reform, and it was this emphasis that gave it its peculiar strength and its inherent weakness. Private morality became the key to all reform. Charles C. Cole in *The Social Ideas of the Northern Evangelists* described the conservatism of the northern evangelists.[32] Charles G. Finney expressed this conservatism very succinctly. He condemned personal vices like card-playing, drinking, and theatergoing, but his zeal for personal piety blinded him to more complex problems. In politics, he decreed: "Christians must vote for honest men, and take consistent ground in politics or the Lord will curse them . . . ."[33] He warned against voting for a man because he belonged to the same party, was for or against the Bank of the United States, or was a Jackson man or not. Instead, one must ask: is he honest, upright, fit to be trusted? "They must let the world see that the church will uphold no man in office who is known to be a knave, or an adulterer, or a Sabbath breaker, or a Gambler."[34] To Finney, idleness was sinful; man's station in life was proscribed by God, and he must cheerfully submit to his lot, even if that lot was poverty.[35] He opposed poor relief, he did not support limitation of child labor, and he felt that the eight-hour law was psychologically, economically, and socially absurd and would bring evil to the world.[36] He opposed any union or labor on the grounds that unions channeled workers' energy away from their jobs and more devout pursuits. Strikes, of course, were anathema. Every issue was seen in terms of personal piety and morality, and the broader problems of society and social change were simply not perceived.

In Philadelphia this conservatism of Finney was matched by the conservatism of revivalist ministers. Patterson opposed poor laws on the grounds that intemperance was the real cause of poverty; Barnes was sure that nine-tenths of all crime was due to intoxication. In Philadelphia, as in the nation, revivalists engaged earnestly and hopefully in what they conceived to be reform, certain that with man's regeneration would come regeneration of the world.

6

The Sectarian Response

The reception accorded revivalism by the various Protestant denominations was neither unanimous nor unreserved, but the thrust was toward a recognition of revivals as an accepted means of grace. Denominations responded in terms of several factors—social class, age, and strength of historical tradition. Often it was a simple matter, like the language in which the religious service was conducted, that determined the vulnerability to revivals. Sometimes it was clerical leadership that determined the way in which the denomination would react. But as decade followed decade, although the fever of revivals subsided, the revivals were transformed from "New Measures" into conventional measures.

Methodism in Philadelphia had foundations stretching back to the coming of George Whitefield to the city in 1739, when Whitefield had preached to great crowds in the Society Hill area at Front and Pine Streets. For three nights successively the great revivalist preached on the Court house steps and later from the balcony of a house on Second Street. As a result of these labors, a dancing school and concert room were shut as inconsistent with the Gospel.[1]

Organized Methodism, of course, was an outgrowth of the Protestant Episcopal Church, earlier the Church of England. Early Methodists remained within the Episcopal church, while holding prayer meetings with like-minded members. Theirs was a reaction against ritual and form, an attempt to reemotionalize religious worship. In Philadelphia, Methodism began in 1767 with the founding of the John Street and St. George's Societies.

The Methodist tradition was warmly responsive to revivalism; indeed, many felt that Methodists started revivalism. This denomination, with its emotional approach, its Arminian theology, its antipathy to educated ministers, and its circuit preacher, had been dominant in the camp meetings of the West. Charles Grandison Finney had often expressed admiration of the "ignorant Methodist circuit rider" for his effectiveness, and had drawn extensively from Methodist theology and style.[2] In this denomination, the distinction between the itinerant preacher and the minister who was settled into a congregation was blurred, for ministers often alternated a settled ministry with a circuit. All early nineteenth-century Methodist churches had free seats and appealed generally to plain people of small means. Ministers used revival techniques routinely, but there were also periodic revivals wherein a single church showed a large number of converts. Jacob Gruber, the minister of St. George's Methodist Church, the major Methodist church in Philadelphia, had traveled several circuits before being assigned to St. George's in 1828, where he worked with three other ministers to bring spiritual sustenance to Philadelphia Methodists. Presbyterian revivals met with his scorn for their borrowing of Methodist forms:

> The Presbyterians in this country have sacrament meetings, anxious meetings, and anxious seats. Some who have been at them say they carry on their meetings just like the Methodists . . . . Why they preach Methodist doc-

trine, then they invite anxious persons to come and sit down on the anxious seats; then someone speaks to them; then some sing; then one stands up and prays, while the anxious persons sit on the anxious seats. So this is just like the Methodist plan as much as an ape is just like a man. I do not like nicknames; everything should be called by its proper name.[3]

Philadelphia was constantly worked over by Methodist itinerants, many of them lost in historical oblivion. A few, however, remain visible. The Reverend James Caughey, an eminent Methodist revivalist, had fruitful campaigns in Philadelphia. His tours usually began in the autumn and continued to April or May, the extreme heat of Philadelphia summers compelling him to refrain from revivals in that season. He was a volatile speaker, rising to heights of eloquence under the pressure of animosity, which his preaching sometimes caused. The Rev. Caughey was committed to itinerant revivalism, "In one revival of religion, a man will learn better how to preach the truths of Christianity in such a manner as will awaken and convert men than he could in many years close study in connection with his ordinary ministry."[4]

John Newland Maffitt was another Methodist itinerant revivalist who worked over the cities of the East. Maffitt had burst upon the country in 1822. Born in Dublin, Ireland, in 1794 into the established church, he was drawn to the Methodist party in the church for its warmth of spirit and rejection of ritual. His parents were people of wealth and he was educated at Trinity College in Dublin. A revival in Dublin brought about a cataclysmic conversion and opened the way for the exercise of his gifts. He came to America, settled in North Carolina, and in 1822 became an itinerant preacher. A handsome man, strongly emotional in nature, and with a powerfully melodramatic style, he traveled as an itinerant preacher for ten years. He was in constant demand, and large audiences thronged to hear him. He spoke in Philadelphia, at the crowded Salem Street Church in New York to 3,000 people, and in Washington, D.C., where he had to be lifted into the building through a window over the heads of the waiting crowd.[5] In 1841 Maffitt reached the pinnacle of his career, being elected chaplain of the House of Representatives. It was a highlight in a life dedicated to revivalism.

Philadelphia Baptists, having gone through the bitter disputes of the "period of contention," settled into an acceptance of revivalism. In general, Baptists and Methodists represented less-well-educated and poorer churchgoers than did the Presbyterians and Episcopalians. Although a stubborn minority resisted, revivals came to be regarded as among the established means of grace.[6] Revivalists Jabez Swan and Jacob Knapp kept revivals activated for fifty years. Both had to fight fears of "New Measures," and both freely gave credit to Charles G. Finney for teaching the Baptists to "discern the connection between the means and the end" in religion.[7]

Jacob Knapp was perhaps the first Baptist in the Northern states to devote himself exclusively to the work of conducting protracted meetings. He was born in Otsego County, New York, on December 7, 1799, of Episcopalian parents. As a youth, he tells us, he experienced much anxiety over the future welfare of his soul, and spent much time in secret prayer. He was licensed to preach and spent the next three years at the Literary and Theological Institution at Hamilton, New York. In the 1830s, the New Measures had entered the Baptist churches, although they were viewed with distrust. Knapp was one of the earliest Baptists to champion revivals. After eight years in two settled pastorates, he took his first tour in the autumn of 1833 and worked until his death in 1874. Knapp paid homage to Charles Finney, who he felt had broken up the set forms and stereotyped prayers that had characterized the Presbyterian congregations and other established churches.[8] His entry into the ranks of the itinerant revivalists he felt to be an important step: "I felt that I was entering upon a path that had not been trodden before me."[9] He was to be followed by other Baptists: Jabez Swan, A. C. Kingsley, and Lewis Raymond, among others. Knapp's preaching met with great success. He was a short, plump man with a thundering voice, who often pounded his fists on the pulpit. He had few educational advantages, and spoke in an ungrammatical style, especially in moments of excitement, but his knowledge of the Scriptures was immense. His preaching was coarse and severe, but said to be enormously effective.[10] Like other revivalists, Knapp was involved in many of the moral reforms of his time. An avowed antislavery man, he often spoke out against slavery. He was a pioneer in the temperance movement, and an officer in several temperance organizations. His concern with private habits of morality was characteristic of revivalists. "Tobacco," he felt, "softens the brain, weakens the intellect, enfeebles the body, vitiates the appetite, and hurries its victim to the grave."[11] He inveighed against light reading as a "waste of time," in that it weakened the mental powers, gave a false view of life and created distaste for the matter-of-fact duties and realities. He thus concluded that " . . . the practice of reading novels was a serious hindrance to growth in grace."[12] So strong were his views on inappropriate literature that, when he closed his meeting in the Baptist Tabernacle in New York City he said, "I called upon the congregation to bring together all their novels and other pernicious books. A great heap of books was collected, which for once were made useful in furnishing material for a brilliant bonfire."[13] One can but wonder what was the nature of the "other" pernicious books!

To Knapp, poverty and distress were evidence of the hand of God punishing men for impiety.

There are many thousands who never understand that
all their stripes come from God, their rightful owner . . .
when God chastises us, and lays his rod upon us; when we
find sickness and death entering our families and we are
compelled to sustain heavy losses in our fortunes; when
He is thus dealing with us to make us wiser and better,
how many of us fail to see God, to hear his voice, and to
recognize him in all his dealings with us.[14]

Unfortunate events, however, marred his revivals. His
habit of publicly singling out individuals as sinners caused
enormous dissension. In January 1839 in Rochester, New
York, he "felt it his duty to make known to the public, facts
which had been disclosed to him about moral shortcomings
of members of the congregation." As a result of this public
vilification, the meeting was broken up by violence, and
Knapp was attacked and forced to retreat hastily. He failed
to appear at the trial, and the matter was allowed to die.[15]
Another such incident in Providence, Rhode Island,
brought suit for defamation of character from the pulpit.
Knapp evaded police who came to church to arrest him, and
when he was finally arrested, his bail was paid by several
Baptist and Congregational members. Again, in 1841 in
New Haven, Connecticut, a disastrous meeting ended with
a mob threatening his life. Knapp never succeeded in quiet-
ing suspicions about his character, and he seldom ventured
into New England again, but he was able to continue his
work elsewhere.

Knapp worked in Philadelphia later in his career. In 1865
he came to the Bethel Baptist Church in Philadelphia to
work with the Reverend J. M. Perry. It was a small congregation, many of whom were involved in naval activities and
stayed away for extended periods of time. Knapp termed it
a "floating church," its members to be found in every part of
the globe, but some of them remained always on land and
attended Knapp's meetings. He preached at Bethel for five
weeks, during which time 75 persons wers baptized, and

after he left, the work continued under the guidance of the minister until nearly 200 converts were added to the church.[16] Later, in December of 1865, he started a revival at the Fourth Baptist Church in Philadelphia, under the Reverend R. Jeffery. Here he preached for seven weeks, every night at 7:30, and included a prayer meeting both before and after the sermon. During this time, 93 persons were added to the church, and after he left, the work continued until "200 souls were converted and added to the church."[17] But Knapp, like other revivalists, was disappointed in Philadelphia:

> When I came to Philadelphia, I was strongly in hopes that the way would be opened for my remaining until the whole city was raised up, and at least twenty thousand souls were converted. But I found the people of Philadelphia slow to move, tenacious of their own way of doing things, and satisfied to trudge along in the way their fathers trod . . . . Some other of the churches talked somewhat of asking me to visit them but were so long in coming to a decision that I was unable to wait their movements.[18]

Knapp worked in revivals all his life. By the 1860s he felt that revivals were "an established means of grace; and in numerous instances, the conducting of them is considered among the regular services of the pastor, and his own acceptability, in great measure, is determined by his success in carrying them on."[19]

Another prominent Baptist revivalist, Jabez S. Swan, was noteworthy for the emotional zeal of his revivals. Born in Stonington, Connecticut, in 1800, he was the son of a Baptist deacon's daughter, who was noted for her exhortations and singing at church. He was converted at age 21 in a highly emotional experience, amidst an all-night thunderstorm.[20] He prepared himself for the ministry at Hamilton College. Although he was more cultivated than some revivalists, the news of Swan's emotional revivals spread. He was active primarily in New England and New York State, but wherever he went there was a continued series of revivals. Swan preached that baptism by immersion was the only door to the visible church. Those who believed but had not been baptized were on dangerous middle ground.[21] Baptists, then, despite dissent, became increasingly involved with revivalism, and for many Baptists revivals were an established part of their religious experience.

The response of the Episcopal Church in Philadelphia to the revivalism of the Second Great Awakening was a bifurcated one, reflecting the dichotomy that Episcopalianism had long contained. That denomination had long been accustomed to a "low-church" party within its midst and had accommodated itself to such differences. John Wesley had begun his ministry as a high churchman in the Episcopal Church, and never officially left that church. His beliefs in sudden conversion as the starting point in religious life, in emotional preaching, and in less ritual formed the basis of the Methodist development, and in America most Wesleyans became members of the Methodist Church, but some remained within the Episcopal Church to form an influential group, the Evangelicals or the low-church party. The Evangelicals of the Episcopal Church accepted the new measures and utilized prayer meetings and emotional preaching. They tended to resemble other evangelical denominations in morals, condemning all forms of self-indulgence and looking with disapproval upon all of the lighter social amusements such as dancing, card-playing, and theatergoing. They differed in degree rather than in kind from the evangelical denominations, because they were always sensitive to criticism from the high-church party. Their emotionalism was thus inhibited. For this reason, and because class differences made them uncomfortable with other denominations, Episcopalian evangelicals generally held their own revivals and were not willing to

join in interdenominational revival services.[22] Episcopal
Evangelicals were more likely than high churchmen to participate in reform movements. They championed the temperance movement in its earlier voluntary phase, withdraw-
ing as it moved on to legal prohibition. They were more
active in tract societies, Sunday School unions, missionary
societies, and the interdenominational Bible societies that
developed out of the Second Great Awakening.

The high-church party looked to gradual development
of the Christian, rather than sudden coversion, as the pref-
erable pattern for religious growth. While their moral outlook was by no means lax, they were disposed to be more
tolerant of the social amusements on which evangelicals
frowned. A liturgy, they felt, was necessary to prevent improper and unguarded language before God and to ensure
correct doctrine. "Worship should be both holy and beautiful," stated the *Protestant Episcopalian and Church Register*,
the official organ of the church.[23]

In Pennsylvania in the early decades of the nineteenth
century, high churchmen and evangelicals were more
nearly balanced than elsewhere, and the conflict was
sharper. In Philadelphia, the same situation held true. The
six Episcopal churches in the city were overseen by Bishop
William White, who had become Presiding Bishop in 1795,
and continued as such until his death in 1836 at the age of
89. A prominent churchman, Bishop White founded the
Episcopal Academy in 1785 and the Missionary Society in
1816, and he sponsored the Reverend Absalom Jones as
head of the first Negro Episcopalian congregation. He was
a high churchman, yet he trod the conciliatory path that
enabled both parties to coexist while differences persisted.
The openness with which evangelicals in his church discussed their spiritual experience conflicted with his habitual
reticence on all private matters, and the freedom with
which some of them introduced extemporaneous prayers
into the services of the church offended his sense of order.

He was attached to the institutions of the church and critical of any serious breach of church canons. To those who defended certain violations with the plea of piety, he replied that piety that led to disorder must be mixed with a serious amount of error, adding, " . . . where piety of any sort is the motive: . . . in the greater number of instances falling under my observation, I have been compelled to ascribe it to mere vanity and the exaltation of self."[24] On the other hand, he was willing to accept association meetings similar to the protracted revivals of other denominations, providing care was taken to violate no law of the Church in the conduct of them.

The Protestant Episcopalian and Church Register, however, took the high-church stand, ridiculing the proceedings at revivals:

> At an "anxious" or "inquiry" meeting, they can measure their spiritual growth with much apparent meekness, and confess the vileness of their nature and the enormity of their sins, with much real pride; and while they are calling themselves worms, they mean all the time that they are the "chosen of God's creatures."[25]

Vanity was the cause of these feverished activities, as well as love of excitement and a feeling that incessant attendance at religious meetings will atone for other negligence and weaknesses. An evangelical woman takes all her religion to church and lets her own house burn "while she is dissolving in tears at some shocking story about the Hindoo [*sic*] widows who burn themselves."[26]

Among the Philadelphia Episcopal churches most involved with revivals was St. Paul's Protestant Episcopal Church at 225 S. Third St. The church had been started by followers of the Rev. William McClennachan, a disciple of George Whitefield.[27] Its minister was an uncompromising Evangelical divine, the Reverend Stephen Tyng. Born in Massachusetts in 1800 and a graduate of Harvard, the

Reverend Tyng studied theology at Andover, and was ordained into the Protestant Episcopal Church in 1821. In 1829 he came to St. Paul's. A tall, dignified man with a massive brow and well-chosen, graceful movements, he was nearly as independent an Episcopalian as could be imagined. He felt rituals necessary to proclaim the Gospel, yet he allowed, even encouraged, the offering of testimony at the prayer meetings that he introduced to Philadelphia Episcopalianism. While St. Paul's had always been an evangelical parish, there was a high-church minority that had vigorously opposed Tyng's election in 1829, and they even posted placards against him in the church when he arrived.[28] Nevertheless, in 1831 he held a revival that counted among the converts both old and young and some of the best educated in the congregation.[29] For two years he held daily prayer meetings at 6 A.M. and soon became one of the national leaders of the evangelical party within this denomination.

Another flourishing Evangelical church was known as the Church of the Evangelists, on Catherine Street between 7th and 8th (later sold to Samuel S. Fleisher, a Philadelphia art collector who established an art school and collection). But evangelicals existed in every Episcopalian church, causing a certain amount of friction. By the middle of the nineteenth century, conflict diminished as Episcopalianism came to be almost exclusively an urban upper-class denomination, and the lower classes drifted into Methodism or other denominations.[30]

Philadelphia Quakerism did not remain untouched by the evangelical waves that swept over Philadelphia during the early decades of the century. Its response to revivalism was intimately connected with what is considered by Friends as the greatest tragedy in American Quakerism—the Hicksite or Great Separation of 1827-28.

Early Quakerism had been born out of a "mighty protest of the soul," against turning religion from a personal experience into a ritual. English Quakers had rejected the ritual and doctrine that had developed in the English church and that were pronounced necessary for salvation. It was a double rejection, for English craftsmen, yeoman farmers, and servants turned against a church that reflected the class structure of English life. Quakers, in sect fashion, were rigid in their moral strictures, and in their attitude toward levity and display, drunkenness, and all the sins of the lower classes. George Fox's Quakerism emphasized individual experience, the "Inner Light," as the source of all revelation. It was this Inner Light that liberated Quakers from the established church of the day. One tends to forget that seventeenth-century Quakerism had been boisterous, enthusiastic, even fanatic in its stance toward established religion. But by the time of the Great Awakening in America in the eighteenth century, the Quaker movement was nearly a century old, and had left behind the extravagances of its earlier period. It had matured into a less prophetic ministry, and its aggressive spirit had softened into an inward-looking piety. Doctrine had crept into Quaker thought to correct the anarchic tendencies inherent in the Inner Light. Quakerism had become socially acceptable; the sect had become a church. Consequently in 1739, when George Whitefield, the itinerant revivalist, spoke in Philadelphia, Quakers watched with tolerant amusement the religious antics of evangelistic revivals. Whitefield, on the other hand, was shocked at Quaker concern with the Christ within almost to the exclusion of the historic Christ.[31]

There is no evidence that any significant number of Friends were torn away from their traditional moorings. The records of the Philadelphia Monthly Meeting between Whitefield's arrival and June of 1743 show only five people dealt with for joining other societies in their way of worship.[32]

But by the early nineteenth century, Quakers had moved further into conformity with American life and into the patterns of an established institution. Consequently,

Quakerism felt the impulse of the revivalism that had been infecting other denominations, and this conformity with American religious developments caused a new eruption of those who rejected the compromises that institutionalization involves. The Hicksite Separation, occurring in Philadelphia at approximately the same time Charles Finney was there, represents the divergence of two basic themes in Quaker thought: personal experience or the "Inner Light" as opposed to doctrine or Scripture.[33] Quakerism had contained these two tendencies and the ambivalence therein had given Quakerism a strength and resiliency. But matters came to a crisis in 1828, and the Society of Friends was unable to contain the two divergent streams. Orthodox Quakers, more urban and better educated (in Philadelphia, the majority of Quakers were orthodox), saw the dangers inherent in the Inner Light and defended the institution of the church and of tradition. The Hicksites, followers of Elias Hicks, resisted the institutionalization of Quakerism and looked to the Inner Light as the ultimate authority. The Bible was relegated to a subordinate place, as was Jesus. For Hicksites, Jesus was a model man who lived in Palestine at a definite date, a Jew who brought to culmination the work of the Prophets of Israel. But this historic, outward Jesus was not the Savior. The inner spirit in Jesus was the Christ; Jesus was different from other men in that the eternal Christ was in him to a greater degree than in other men. Hicks rejected original sin: every new-born soul starts clean from the hands of God and each person is responsible for his own failures and shortcomings as determined by the Inner Light. Hicks opposed studied preaching and placed little value on education: "A great deal of learning is rather a hindrance than a help."[34]

The Hicksites, strongest in rural areas and among poorer Quakers, rejected the evangelism that pervaded the religious establishment of the day.[35] Orthodox Quakers, more often richer, better educated, and city bred, were more involved in revivalism. They had grown by now from a sect into an institution, and were conforming with religious currents about them.[36] It was an anomalous twist: revivalism generally undermined doctrine and emphasized personal experience. Instead, in Quakerism, revivalism and doctrine went hand in hand. There was yet another difference: revivalism was generally bred in rural areas and was less acceptable to urban dwellers. Yet it was the urban Quakers who accepted revivalism more readily than the rural Hicksites.

The separation was precipitated by a visit of English Quakers to America in the autumn of 1826. Thomas Shillitoe, an outstanding English evangelist, preached doctrine over Inner Light, and was the foremost opponent of Hicks. The parties drew further and further apart, the crisis coming in the yearly meeting of 1827 in an attempt to decide on a clerk, between John Comley, a Hicksite, and Samuel Beetle, an orthodox Quaker. According to Quaker practice, no votes were taken, but the unity sought could not be reached, and in tumultuous disorder the parties polarized. What happened at Philadelphia was only the beginning of a widespread movement, and there were stormy separations in New York, Ohio, Indiana, and elsewhere. Each group claimed to be primitive Quakerism, the genuine, unalloyed Christianity. Many Hicksites, alienated from their meetings, joined the Unitarians, and by 1830 the Unitarians had enjoyed a strengthening and enlarging of their denomination as a result of the Hicksite separation.[37]

Revivalists were active among orthodox Quakers, and there were some notable examples of itinerant revivalists in this denomination. It was among Quakers that women evangelists were most often found. Since there was no paid ministry among Quakers, women as well as men were duty bound, when the spirit urged them, to rise up in meeting to "instruct, exhort, convince or console."[38] Women's souls were considered equal with men's in the eyes of God. The prohibition against women's preaching came from Paul, who commanded women to keep silent in church, and, if they wanted to know anything, to ask their husbands at home. But Joseph John Gurney, evangelist and husband of a well-known woman evangelist, Eliza Paul Gurney, expressed the Quaker position. He stated that women or men preachers are not in themselves important, but are instruments of the Holy Spirit, and thus women who speak in meeting assume no personal authority over others. "Friends believe it right, freely and EQUALLY, to allow the ministry of both sexes."[39]

Eliza Paul Gurney, the best-known Quaker woman revivalist, was born Eliza Paul Kirkbride in 1801 into the conservatism of Philadelphia Quakerism. She suffered the death of her mother and father while a young child, attended Westtown School (then called Weston), and made her home among various members of her family. It was a lonely girlhood, but in 1830 she met the English couple Jonathan and Hannah C. Backhouse, in America on a Gospel mission. Eliza Kirkbride worked with them for five years in Canada and America, forming a deep and lifelong attachment to them. She accompanied them on a religious journey to England in 1836, where she met Joseph John Gurney, an evangelical from a highly cultured and influential family, a family noted for its piety. He returned to America with her in 1837. By 1838, on October 7, Eliza P. Kirkbride appeared as a minister in her own meeting in Philadelphia, beginning her long ministry. Her marriage to Joseph John Gurney in 1841 lasted until his death six years later, and Eliza Gurney, with ample means at her disposal, traveled and preached throughout the Philadelphia and New Jersey areas.[40] Her ministry was characterized by clear exposition of the Gospel truth and by a direct appeal to the emotions.[41] She seldom spoke at great length, but always with great dignity and solemnity of manner. Her sermons were especially attractive to the young. Eliza Gurney shunned controversy, and she circumvented points that would create it, as well as all radical views in doctrine or church polity. "Extremes," she wrote, "are painful and oppressive to me, be they on which side they may. I prefer the middle . . . way."[42] Eliza Gurney settled in Burlington, New Jersey but, disliking the New Jersey summers, she built a large cottage in Atlantic City where grew an important Friends meeting, attracting gay and fashionable visitors from various hotels. She enjoyed a 42-year ministry, and became a well-known speaker among Friends and among other denominations as well.

In later years, another Quaker woman revivalist, Sarah Smiley, traveled and preached to Methodists, Baptists, Congregationalists, and Presbyterians, as well as her own Quakers.[43] She worked in Boston, New Haven, Westchester, Rochester, and Philadelphia. In 1866 she was recorded as a minister and she preached the faith with great vigor and enthusiasm. In 1872 she withdrew from the Friends and received water baptism in New York, without, however, joining any other denomination. Eliza Gurney and Sarah Smiley are examples of itinerant revivalists among the orthodox Quakers. Philadelphia Quakerism, although it may have been distinguished by the most fashionable people in Philadelphia and although its customary service was in the traditional, hushed atmosphere we know today, by mid-nineteenth century had incorporated some of the attributes of evangelical revivalism, with occasional revivals that had strong sermons, much tear-shedding, and highly emotional meetings.[44]

Philadelphia and Germantown Lutherans experienced revivalism in the early nineteenth century, both of the pastor-led type and the more spectacular itinerant revivalist meetings. The mass German immigration in America that started in the 1730s swelled the earlier Dutch and Swedish Lutheran population. Arriving in great numbers through the port of Philadelphia, most German Lutherans pushed into the interior of Pennsylvania, but Philadelphia had a sizeable Lutheran population. Heinrich (Henry) M. Muhlenberg, the able colonial leader of the Lutheran church in America, organized Philadelphia Lutheran churches. Arriving during the Great Awakening, he was sympathetic to George Whitefield's pietistic intensity, and he carried ths revival spirit to his non-English-speaking congregations who otherwise would have been isolated from the movement. In his journal he wrote of "old Father [Gilbert] Tennent," whose sermons he appreciated, and George Whitefield, whom he greatly admired.[45]

As with the Germans in the Reformed Church, however, the language barrier kept Lutheran congregations aloof from the evangelical movement. There was, as well, a conservatism in doctrine and practice that looked askance at the new measures. But Lutherans were not long able to resist the momentum of revivalism. They were, after all, heirs to the seventeenth-century pietistic movement in Germany, and the inward-looking piety of the revivals was congenial to their mind-set. Large numbers of Lutherans participated in the extravagances of the camp meetings. The frontier was a lonely and isolated existence, and camp meetings provided a joyous release. In the cities, more resistance was met among Lutherans, and, as in the German Reformed Church, it was connected with language problems. The desire among some to abandon the mother tongue alienated many Lutherans who felt that the German language was the bulwark of their faith. There were persistent efforts to hold services in English, supported, as in the German Reformed Church, by many of the younger people. In frustration over their inability to have English used in church, many were driven into Methodist, Presbyterian, and Episcopalian churches. In Philadelphia the parties were equally divided, and the annual election of officers caused great tensions between the two sides. In 1806 an

English-speaking group withdrew from their church and founded St. John's, the first exclusively English-speaking Lutheran church in Pennsylvania.[46] By 1807 English had become the official language of the body, but for some years the language problem plagued American Lutheranism.[47]

It was in the English-speaking congregations that revivals were more readily accepted. Those who favored the new measures were called "American Lutherans." They sought to modify historic Lutheranism, to infuse it with the vigor of Presbyterianism and the warmth of Methodism. All liturgical worship was denounced and personal piety exalted. American Lutherans strongly favored revivals, and both clergy and laity of this group gave cordial support to undenominational Bible and Tract societies, as well as forming Lutheran missionary societies of their own.[48] Dr. Benjamin Kurtz, editor of the *Lutheran Observer* from 1833 to 1861, used this journal to champion the new measures. Those who opposed the new measures were called "Head Christians" or "Catechism Christians." They were those who adhered to the Augsburg Confession and persisted in favoring slow Christian growth as the means to salvation.[49]

In spite of the opposition of the "Head Christians," the 1830s were notable for renewed spiritual life in Philadelphia Lutheranism and the pulpit was marked by great expressions of piety and zeal. Informal expression of religious experience often took the place of liturgy. But as had happened with the German Reformed Church, by the 1850s the accommodation began to wear thin, and the historic doctrines of Lutheranism reasserted their old pull. Advocates of American Lutheranism lost favor, the Lutheran church retreated to its old tradition, and revivals were greatly diminished.[50]

The denominational acceptance was neither unanimous nor unreserved. Yet, the tendency was for revivals to become a regular part of church procedure. More and more churches were including periods of revivals in their annual calendar. More and more people were touched by periods of revivals in their churches, and by the revivalist mentality.

7

Black Revivalism

The response of the Negro population of Philadelphia to revivalism was, not unexpectedly, warmly enthusiastic. Black religion had always been highly emotional and revivalistic. But an examination of the Philadelphia black community reveals fundamental differences in many aspects of their religious culture as well as economic and political differences. One major difference was the centrality of the church in Negro life. Indeed, as a social group, the black church antedates the Negro family on American soil.[1] The Negro church is the center of social life and performs philanthropic and other functions. The Negro preacher has always had an important role in black social life, and from the clergy have come political and civil rights leaders.

Besides the importance of the black church for understanding black revivalism, there is the nature of the population and its position in mid-nineteenth century society. W. E. B. DuBois suggests that several social developments from 1820 to 1840 were critical for the nation and for Philadelphia Negroes. Industrialization, the rapid increase of foreign immigration, the influx of free Negroes and fugitive slaves, especially into Philadelphia, and the rise of the slavery controversy, caused changes in the position of Philadelphia blacks, changes in a downward direction. Philadelphia was a natural gateway between North and South. A stream of free Negroes and fugitive slaves had long passed through the city from the rural South. By 1820 this stream had increased. Newly freed blacks and their children flocked to Philadelphia.[2] The Negro population in 1820 was 7,331; by 1830 the black population of the city and districts had increased to 15,624, an increase of more than 50%. But the rise in black population was soon outstripped by the white increase, much of it in the form of foreign immigration. By 1840 the black population was up to 19,833, but the rate of increase had dropped, while the rate of increase of whites to the city rose dramatically.

TABLE 7.1
Population of Philadelphia County[3]

Year	Whites	Negros	%Negro
1790	51,902	2,489	4.6
1800	74,129	6,880	8.5
1810	100,688	10,552	9.5
1820	123,746	11,891	8.8
1830	173,173	15,624	8.3
1840	238,204	19,833	7.7
1850	389,001	19,761	4.8
1860	543,344	22,185	3.9
1870	651,854	22,147	3.3

A fierce struggle between Irish and German immigrants resulted in the displacement of Negroes by foreign immigrants in economic life. This took place amid riots against Negroes, which began in 1829 and recurred frequently until the 1840s, and did not wholly cease until after the Civil War. An effort to deprive free Negroes of the franchise was successful, and when the Pennsylvania Constitution of 1837 inserted *white* in its qualifications for the franchise, a right of suffrage engaged in for nearly fifty years was rescinded. The period of 1820 to 1840, concludes DuBois, was a time of retrogression for the mass of blacks.

In the history of black occupations, it was the custom in early Pennsylvania to hire out slaves, especially mechanics and skilled workmen.[4] Free white workmen often objected, but the habit persisted because influential slaveholders insisted. Thus, before and after the Revolution, although many blacks were servants, there was a diversity of occupations among Negroes. But the period of 1820-1840 removed many Negroes from occupations previously open to them. By the end of that period, Philadelphia blacks were overwhelmingly in domestic service, with a small minority of laborers, artisans, coachmen, expressmen, and barbers.

Residentially, by the mid-nineteenth century, the black population had grown increasingly concentrated. Where in 1790 many had lived north of Market Street and almost a half had lived between Market Street and South Street, by 1847 only a few lived north of Vine or east of Sixth Street. Although many lived with white families, the majority were in the city in a concentrated area of narrow, filthy alleys, riddled with poverty, crime, and disease.[5]

The black family, smaller in cities than in rural areas, was essentially composed of renters, although in Philadelphia there was a relatively large number of home owners. Interestingly, the population had an unusual excess of females, typical of all Negro urban populations.[6] In 1820 there were 5,220 males and 6,671 females, or 1,091 females to each 1,000 males. In addition, there was a disproportionate number of young persons, that is, of young women between 18 and 30 and young men between 25 and 35. This affected the crime rate, for it is the young and untrained in any population who commit the most crime. The nature and condition of the black population have an intimate connection with black revivalism, as we shall see.

Black religion had always been marked by visible expressions of emotion and fervor. There is a twofold explanation for this phenomenon. The religion of the slave, as with that of most dispossessed peoples, was one of emotional release, emphasizing otherwordly rewards for men and women enslaved in this world. It undoubtedly served a survival function for the black slave. Melville Herskovits emphasizes that vestiges of African culture are an important element in black religion,[7] but while these practices may have provided a susceptibility to the emotionalism of the revival, the Baptist and Methodist preachers who evangelized the Negro in the South encouraged this tendency to emotional release and otherworldliness in religious world view.

In the 1780s, most blacks belonged to the white St. George's Methodist Episcopal Church. They were subject to various restrictions in seating and participation and were growing restless under these strictures. Richard Allen came to Philadelphia in 1786 and began preaching by appointment at St. George's church and at several other places in the city: in the commons, in Southwark, in Northern Liberties. He soon felt it necessary that the city's blacks should have a place of their own in which to worship. When in 1787 the seats for Negroes were moved from the wall to the gallery and blacks were ejected from their accustomed seats, a scuffle ensued, and the blacks left St. George's in a body. This resulted in the formation of the "Free African Society," a benevolent and reform association of Negroes, and out of this society grew the first black church in Philadelphia. Some went with Absalom Jones into the Episcopal church, others followed Richard Allen to the Bethel African Methodist Episcopal Church. As Allen describes it,

> I was confident there was no religious sect or denomination would suit the capacity of the colored people as well as the Methodist, for the plain and simple gospel suits best for the people, for the unlearned can understand;

and the reason that the Methodists are so successful in the awakening and conversion of the colored people is the plain doctrine and having a good discipline . . . . The Methodists were the first people that brought glad tidings to the colored people.[8]

The African Methodist Episcopal Bethel Church at Sixth and Lombard Streets was dedicated in 1794 and, by 1816, what had begun as a weekly gathering in Allen's blacksmith shop grew into a large edifice. In the same year Allen was elected Bishop of the A. M. E. Church of Philadelphia.[9] Its Episcopalian counterpart, the First African Church of St. Thomas, with Absalom Jones as pastor, continued to survive, but with its Episcopalian ritual and prayer it was not popular among the masses, who preferred the spontaneity and emotional release of the Methodists. Its small membership, however, included the most cultured, intellectual, and wealthy among Philadelphia Negroes.[10]

Thus, before the end of the eighteenth century, there were Methodist and Episcopalian black churches organized. The first African Baptist church in Philadelphia, at 16th and Christian Streets, dates from 1809, when it began with 13 members dismissed by their own request from the Baptist Church, for the purpose of forming their own church. The black Presbyterian church was founded in 1807 by two Negro missionaries, a father and son, along with 22 people, 9 men and 13 women. There were few black Presbyterians in Philadelphia at the time. While not mistreated, they desired to build a church of their own. A Presbyterian clergyman, Gideon Blackburn, arrived in the city in 1806 with his servant, John Gloucester. The Reverend Blackburn had purchased Gloucester in order to prevent his being sold to an unsympathetic person. He freed the slave, who began to preach wherever he could get an audience—in houses, at schoolhouses, in clear weather on street corners. He was a man of deep piety and had been well instructed by Blackburn in the Presbyterian faith. When he organized the First African Presbyterian Church of Philadelphia in 1807, it was felt that the venture could not succeed, that "it was a waste of time to start a Presbyterian church among Philadelphia blacks who were Methodist at heart."[11] With the help of the white Evangelical Society of Philadelphia, of which Dr. Archibald Alexander was president, the black church struggled along, and in 1811 a small brick church was built with a congregation of 123 members.[12]

By the early decades of the nineteenth century, the black population in Philadelphia was largely Methodist in affiliation, with members in Baptist, Episcopalian, and Presbyterian churches as well.[13] Some were in churches with whites, but most preferred to worship with other Negroes. Churches varied in size from a dozen to a thousand members. The largest church, Bethel (A. M. E.) was composed of the great laboring class, steady, honest, with church and family traditions. St. Thomas, the black Episcopal church, was composed of well-to-do Philadelphia Negroes, descendents of favorite mulatto house servants, well-bred and better educated. Central Presbyterian Church had an older congregation, many with Quaker characteristics. New arrivals in the city and sightseers often attended the Wesley Methodist Church.[14] Black Baptists had the largest rate of illiteracy of any denomination, and their ministers were of a correspondingly low educational quality.

The black church was a social institution first, a religious one afterward. A popular church with large membership meant ample revenues and large social influences. Consequently, every year revivals were held, at which considerable numbers of young people were converted.[15] Even regular Sunday services were strong emotional experiences, with their African rhythms, the frenzy or "shouting" varying from a low murmur to the wild abandon of shrieking, weeping, or stamping.[16] Black religion was revivalist religion. It was steeped in the revivals of the Methodist circuit rider in the South, in the slave religion of the plantation, and in African remnants.

The founders of Philadelphia black churches were themselves strong advocates of revivals. Richard Allen, the most famous Philadelphia black preacher, is the best example. Born in 1760 as a slave of Benjamin Chew, a leading Philadelphia lawyer, he was converted at the age of 17. He bought his freedom, learned to read and write, and sought to bring the word to others. His early contract with Methodist prayer meetings taught him the simple Arminian theology and the warm direct appeal to the heart. Allen was very devout, a man of mystical intensity and imaginative power. He would pray often, "whether sitting, standing, or lying."[17] His sermons were extemporaneous, and therefore few printed sermons remain. Since Methodism was based on itineracy, he began in the late 1780s to travel and to preach to white and black audiences alike. He did not confine himself to church buildings, but held camp meetings in the wooded outskirts of Philadelphia.[18] When he founded the A. M. E. Bethel Church, his revival meetings became normal procedure. His warm emotional sermons, the praying, singing, demonstrations, and excitement caused no opposition, he reported. The Bethel church was crowded and officials had to increase the seating arrangements. "Many backsliders are reclaimed, and old believers are getting more zeal for the glory of God and the salvation of souls . . . . Such a time of the power of the Almighty has not been seen these twenty years here . . . ."[19]

John Gloucester, founder of black Presbyterianism, was another strong revivalist. He was a powerful speaker with a bold manner and a sweet singing voice. During his ministry he earnestly sought to save souls and often many of his listeners broke out in unrestrained emotionalism, although he tried to accustom them to accept more church order.[20] He subscribed to the simple piety and rigid view of personal and artistic expression of other revivalists. A story is told by his biographer that is a case in point. When he arrived in Philadelphia, he boarded with the family of a sailmaker by trade, a man who after his daily toil would spend the evening at home at his hobby, playing the fiddle. A series of prayer meetings in his home at the request of his wife caused the husband to object, but he fiddled in an adjoining room. Gloucester was able to convert the man and he played the fiddle no more.[21] Such was the inability of revivalism to differentiate between simple artistic expression and destructive vice.

Francis Lieber describes a Methodist revival meeting for black people in Philadelphia:

> I shall never forget the impression made upon me by the unbounded excitement and passion of the Congregation. The preacher, a mulatto, spoke incoherently on a variety of subjects ... his gesticulations were violent in the highest degree ... his ideas concentrated upon the constant theme—the torments of the damned, which he depicted not without the eloquence and poetry of high passion .... The people groaned with his vivid descriptions of purgatory. This was the sign for a general convulsion of the meeting, screaming, shrieking, moaning ... weeping, stamping, groaning ... while in contrast with this scene, I observed an old Negro without any signs of violence, over whose dark cheeks rolled the big tears of contrition.[22]

The African Methodist Episcopal Church produced the first black female itinerant revivalist, Jarena Lee. Born in 1783 in Cape May, New Jersey, she spent her youth as a servant, and in 1804, at age 21, she went to hear a Presbyterian missionary preach. Overcome by a sense of sinfulness, she tried to commit suicide by drowning herself. The event was followed by a period of mental distress, and she left her job and went to Philadelphia, still plagued by anxiety. Upon visiting the Methodist church and hearing the Reverend Richard Allen, she embraced the A.M.E. church and three weeks later was converted by Allen. On that occasion, she reports that she leaped to her feet, declared that God, for Christ's sake, had pardoned the sins of her soul, and she then experienced great ecstasy as all her sins were swept away.[23] Jarena Lee then started exhorting sinners and a few years later was called to preach the Gospel. Allen was reluctant to have a woman preacher, for Methodism had no tradition of women preachers. Her marriage in 1811 caused her to move to a small town six miles outside Philadelphia. Tragedy pursued her, with the death of her husband and several of her children, and she was left with two infants. Jarena Lee, again plagued with anxiety and guilt, once more sought Allen's permission to preach. He agreed to allow her to preach at a hired house in the city. She read and sang hymns and gave a sermon. Some wept, she reports, and others shouted for joy. "One whole seat of females, by the power of God as the rushing of a wind, were all bowed to the floor at once, and screamed out."[24]

This initial sermon led to preaching at camp meetings and revivals at private homes in the city, and to white and black congregations in New Jersey, New York, and in Baltimore, Maryland. She spoke to Methodists and Baptists alike, and her tours took her to Philadelphia again and again, where she reported many conversions. She spoke as well at anti-slavery meetings, with impassioned pleas for the freedom of her people.[25] Jarena Lee traveled under the sponsorship and approval of the Reverend Richard Allen, although instead of ordaining her, he gave her "licensed papers." She raised money and started new Methodist groups. In one typical year she covered 2,325 miles and preached 178 sermons, which makes her one of the active itinerant revivalists of the time.[26]

The overwhelming support given by blacks to revivalism was largely due to their own religious tendencies, along with their historic experience. It must also have reflected the preponderance of young people and women in the urban black population. These two segments of the population have traditionally been vulnerable to revivals and dramatic conversions. Women and youth were converted in large numbers in emotion-charged black churches of Philadelphia. The badly depressed state of blacks in that city, and their worsening plight before the Civil War, must also have fostered a need for emotional release in the religious experience. At least on Sunday at church, the Negro could be completely himself.

Black religion has received censure from many sources within the black community. W. E. B. DuBois observed that since Negro ministers are largely chosen by the masses, they must cater to the tastes of the masses. The Baptist minister, he suggested, is the elected chairman of a pure democracy; the Methodist minister, the appointed steward of a large corporation. Consequently, such leaders often court popular approval. In addition, such leaders were and are often uneducated, sometimes illiterate.[27] Booker T. Washington criticized the Negro church for its apocalyptic vision, its otherworldliness, its failure to give the Negro social purpose.[28] Certainly, among blacks, the tradition of revivalism, with its emotional excesses and its pastoral flamboyance, was a mixed blessing. Its otherworldliness enabled the Negro to escape emotionally from the degradation of the slave experience, and from the institutionalized racism of late-nineteenth-century America. But the world view of revivalism was counterproductive of pragmatic change in dealing with economic, social, and political problems of Negroes in this world. Only as the black church became secularized and moved away from earlier attitudes, only as black ministers have perceived the needs of their people, have they been useful in helping the Negro achieve equality. The store-front churches of the lower-class black neighborhoods, with their often illiterate preachers, are a testimonial to the lasting impact of revivalism upon the black religious experience, and the ultimately inhibitory effect of revivalism on the black people.

8

The Outsiders

The religious consensus that developed in the 1830s and 1840s was not without dissenters. There were considerable numbers of people who, because of religious tradition, background or training, or temperament, looked askance at the assumptions and methods of the revival. There were, for example, the Old-School Presbyterians, who continued to voice distress over the new measures. There were parties among the German Reformed and the Lutherans, as well as some Baptists and Episcopalians, who could not accept revivalism despite its apparent success in filling the churches. Foreign visitors, as well, voiced outspoken distaste for revivals. But these were segments of groups, not entire denominations. Two groups lay outside the consensus, a sore reminder of the heterogeneity of American culture. They were the Unitarians and the Jews. In later years, they would be joined by Catholics, but the Catholic presence in the city was not yet sufficiently strong to voice unified objections. Both Unitarians and Jews were tacitly assumed to be in a kind of schism that someday would be healed when they saw the error of their ways, in a grand

137

assimilation to the majority. Nineteenth-century Protestants, the socially dominant group, sought a homogeneous nation, pure, whole, and united. Their vision of America was not pluralistic and they took no pleasure in diversity. They understood the word *American* to mean their own kind, and conceived their sacred mission to be to preserve the nation's inheritance. If deviants refused to conform, they had only themselves to blame for being excluded. Robert Kelley in *The Transatlantic Persuasion* finds this attitude consistent with attitudes in the broader transatlantic community, which he understands as America, England, and Canada.[1] The English were constantly seeking to Anglicize the Irish as well as the Scots and the Welsh; Anglo-Canadians in Canada sought to do the same with French Canadians; evangelical Protestants consistently sought to incorporate dissident religious groups. A pluralistic Britain, a multi-ethnic Canada, a polyglot America was inconceivable. Thus, Unitarians and Jews stood outside the consensus in awkward nonsymmetry. These two groups, small though they were, expressed open hostility to evangelical revivalism.

Foreign observers often voiced sharp criticism of revivals. With her customary sharpness, Frances Trollope condemned not only the camp meetings, but revivals in city churches. She decried itinerant ministers of all persuasions, but usually Methodist, Baptist, and Presbyterian, with their "offensively familiar manners and disgusting descriptions in minute detail of the last feeble moments of human life and the gradual process of decomposition and decay after death."[2] The Reverend G. Lewis, making a trip from England during the first half of 1844, found much to criticize: "Got up revivals are but the animalism of religion—a gush and all is over—floods in the desert—a succession of warm and cold fits that end in fanaticism or infidelity."[3] The Reverend Lewis was of the opinion that revivals were increased and spread by the activity of the religious press, which reported everything connected with a congregation in great detail. This publicity, he felt, encouraged the getting-up of revivals even where they did not arise naturally. It was true that the religious press had proliferated greatly. Each denomination had at least one organ expressing its point of view and containing denominational and congregational news, theological discourses, and disputes, and these were widely read and distributed in religious circles.

Not only were foreign observers critical, but the two major dissenting groups, the Unitarians and the Jews, were actually hostile. Unitarianism was a consistent and articulate enemy of revivals. Unitarianism was the theological offspring of Congregationalism, but the intellectual child of the Enlightenment. Unitarians preferred a more rationalistic approach to religion, and consequently rejected the whole pietistic emphasis on the religion of the heart. In turn, they were the frequent target of revival diatribes.[4] They favored a well-reasoned and rational sermon, and their appeal was to the educated and upper classes. The unlettered and those who preferred a warmer, experiential religion usually drifted away to the Congregationalists, Baptists, or Methodists. Unitarians rejected the Westminster Confession, man's apostasy from God, and his dependence on mere grace for salvation. They rejected the necessity of an atonement by the blood of Christ. The conversion experience was not essential to a Christian life, they felt. They wished no sudden conversions, preferring instead that Christian development should take a gradual path. Arminian in attitude, they insisted that man worked out his own salvation and suffered his just desserts. Perfection, however, was attainable in this world. Man must obey his own best impulses and the world would grow more rational and more humane. Unitarian perfectionism joined the wider perfectionism in antebellum thought and helped give that period the optimistic, buoyant mood that was its most pervasive characteristic.

By 1825 the number of Unitarian congregations in the United States was estimated at 120, and the year marks the formation of the American Unitarian Association.[5] Philadelphia Unitarianism had never been so active as its Boston counterpart, yet it boasted adherents from among the wealthiest, best-educated, and most influential civic leaders in Philadelphia. During the late 1820s and for 50 years afterwards, Philadelphia Unitarianism was under the inspired leadership of William Henry Furness, one of the most forceful and attractive human beings in Philadelphia. Born in Boston in 1802, he attended Harvard, the bastion of Unitarianism, and became a minister, preaching his first sermon in 1823. He was called to Philadelphia in 1825, where a small Unitarian society had gathered in 1796 and had been together for 30 years without a pastor, relying upon lay services. Dr. Furness was installed in 1825, married in the same year, and for half a century he guided Philadelphia Unitarianism. A man of exquisitely cultivated tastes, he enjoyed drama and the fine arts. He often translated poems and tales from the German into English. He was a member of the Philosophical Society and active in the intellectual life of the city.

The Reverend Furness clearly despised the revivalism that swept through many Philadelphia churches in the early nineteenth century. Preaching in 1828 at the dedication of a new church edifice in Philadelphia, he noted with some satisfaction the absence of evangelism in Unitarianism, and took the opportunity to denounce revivalism as appealing to the baser elements of human nature:

> If it [evangelism] readily affected the minds of the generality of those whose previous self-regulation has been in no wise remarkable, we might suspect that it purchased

its success by yielding something to the lower tendencies of our nature.[6]

The undeniable connection between revivalism and reform has been made earlier. But reform was not limited to evangelicals. William H. Furness believed that abolitionism was a profoundly religious movement. He eschewed, however, the Theodore Weld group of abolitionists, believing instead that the Garrisonians had the best program for arousing public opinion in favor of abolition. From the 1830s to the 1850s, the tempo of violence in Philadelphia increased. In 1836 the city council had to provide city funds to reimburse victims of mob violence for damage to persons or property. In May 1838 a mob burned down Pennsylvania Hall, built as a meeting place by antislavery forces and dedicated four days earlier. Furness delivered a sermon decrying the violence, and a year later he enlisted in the antislavery struggle and never gave it up.[7] The long and untiring activity of William H. Furness in the antislavery struggle is a subtle reminder of the varied components of the movement.

There was in Unitarianism none of the sectarian insistence on personal habits of piety, abstinence, or refraining from activities that evangelical groups considered vices: novel-reading, theater-going, smoking. There was not in Unitarianism the single-mindedness, the certitude, nor the intolerance of others' religious views. Furness, for example, opposed Bible-reading in schools, considering that " . . . a form of religious observance, and against religious liberty, the practice of reading the Bible in public schools should be given up."[8] Perhaps it was this open-minded attitude of Unitarians that made them philosophically congenial to Jews, for both were part of the tradition of ethnic pluralism. Rebecca Gratz, for example, a prominent Jewish philanthropist of nineteenth-century Philadelphia, was a warm friend of the Reverend Furness and his wife. She often attended his sermons with her nieces, and shared lively intellectual debates with the learned minister. She reported, "... in religion we're not *very* different."[9] She commented upon the sectarian jealousies toward Unitarians. Miss Gratz had promised her friend Mrs. Furness to apply for a little girl from the Orphan Asylum. She was then secretary of the organization, which was officially nonsectarian but dominated by Presbyterian women. The application was rejected on the ground that Mrs. Furness was a Unitarian. The ladies of the Orphan Asylum patiently explained to Miss Gratz that they could not consent to putting the child under the influence of a Unitarian.[10] Between Unitarians and Jews was the bond of the disaffected. The bond may have been amplified by the fact that Unitarians, like Jews, did not seek conversions. The result was an attitude of mutual respect.

Perhaps because of its lack of aggressiveness, or perhaps because its appeal was strictly to the educated and the upper classes, Philadelphia Unitarianism never reached the heights of Boston Unitarianism. Philadelphians were conservative and tended to belong to churches into which they had been born, and, as with political allegiance, gentlemen changed neither. Since Philadelphia Unitarianism had no established base from which it could grow, membership was a matter of personal choice. When children married non-Unitarians, since the denomination fostered no denominational spirit and did not proscribe such liaisons, many turned to the partner's faith. Thus, while the Philadelphia population grew from 70,000 in 1800 to 568,034 in 1860, and while Unitarians included the finest men and women in the city, leaders of cultural life, business, the professions, and government, in the latter year there was but one large congregation and one small struggling one. Clearly, Unitarianism was not for everyone, and no one knew this better than Unitarians themselves. In forgoing the diversions and the enthusiasm of revivals, the Unitarians were forced to deny themselves also whatever growth might derive from them.

All his life William H. Furness detested revivals. When, in 1858, Philadelphia was in the midst of a new evangelical outburst, sponsored by the newly organized Young Men's Christian Association, Furness attacked revival activity anew, as a "paroxysm wasting the religious feeling of this generation," and prayed that "God, in his mercy, may bury it deep beyond the possibility of a resurrection."[11] Philadelphia Unitarianism, like its counterparts elsewhere, differed from the evangelical denominations in philosophical assumptions and historical development, and consistently opposed revivalism in American church life.

Philadelphia Jews also expressed some anxiety about revivals. This anxiety developed into a clearly defined antipathy as soon as the goals of revivalists became clear to Jews. Paradoxically, revivalism had the effect of producing in Philadelphia Jewry a renewed sense of common destiny and purpose that was salutary to that group.

During the early decades of the nineteenth century, there were only a small number of Jews in Philadelphia. The city and adjacent suburbs of Northern Liberties, Southwark, Kensington, Moyamensing, and Spring Garden, out of a general population of 114,410 in 1820, had about 450 Jews. They were 1% of the white population and were concentrated in commercial activity.[12] In the entire nation, out of some 9 million people, there were about 2,700 Jews. They were concentrated in New York, which had about 1,000 Jewish inhabitants, and cities like Philadelphia, Charleston, Savannah, and Baltimore. Most rural and small-town Americans knew the Jew only by hearsay or as an occasional itinerant peddler.

This was a transitional period for Philadelphia Jewry. The earlier Jewish settlers, the Spanish-Portuguese

(Sephardim) of colonial times, along with some early German immigrants, had risen in position and affluence and had been largely absorbed through intermarriage. Whereas the elder Gratzes, Mordecai Mordecai, and Jonas Phillips joined in the birth of the nation, their children, with no language barrier, became doctors and lawyers, were on the boards of the largest Philadelphia companies and banks, founded art academies; in short, they were fully accepted into the economic, educational, and professional life of Philadelphia. In addition, they intermarried with Christians and became Christians at an alarming rate. Some of the oldest and most distinguished Jewish families followed this path. While there were a few important Sephardic families in Philadelphia persisting in their Jewish tradition, the hospitable social environment for Jews in America had weakened their sense of identity and their desire for continuity.

The trickle of German Jews was beginning, however. While in 1822 roughly half the Philadelphia Jews were foreign-born, by 1830 the recent arrivals outnumbered the native-born. The wave of German Jews, or Ashkenazim, which reached its peak in the 1870s, was to transform American Jewry, both culturally and theologically, and infuse it with new vigor and commitment. The older Jewish segment clung to Mikveh Israel synagogue, built in 1782, but the new arrivals sought a synagogue in which they could be comfortable in ritual and tradition. Consequently, they organized formally as early as 1802, and survived in inadequate rented quarters until the larger German migration of the 1830s gave them adequate support and they were able to build a new synagogue, Rodeph Shalom.[13] It was the only congregation in America to follow Ashkenazic (or German) ritual. Among both Sephardic and Ashkenazic Jews, however, the biggest threat was assimilation through intermarriage. Newspapers announced mixed marriages with such significant frequency that Mikveh Israel, after long and bitter debate, was forced to bend and allow Jews who married Christians to partake of religious honors in the synagogue. Rodeph Shalom, likewise, withdrew a punitive provision three years after it was introduced, ruling instead that if members raised their children as Jews, they were not to be expelled.[14]

In the nonthreatening American ambience, with wide economic opportunity open to all who would avail themselves of it, with religious freedom unprecedented in the Western world, many Jews forgot their traditions in an attempt to incorporate themselves wholly in American society, and assimilation became the biggest threat to the continuation of the Jewish people.

But the 1820s brought a new danger to Philadelphia Jews—the aggressive evangelism that rose out of the revivals threatened Jewish survival, causing, paradoxically, a strengthening of the Jewish community. Evangelization of the Jew had a long and bloody history in Europe. In America, with its multiplicity of religions and its developing philosophy of religious pluralism, attempts to convert the Jew had to be more subtle than in Europe. These attempts started early. Cotton Mather, as well as his father, Increase, had written tracts to convert the Jews.[15] All attempts to convert the Jew were based upon the millennial vision and the biblical prophecy that the dispersal of the Jews to every land on earth would end with a calling of the Jewish nation back to their own land, and their conversion to Christianity would bring about the millennial perfection. There was some debate as to whether the conversion of the Jews was to be by individuals or as a group, but the result would be the same—the hastening of the Kingdom of God on earth. It was necessary that Jews accept Christ in order for human history to enter its final phases. Despite the concern of some Christians regarding the salvation of the Jews, there was no organized missionary work directed toward him in eighteenth-century America. It was with the Second Great

Awakening that the Jews became the object of evangelical efforts. Converting the Jew became an essential part of the spectrum of activities that were fueled by the energy of the revivals.

It was concern over the persistent stubbornness of the Jew in resisting conversion that led to the founding of an organization dedicated to that purpose. The Society for Meliorating the Condition of the Jews was started in 1820 and existed intermittently through to the Civil War. The organization, often referred to as the American Jews Society, had its start in connection with the arrival from London in 1816 of the Reverend Joseph Samuel C. F. Frey, a converted German Jew. Frey, born Joseph Samuel Levi, had been active in the London Missionary Society, and when that organization foundered, he turned to America.[16] He preached as a Congregational minister in New York, then became a Baptist and ministered a Baptist Church in Newark, New Jersey. Frey's autobiography, *The Converted Jew*, interested groups in New York and Boston. He had a plan to establish a colonization society for Jews. He proposed to find a place where converted Jews and their families could go to leave the censure of the Jewish community, where they could live together and receive instruction in the Christian religion.[17] The American Society for Evangelizing the Jews was formed in 1816 in New York, but the organization languished. Frey finally interested the Reverend Elias Boudinot, well-known philanthropist and president of the American Bible Society, in his proposal, and the late American Society for Evangelizing the Jews was revived. At a meeting on February 8, 1820, the new Society for Colonizing and Evangelizing the Jews was formed. Frey was charged with seeking a charter from the New York State legislature, where he met some objections to the words *colonizing and evangelizing*.[18] The offending words were removed from the title and the word *meliorating* substituted, whereupon the charter was granted in April of 1820. The

Reverend Philip Milledoler was the first president, and among the vice-presidents were John Q. Adams and Dr. Jeremiah Day, president of Yale College.[19]

The society felt that colonizing would be more effective than just evangelizing:

> If we continue to employ former means for the conversion of the Jews namely the sending them Missionaries, the putting Christian writings into their hands ... we may hope at most to have occasional and individual conversions .... But by forming a Jewish Christian colony we lay the foundation or prepare the way for national conversion.[20]

Little was done by the organization for two years, for funds were slow in coming in and expected converts from Europe failed to appear. In 1822 Boudinot died and left the society the sum of $1,000. With this, the society leased a small tract of land 30 miles from New York City, in New Paltz, New York. It contained 500 acres of woodland, 100 of which were cleared for cultivation, and had a good house, a barn, and an orchard. Frey resigned from his pulpit and became the general agent of the society. He traveled thousands of miles and lectured to hundreds of church groups in an effort to raise money. By 1823, when the Society presented its first report, it claimed to have 150 auxiliary societies in various cities, and donations were coming in.[21]

The Philadelphia Auxiliary Society for Meliorating the Condition of the Jews was started in 1823.[22] Its president was the Reverend George Boyd of the Episcopal Church. Episcopalians had long been involved in seeking Jewish converts and, along with the Presbyterian Church, took the lead in the American Society for Meliorating the Condition of the Jews. The Reverend Boyd was rector of St. John's Church in Northern Liberties for 36 years; it was his first and only parish. Born in New York City and brought up in the Associate Reformed Church, upon his marriage he became an Episcopalian. He was a graduate of Columbia College, where he studied law; then he entered the ministry. He accepted the doctrine of the millennium, which looked for a literal restoration of the Jews to their own city and then the personal reign of Christ and his saints on earth. He was active as the secretary and general agent of the Board of Missions of the Episcopal Church as well as president of the society to convert the Jews.[23]

When the Philadelphia branch held its annual meeting on Tuesday evening, April 1, 1824, the large session room of the First Presbyterian Church of Philadelphia was crowded and hundreds were turned away. The two-hour meeting was addressed by Philadelphia ministers interested in the work, among them the Reverend Ballentine, a Baptist minister, and Dr. Ashbel Green, the distinguished Presbyterian clergyman. Green had been president of the college of New Jersey (Princeton) until 1822, when he resigned because of age to edit the *Christian Advocate*. During his term at Princeton, he had been involved in the revivals of 1815 at that college. Green was to move toward the Old School Presbyterianism when the denomination polarized a decade later. But he had always been a moderate revivalist and held a long-time interest in missions. Now a resident of Philadelphia, Dr. Green hoped

> that there [would] be a zealous interest taken by friends of the Jewish cause in this city, in support of the measures now in operation to meliorate the condition of that long neglected and persecuted people whose time of restoration to the church of God, the signs of the times strongly indicate to be rapidly approaching.[24]

The first president of the national organization, the Reverend Philip Milledoler, had ties to Philadelphia as well. He had been for a time minister of the Pine Street Presbyterian

Church and was active in the Philadelphia branch of the organization. Milledoler was a revivalist minister whose congregation remembered "an almost constant revival of religion in the Pine Street Church of Philadelphia during his connection with it."[25] Born in Rhinebeck, New York, of a Swiss-German family, ordained in 1794 into the German Reformed Church, he was greatly influenced by the Methodist camp meetings he attended. Although there were irregularities that he felt obliged to condemn, the camp meetings produced a marked, enduring change of feeling. In 1800 he transferred from the German Reformed Church and became a minister of the Pine Street Presbyterian Church, where he remained until 1805 when illness forced him to leave. It was an eminently successful ministry, with constant revivals remembered with great affection. The Reverend Milledoler was impressive in the pulpit. His sermons were designed to bring the sinner to an awareness of his sinful condition. "He often rose to heights of eloquence . . . emphasizing the plain truth of the Gospel, a simple and unostentatious piety."[26] Like many of the others in the ASMCJ, Milledoler's interests went beyond the conversion of Jews. He was also a founding member of the American Bible Society.

Another Philadelphian active in the society was the Reverend Archibald Alexander, the minister of the Pine Street Presbyterian Church after Milledoler. Born in 1772 in Virginia, he became converted during a student revival in 1790 and returned home with a new religious attitude. Shortly thereafter, he led a revival in his Presbyterian church. He entered the ministry, becoming active in the Presbyterian General Assembly. In 1806 he was called to the Pine Street church in Philadelphia after Dr. Milledoler's health forced him to leave. The naturalness of his sermons, with direct and colloquial speech, was very appealing to his congregation. "He could awaken religious emotions with great power," reported a colleague, the Reverend Henry

Boardman.[27] Dr. Alexander was interested in revivals all his life, and in his later years was involved in the revivals at Princeton in the spring of 1850.[28]

The Philadelphia organization, along with the others that made up the national society, supported the farm at New Paltz. But there were problems: converts were few and those who came rejected the rules as too rigid. They were the rules of an almshouse or an asylum rather than a free community, they complained. They were not free to manage their affairs. "What well-educated and enlightened Hebrew would wish to join the settlement under such an aspect?"[29] In addition, some Christians opposed colonization on the grounds that Jews should mix freely in the broader Christian life of America rather than be sequestered. Still others pointed out that Jews were not accustomed by long tradition to cultivating lands, and to force them into agriculture would be unwise.[30]

By the latter part of the 1820s the society was beginning to abandon its plan for colonizing and to concentrate on converting Jews. *The Messenger* in 1828 reported that at the time of publication there was not one Jew at the farm at New Paltz.[31] The farm was sold at auction in 1835 (a farm had been purchased in 1827, replacing the earlier one that was leased) after it became an acknowledged failure. It was described at the time of its sale as " . . . not only wholly unproductive, but going rapidly to decay for want of repairs . . . . The settlement had fallen through beyond resuscitation."[32] The society, shorn of its colonization plan and often shrouded in controversy, appeared and reappeared throughout the next decades, by now frankly evangelical.

The one great, and sole object of this Society is to bring Jews, not to the profession of any particular creed, nor to the practice of any particular form of denominational Christianity, but to the faith and love of Christ himself . . . . With what denomination any convert, in the expression of his Christian liberty, may afterwards choose to connect himself is a matter of perfect indifference to the Board, and of comparative indifference, as we believe, to every member of it. There is scarcely one of our evangelical sects that is not represented in the directorship of the Society.[33]

The millennial basis for the conversion of the Jews was clearly evident. "Let it never be forgotten," said the Reverend Cone to the Society, "that there is a profound connection between the salvation of Israel and the salvation of the world."[34] The Society expressed gratitude to the Jews for giving to the world the Bible, the Prophets, Christianity itself. "Who but the Jews preserved and transmitted to us the treasures of the Old Testament? Who but the Jews first brought the Gospel to our Gentile ancestors?" Why, in spite of this indebtedness, single out the Jews?

Because God has singled them out. They have been kept distinct by wonderful providence for so many ages, so that they might become the distinct attention of the Church. The restoration as a distinct nation to the bosom of the church will be one of the most important events in the history of mankind . . . . [Their restoration] will do more to convince mankind of the truth of Christianity than a thousand volumes of arguments. The lectures which they will preach from Mount Zion will be more efficacious than the sermons of half the Gentile world. Even in this view the moral influence gained by their restoration will be cheaply purchased by ten times the sum expended on Gentile missions up to that day. Thus if you would hasten the conversion of the world, urge forward the restoration of the Jews.[35]

Griffin regretted the injustice and cruelty that Jews had received from baptized nations as "an everlasting blot on the Christian world," yet "the nominal followers of Christ have been executing the divine sentence," he concluded.[36]

The American Society for Meliorating the Condition of the Jews was aided in its work by its organ, *Israel's Advocate, or The Restoration of the Jews Contemplated and Urged.* This deceptively named missionary journal, whose title was supposed to induce Jews to buy and read it under the mistaken notion that it expressed a Jewish viewpoint, was a collection of articles on converted Jews, biblical arguments for conversion, and reports from branch societies. It emphasized, however, Jews in Europe, no doubt being vulnerable to complaints about undercutting religious freedom in America. It first appeared in 1822 and by 1826 it appeared for the last time, being succeeded by the *Jewish Chronicle* in 1836-1841.

In addition to these interdenominational missionary groups, individual denominations had their own societies. The Protestant Episcopal, Baptist, and Presbyterian churches, for example, formed agencies to convert Jews.[37] Denominational periodicals assisted in the work, often containing stories of converted Jews and arguments for conversion.[38]

Attempts to convert Jews in America, however, met with meager success. In a commentary of a colleague after Frey's death in 1850 came the admission: "It must be acknowledged that Mr. Frey's labours, so far as respects his own people, never seemed to mature into very much of abiding fruit . . . ."[39] Continued failure to convert more than a few scattered Jews, however, did not inhibit these societies, but made it necessary for them to justify their existence. "Our duty does not depend on results. Our duty is to sow the seeds and leave it to the Spirit of God to bring them out."[40] The Society formed and reformed, seeking funds and converts, convinced that they were doing God's work and oblivious of the resentment they were causing among their chosen objects.

The Jews deeply resented these attempts to convert them to Christianity. In America they had encountered a religious freedom unparalleled in their long history, and they wished to be free to worship in their own way within the religious pluralism of America. When revivalism turned from the West, where it had little impact upon them, to the cities where most Jews made their homes, they found it intolerable to be considered the object of an open missionary effort. This resentment in the Jewish community caused the emergence of the first Jewish periodical in America, *The Jew*. It was short-lived, lasting from March 1823 to March 1825, but during that time it was devoted fully to an attack on the efforts to convert Jews to Christianity. It was edited by Solomon Henry Jackson, a Jew born in England who had come to the United States in 1787 and settled in Pike County, Pennsylvania. He married Helen Miller, the daughter of a Presbyterian minister, and after her death, he resettled in New York, raising his five children in the Jewish faith. He was later the publisher of an English-Hebrew prayer book and, in 1837, of the first American edition of Passover services in English and Hebrew.[41] *The Jew* refuted the missionary attacks of *Israel's Advocate*. Jews wanted, it insisted, religious freedom and equality to be on an equal footing with other religions and were not to be considered a field for missionary activities. "You mock us by offering to bribe us like children with toys; you offer us farms; keep your toys, keep your farms; give us the pearl of great price that we want."[42]

In addition to *The Jew*, the Jewish point of view was expressed in a book published in 1820 by George Houston called *Israel Vindicated*, which consisted of a series of discussions cast in the form of letters, and aimed at correcting the view of Jews presented by the American Society for Meliorating the Condition of the Jews.[43] The Society, says Houston, is contrary to the spirit of the Constitution, for it puts the Jew below the level of Christians and presupposes the former to be in a degraded and uncultivated state and the latter completely civilized. All religions are equal in the sight of God, he insists, and have equal claim to the protection of the Constitution.

It [the Society] recognizes the impolitic principle, evidently discountenanced by the constitution, that Christianity ought to be the predominant religion; that those who do not profess it must necessarily be immoral persons, undeserving of the rights of citizens . . . . The Jew is as competent as the Christian to discharge the duties of civil society, and entertains as high a respect for all the social virtues.[44]

Houston noted that the missionaries were usually "of a low origin, and of indolent habits . . . . They affect a sanctity of manners and aspect which passes with the vulgar as proof of holiness . . . . They boldly pretend to divine illumination, to be the inspired of heaven, the peculiar favourites of the Almighty . . . ." In addition, the Society was composed largely of females, said Houston, "whose temperament renders them more the dupes of craft and fanaticism than the other sex . . . . Girls, scarcely arrived at the age of puberty engage in this task of 'soul-saving' as if this was the only end of their creation . . . ."[45]

He concluded that the attempts at conversion were an "underhand and masked system of persecution, not only of the people of our nation, but of Christians toward Christians, of men calling themselves fellow-worshippers of the same God . . . . But it is chiefly against men of science, intelligence, and liberal sentiments that these fanatics employ their secret weapons . . . . They abandon rational discussions and demonstration and substitute the most absurd theories and the most ridiculous observances, well-assured that they will always find admirers and supporters among the stupid and the vulgar."[46]

The often aggressive attempts to convert Jews caused much consternation in the Jewish community. Agents of the American Tract Society would come to a Sabbath service, post themselves at the entrance, and hand out copies of their tract as people left.[47] Even prominent and wealthy people were not immune to conversion attempts. Rebecca

Gratz reported that a neighbor sent volumes of Christian literature, urging her to study them and to examine her soul daily. In her characteristically humorous manner, Miss Gratz commented that the woman wished "to canonize herself by my conversion . . . ." In addition, she received anonymous letters and tracts, zealous in nature but not very eloquent, communications that she found irritating and in bad taste.[48]

As the activities of the American Society for Meliorating the Condition of the Jews persisted, albeit weakened, into the 1840s and 1850s, they met with the articulate resistance of Isaac Leeser, the leader of the Philadelphia Jewish community, and publisher of *The Occident*, the most influential and widely read national Jewish magazine in the United States.[49] Isaac Leeser was the most important and most influential American Jewish religious leader of the antebellum period, not only of the city but of the nation. He was a religious leader who in 1843 established the first effective Jewish periodical in the country. Brought to America from Germany by his uncle, he settled in Richmond, helping teach Jewish children in the Richmond congregation. Called to Philadelphia's Mikveh Israel in 1829 as its hazzan (cantor-minister), he found Philadelphia Jewry highly individuated, lacking the hostile pressures that often kept them loyal to their faith. He worked to set up Jewish hospitals, orphanages, charity federations; he translated basic Jewish books into English and set up the first Hebrew high school in 1849. Perhaps his greatest single achievement was *The Occident*, a monthly journal that gave a sense of purpose to the scattered Jews of the United States.

Leeser advised the Society not to employ converted Jews as their agents to visit Jewish houses, because this was particularly obnoxious to Jews. "Many of us are averse to holding any intercourse with them and hence it is almost an insult to send these persons although we will gladly receive Christians by birth . . . ."[50] Agents of the Society were in the habit of conversing with Jewish families in cities, finding them in front and back buildings, basements, garrets, and alleys. Most of these Jews were poor, they admitted, because they had little access to those who were not.[51] Leeser warned that while both rich and poor were vulnerable, it was the poor who were more frequently approached.

> The access somewhat difficult to the high, is easily obtainable to the low in station. Intercourse with the conversionist cannot be avoided when he appears as a customer, moreover as a benefactor. He will introduce himself into the homes of the poor, and by simulating disinterested love for the descendents of the patriarchs, insinuate himself, gain their esteem and confidence, and gradually ensnare the unsuspecting, the ignorant, and the young.

The young were particularly susceptible:

> Look with what glee the overjoyed child holds up to the admiration of the grateful parent the handsome present just received! It is a Bible, so neatly bound, and with such a pretty book-mark in it, on which are embroidered some endearing Hebrew words. How kind, how thoughtful it was to make such a present! ... Of course, at the next friendly meeting, the question is put whether and what part of the word of God was read, and in due time the tract completes its work.[52]

The success of conversion attempts, said Lesser, depended upon the length of time the individual was exposed to the conversion processes, the amount of natural intelligence possessed, the previous religious instruction, and the intensity of Jewish feeling. He warned of benevolences as hardly disinterested—they always sought a return: "If they give a poor Jew money—they want him to think well of the benevolence of Christians and open his heart to Christianity."[53] Isaac Leeser summarized his views toward the conversionists thus:

Conversion of Jews, therefore, means the destruction of the Jews; and if any one believes, therefore, that the Jews must be converted as a thing demanded by his religion, and he believes that everything save violence is permitted to compass this result, he cannot be looked upon otherwise than as an enemy of the Jewish people.[54]

Despite decades of activity, it is clear that the missionary societies failed to convert more than an occasional Jew here and there. Undaunted by failure, they continued to speak, to work, to collect funds. In 1856 Robert Baird admitted the few instances of conversions, blaming this upon the fact that " ... the attention of Christians ... not having been sufficiently turned to that object."[55] The American Society for Meliorating the Condition of the Jews was revived for the last time in 1858, to collapse in 1860 for the last time, in indifference and financial distress. Its 40th report of 1960 tells us that "The Society meets in a condition of feebleness and of almost inaction."[56]

To the Jewish community, the attempts at conversion in the antebellum era represented an irritant that brought to Jews a renewed sense of common destiny. They realized that even in the comfortable American milieu they must educate their children to their own tradition and maintain an awareness of the evangelical threat to their existence. It is paradoxical that Jewish survival was more threatened by the comfortable acceptance of the pre-evangelical period than by frank attempts at conversion. The threat of evangelism, ineffective as it was, caused a coalescence of Jewish feeling and a drawing inward that strengthened the Jewish community. To the Christians who so earnestly sought to convert the Jews to Christianity, evangelization represented but one dimension of the millennial hopes. To bring the Jew, the original recipient of God's promise, who obstinately refused to accept their Savior, into Christianity would bring the world significantly closer to God's kingdom on earth, they felt, and such was their certitude, their righteousness, that none could dissuade them. At deeper levels, the Jews represented a group of alien, unassimilated people who must be converted to achieve ethnic and cultural uniformity. The continued existence of the Jews as a separate people was a reproach they could not accept. While America had no church-state tradition, the habits of control by a dominant group die hard, and the desire for religious homogeneity was a hallmark of the age.

The various missionary and tract societies and the American Society for Meliorating the Condition of the Jews found supporters among Christians of all types. But it was with the evangelical denominations, the heirs of the revivals, that the need to convert Jews had a particular urgency. New School Presbyterians, for example, were more active than the Old School.[47] The Reverend Archibald Alexander and the Reverend Philip Milledoler, both active in the Society, were ardent revivalists. Later revivalists also sought to save Jewish souls. The Methodist revivalist James Caughey, in a sermon called "The Great Test," saw the Jewish religion has having reached a crisis in its history.

> Signs of death were everywhere visible. Rabbinism and tradition had overlaid everything—had almost smothered the last spark of spiritual life . . . . They were now put on trial, to determine whether they would show signs of life, or signs of continued death . . . . The axe of God's judgements was now laid to the roots of these human trees, and ready to be set on against them when the occasion demanded. If they showed signs of life in the bud, blossom, and fruit of true repentence, then they were allowed to live and enjoy the sunshine, the shower and the breeze of the New Dispensation . . . . But if no such signs of life appeared, they were to be hewn down and cast into "fire unquenchable."[58]

Revivalism, then, gave urgency and zeal to the millennial suppositions and to the biblical prophecy that was part of Christian tradition. It buttressed attempts to convert the

Jews as one of the host of religious objectives that were part of antebellum social life. If the Jews considered these efforts as less than a reform, they were in the minority, and, along with other dissidents, provided a steady, if often unheeded, objection to the zeal of the evangelicals.

9

The Smoldering Fire

By the late 1830s the revivals had touched every religious denomination in Philadelphia, and had made some significant changes in many of them. By and large, they had become an established means within the institutional church. But although they continued, it was at a slower pace; the blaze had quieted to a gentler glow. Historians are always eager to attach finite causes to events; they seek to assign specific causality. As David Hume once explained, few things are more elusive than what "causes" something else. Perhaps we might be better served to understand relationships and characteristics, and be satisfied with something less concrete than we might wish. No one really understands why it is that periods of revival have been short-lived, or what brings them on at all. William McLoughlin asserts that there is no simple explanation—it is not economic or political crisis, nor wars or depressions that produce revivals. He suggests, however, that one common characteristic is a reexamination and redefinition of the nation's social and intellectual values—an attempt to maintain balance between tradition and change. This analysis is echoed by Perry Miller in *The Life of the Mind in*

America, his study of pre-Civil War America. Miller speculates that the dominant theme in America from 1800 to 1860 is the persistence of revivalism—sometimes smoldering, sometimes bursting into flame. He explains it in terms of the need of a society to find for itself solidarity and meaning. Revivals, I think, should be viewed as a response to changes in American society—to urbanization and industrialization, and to the dislocations produced by those changes. These changes caused a national "identity crisis," an anxiety to relocate the national soul.

Revivals, like the flames that are often used to describe them, flicker into blazing life for a short time, then diminish into a little more than embers, never wholly dying. Perhaps it is that they demand so much of the human psyche that they cannot be sustained for long periods of time. Perhaps it is that they speak to only one aspect of the human condition and leave so much untouched. But again and again, we see the transiency of periods of revival.

As early as 1835 there were signs that the well-springs of revivalism were drying up. The General Assembly of the Presbyterian Church noted that since there had been a decline in evangelical piety, all members, ministers, and elders should pray for a revival of genuine religion.[1] The *New York Evangelist* believed that revivals of religion were not so numerous as before, and a year later noted that revival interest had steadily declined.[2] Philip Schaff concluded that

> the flourishing period of new measures is now, in general, pretty much past and even among the Methodists the swollen stream of religious excitement seems to be again seeking its natural, fixed channels, especially in the more cultivated city congregations, which have never really approved those unwholesome excesses.[3]

Indeed, the Methodists, chief authors and promoters of revivals in the West and in the cities of the East, were experiencing changes that could only occur with the decline of revivals. The maturing church, which earlier had boasted of ministers who had never seen the inside of a college, was establishing colleges and seminaries, and by the 1850s was publishing scientific periodicals and entering the culture of the age.[4] Denominations like the German Reformed and the Lutherans were drawn back to their traditional patterns and they turned away from revivalism in the 1840s and 1850s.

Finney himself in these years expressed a new caution concerning the efficacy of revivals. The work in urban centers of the East had sobered him, and his attitude had perceptibly changed. In 1835 he had expressed boundless enthusiasm:

> So in revivals of religion, it is found by experience, that in the present state of the world, religion cannot be promoted to any considerable extent without them. The evils which are sometimes complained of, when they are real, are incidental, and of small importance when compared with the amount of good produced by revivals.[5]

As early as 1836, and increasingly after that time, he expressed disappointment in the ability of revivals to produce adequately trained Christians. In a lecture published in the *New York Evangelist*, he said that of all the converts of the revivals in the preceding ten years, "the great body of them are a disgrace to religion."[6] By 1845-46, in a series of lectures on revivals that appeared in the *Oberlin Evangelist*, he was saying:

> The more I have seen of revivals, the more I am impressed with the importance of keeping excitement down.... I have learned to ... feel much more confidence in apparent conversions that occur where there is greater calmness of mind.[7]

and

> Efforts to promote revivals of religion have become so
> mechanical, there is so much policy and machinery, so
> much dependence upon means and measures, so much
> of man and so little of God, that the character of revivals
> has greatly changed within the last few years.[8]

Finney had come to understand the limited value of conversions accomplished under the emotional pressure brought
about by his new measures. There is a poignant sense of
regret in his words. They are the lament of a man question-
ing the value of his life's work.

> I erred in manner and in spirit . . . . I fell short of secur-
> ing all the desirable results which might have been se-
> cured . . . . For the past 10 years, revivals of religion have
> been gradually becoming more and more superficial . . . .
> [Ministers] have seen the disastrous results of modern
> revivals so frequently that they honestly entertain the
> doubt whether they are upon the whole desirable.[9]

Friends of revivals, on the other hand, regretted Finney's
loss of heart. They complained that his preaching was losing the "soul stirring appeals to the heart" of earlier time:
"your preaching a few years ago was better . . . you reason
more than formerly."[10]

Still, revivalism was far from dead. Robert Baird in 1843
reported that in the period since 1800 revivals had become
a constituent part of the religious system of our country and
"he who should oppose himself to revivals as such would be
regarded by most of our evangelical Christians as ipso facto,
an enemy to spiritual religion itself."[11] While there was a
decline, revivals never really stopped. In Philadelphia the
decades of the 40s, 50s, and 60s saw a steady stream of
revivalists exhorting their audiences, as well as established

ministers who persisted in their belief in revivals. In 1841, for example, the Reverend Albert Barnes gave his series of sermons "Revivals of Religion in Cities and Large Towns." These were published and received a wide distribution and much acclaim. Maggie Van Cott, the Methodist evangelist, plied her trade during this time, as did the Reverend James Caughey, who excited audiences with his provocative sermons. Among the Baptists, Jacob Knapp and Jabez Swan kept revivals activated for 50 years, paying homage to Finney, who had long since lost his confidence in revivals. Knapp held revivals in Philadelphia in 1865 at Bethel Church for five weeks and at the Fourth Baptist Church in Philadelphia for seven weeks. After he left, work continued among his followers. Quaker itinerants Eliza Gurney and Sarah Smiley were active in the Philadelphia and New Jersey areas during this period. Revivals persisted as well among the Negro population, and provided the major religious experience for blacks.

Yet, although revivals continued, the fires burned lower. Much of the energy of revivals had channeled itself into various reform societies. The reforms selected by evangelicals were, of course, determined by their particular view of sin as an individual matter. Hence there was little interest on the part of evangelicals in the political or social life of the nation, but much concern with personal habits of piety and morality.

In Philadelphia, revivals had a more difficult acceptance than elsewhere and never, even in their zenith, received the great support that they received in the countryside or in some other cities. Attempts to establish a revival church died, not from hostility but from disinterest. Herein lies an important clue to the understanding of revivals in the city. We are inclined to accept the rhetoric of either the ardent revivalist or the equally ardent anti-revivalist. But there was a vast middle ground of people who, by disposition, or background, or by preoccupation with matters other than religious, simply did not care. They were immune to the religious activities of the time. Thus it is a mistake to view the revivals in terms of a polarity; one should instead perceive the matter in terms of a triangle, with perhaps the largest element of that triangle as the large number of Philadelphians untouched by what seemed to participants a major religious and social struggle. Thus, while denominations endorsed, or fulminated against revivals on an individual level, there was a good deal of indifference to them that went unchronicled. Finney noted this indifference, as did Knapp and later, Dwight L. Moody. As in most cities, opportunities for advancement were abundant, and these matters absorbed many people. In addition, cities have throughout history contained a diverse population and diversion of many sorts to occupy the minds and time of their inhabitants. Philadelphia's coolness to revivals may also perhaps have been due to a strong cultural and intellectual tradition. New York, it may be remembered, was able to establish a revival church for Finney, but that city had a large infusion of inhabitants from New York State, long a center for enthusiastic religion. Thus, while its religious life was disrupted, Philadelphia was relatively cool to revivals and offered greater resistance to attempts to universalize them than did other cities or the rural areas.

What, then, were the results of decades of revivals in Philadelphia, and in other urban centers? The simplest result was that church membership and attendance were increased, at least for the period of the revival and directly afterward. This increase, at the expense of church discipline and meaningful membership, was a dubious blessing, and perhaps contributed to the fascination of American churches with numbers, as though numbers were representative of truth.[12] But along with increases in church membership and attendance, bitter schisms rent churches and congregations. Loyal and hard-working ministers were disposed of at the urging of Finney and other revivalists for their "lukewarm" attitude to revivals. Some churches, such as the German Reformed Chruch of Philadelphia, took years to recover. Others simply fragmented and sought membership consistent with their outlook. Revivals encouraged a proliferation of churches wherever they occurred. In urban areas revivals were used to meet the problems that arose as a result of urban growth and spread. Churches that were vacated as a result of ever-widening circles of growth looked to revivals to rebuild their popular base.

Revivals had an important effect upon the religious life of the nation in other ways. The style of the ministry was appreciably changed by Finney and his followers.[13] The informal, unstudied sermon with its conversational tone and appropriate gestures became the American norm, replacing the carefully designed, closely reasoned sermon of the past. Even nonrevival ministers of the most educated sort realized that they must reach their congregations in a more personal way, and they adjusted their pulpit style accordingly. While they often continued to write and read their sermons, they attempted to make it appear that they were extemporaneous. In addition, the revivals infused American religious life with a large dose of lay participation, which was to become a pattern for decades to come. With piety rather than training made the utmost in importance, dedicated laymen were often most successful in church affairs, and the laity was elevated to great power in American church life. In this sense revivalism was consistent with Jacksonian democracy, which increased the power and importance of the masses in the political life of the nation. Revivalism and Jacksonian democracy, so hostile to each other politically, shared a common view of the importance of the common man in American life. In addition to the common man, women were given a larger role in church life. Evangelical churches, with their lay participation, were more ready to accept women's testimony and participation than the more ritualized churches, where insistence upon training and ordination would have limited them. The frequency of women revivalists attests to this fact.

A significant amount of the pressure in the abolition movement and in the early temperance movement is attributable to the fervor and activism of the revivals. There was a sincere effort to improve conditions for the insane, the orphan, the incarcerated. But much energy went into activities, that attempted to impose on society a narrow, sectarian view of life. The Bible and Tract Societies and the attempts to convert Jews to Christ were at variance with the freedom of conscience that had developed in American society. Revivalists were unable to understand that there was validity to religious experiences other than their own.

It was in the influence on the mass mind that antebellum revivals were most pervasive and long lasting. Revivals left an intellectual residue on vast numbers of Americans that was essentially inhibitory. The mind-set of the revivals, with its tendency to view things in absolutes, cast a Manichaean view on America's national life. Manichaean thinking, derived from an early variant of Christianity, ignores or denies inconvenient facts, and views the world as a great battleground of the forces of good and evil. The Manichaean insists on the need for a decision, but the choice is stacked and practically makes itself—all the good aspects being arranged on one side and the evil on the other. Hence, the often uncomfortable ambiguity of the middle ground is avoided in favor of polarities on either side. Revivals created in the popular mind an inability to understand the "doubtfulness of things," an inability to deal with the complexity of life. This is what made revivalists so dogmatic, so inflexible. As Finney said, "A person's expressing doubts renders his piety truly doubtful. A real Christian has no need to doubt."[14] Unable to see life except in simplistic terms, unable to question its own inherent individualism, revivalism was imbued with a hostility to thought and intellect that crippled it in dealing with recurrent problems of life. It was incapable of dealing with modernity as represented by Darwinian thought later in the century and by new social trends in the twentieth century. It was a heritage whose essential conservatism would flower in later decades.

10

Businessmen's Revivals

The resurgence of revivalism in 1858 occurred in a larger, more industrialized, infinitely more complex city. This revival, shorn of its spontaneity, was a conscious summoning of an old form to subdue new anxieties. It was a recitation of the old evangelical litany of guilt, repentence, and salvation, in order to reassure a disquieted city. This revivalism was new in several ways. It relied heavily upon businessmen, business methods, and the business outlook. It was marked by an increased use of modern techniques of communication. In many ways the Revival of 1858 marked the watershed in the new fusion of business and religion. It was interdenominational and nontheological, a sort of folk expression of middle-class Americans, bred in farm and village, to assuage the anxieties that beset them.

Philadelphia in the 1850s was a city of over half a million inhabitants that was reaching for maturity. The population of the old city between the two rivers from South to Vine Streets, and of Northern Liberties, Southwark, Moyamensing, Passyunk, and Penn Township grew from 96,660 in 1810, to 114,410 in 1820, to 360,305 in 1850.[1] All were really part of the city and the feeling that the districts should

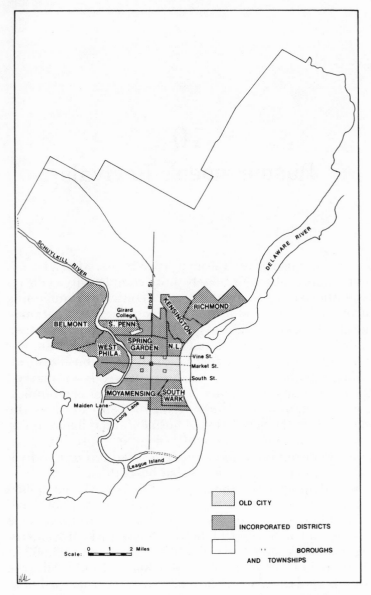

Philadelphia, 1954, showing incorporated districts

be consolidated had been prevalent for a long time. In 1854 consolidation became a reality, and included West Philadelphia, Germantown, Frankford, and Manayunk. The newly consolidated city was second in number of inhabitants only to New York.

The streets retained their quaint regularity, well paved with red brick or granite; handsome trees lined the sidewalk; the colorful old markets continued on Market Street, now under a covered arcade. The city of culture and science persisted. There were various theaters and halls to provide amusement and culture for Philadelphians. Foremost among the theaters were the Walnut Street Theater, Chestnut Street Theater, and Arch Street Theater. The Musical Fund Hall would present favorites like Jenny Lind and various European opera stars, but these facilities were proving inadequate and in 1855 work was begun on the Academy of Music at the southwest corner of Broad and Locust Streets. This great hall seated 3,000 people in opulent splendor, and its opening was a glittering and elegant event. Public lectures were well attended and Philadelphia public libraries were greatly admired. The city boasted many charitable and educational institutions, the newest and most admired being Girard College on the outskirts of the city. Opened in January of 1848, this institution provided an education and a home for fatherless white boys. With the University of Pennsylvania Medical Department, Jefferson Medical College, the Medical Institute of Philadelphia, the Philadelphia College of Medicine, and in 1849 the Female Medical College of Pennsylvania, Philadelphia considered itself the medical metropolis of the United States.

The Quaker City was proud of its parks. Independence Square, no longer a Potters Field, was now a beautiful and favorite promenade; Washington Square a haven with towering trees and birds. Rittenhouse Square in the western section of the city was becoming fashionable and Logan

Square in the northwest section and Fairmount Park provided open space for Philadelphians to enjoy. The city,
growing into maturity in the years before the Civil War,
although it provided all the amenities of an urban center,
still retained its quiet air of a village with the size of a large
city. English visitors characterized New York by busy bus-
tling and the Quaker city as a more subdued place. One
traveler referred to it as the "village-city."[2]

But in deeper ways, the city was changing and the
changes were unsettling to many Philadelphians. Philadelphia had become a modern big city. There were the beginnings of a downtown and some manufacturing sectors, but
the downtown was still mixed with residences, offices,
stores, and manufacturing. The separation of economic life
from residential patterns was only beginning. Workers
were beginning to commute to jobs, and inner-city transit
was becoming an important issue. Hundreds of omnibuses
or stages, drawn by horses and stopping at regular intervals,
crowded the streets to meet this transportation need. The
introduction of streetcars drawn by horses created lively
agitation. The opposition claimed that narrow streets, un-
sightly appearance, and frequent accidents made the
streetcars undesirable. In addition, the introduction of
streetcars soon led to charges of fraud and corruption in
connection with granting franchises. In spite of all of this,
1858 saw workmen busy tearing up many streets and laying
rails in Philadelphia.

Philadelphia's population was changing not only in size,
but in make-up. New arrivals from surrounding rural areas
and villages flocked to the city seeking opportunity. In
addition to the American country boys, there was the influx
from abroad. In the years immediately preceding the Civil
War the city's population grew to be a 30 percent foreign-
born. The mass of this foreign population was composed of
new immigrants from Ireland and, though somewhat
fewer, from Germany. While the city was still largely Protes-

tant, the years between 1850 and 1880 saw the Catholic church growing at a greater rate than the Protestant churches because of this immigration. This growth increased tensions and, despite attempts to restrain them, violence erupted with alarming frequency. With no large stock of old housing to ghettoize, the poor Irish immigrants flooded every ward in a heterogeneous pattern, as did the Germans, although the latter tended to concentrate somewhat in the northern side of town. By now, Negroes lived largely in their own quarter on Cedar Street, poor and ill-dressed, with separate schools, churches, and even a separate juvenile prison for the Negro children of Philadelphia. Tensions between the Irish and Negroes was high. "Nowhere is the prejudice against race stronger than in Philadelphia, the city of brotherly love," remarked a visitor in 1850.[3]

Added to the tension between Negro and Irish was the plight of the artisan. The decades before the Civil War marked a loss of relative standing in the city on the part of skilled artisans. The craft traditions of a century or more were unhinged by new industrial techniques. Many old crafts were broken down into new specialties, and a significant number of artisans became permanent employees, separated from the owner and shopkeeper class, and working longer hours at a faster pace and in a more socially isolated and economically insecure environment than they had ever labored in before or ever would again. A heightened appetite for consumption joined with very little rise in income to create an insuperable frustration. Psychologically, they were trapped in the painful transition from the eighteenth-century small-scale work to modern, large-scale, speculative production.[4]

The city, now more closely tied to national and international business conditions, began to have peaks of prosperity and depression. Depressions struck in 1819 and again in 1837; in the 1840s business was often slow, and a sharp panic hit in 1857. Philadelphia was beginning to perceive a loss of control over its own fate.[5]

With workers starting to commute to jobs came the beginning of the destruction of informal community. To counter this loss, Philadelphians rushed into associations of all sorts—lodges, clubs, benefit associations, even firehouse gangs and gangs of hoodlums. It was a symptom of a maturing community. With consolidation, both fire and police departments were coming under some regularization. The police department was divided into four districts and functions divided into constables, policemen, and watchmen, as well as lamplighters who could be called to service as policemen.[6] A newly installed police and fire alarm telegraph was very helpful in apprehending criminals, but was unable to deal with gangs of young thugs, largely in the outskirts of the city. These gangs, with colorful names like the Schuylkill Rangers, Rats #1, and Reed Birds, prowled the streets, terrorized citizens, and were exceedingly difficult to control. Fire protection was provided by boisterous volunteer fire companies. In 1858 there were 45 engine companies, 42 hose companies, and 5 ladder companies, 92 in all. Their rivalry and fighting made living with them unbearable, while need made them indispensable.[7]

The social environment of Philadelphia in 1857, then, was that of change and displacement. The old artisan class suffered dislocation, the influx of Irish immigrants brought controversy over use of the Bible in schools, and aroused the specter of an ancient enemy—the popish church. Periodic depressions caused people concern over the control of their lives. In addition to this free-floating anxiety was the agony of the slavery dispute, rapidly coming to a crisis. Anxiety about slavery disturbed the public and private conscience, but few spoke out for abolition. The city had a large trade with the South and large numbers of medical students from that area as well. Those who did advocate abolition were called by the Philadelphia *Public Ledger* "fanatics" and "incendiaries." Nevertheless there were antislavery meetings taking place throughout the city, and the confusion and bloodshed in Kansas had cast an ominous note regarding the future.[8] The churches were one way in which people attempted to deal with their anxieties. In 1857 the city directory reported 62 Presbyterian churches (including Old and New School Presbyterians as well as unaffiliated denominations), 50 Protestant Episcopal churches, 42 Methodist Episcopal, 31 Baptist, and 15 Lutheran churches, 11 Friends meeting houses, 5 German Reformed, and 4 Dutch Reformed, as well as numerous smaller groups, among them Unitarians, Universalists, Moravians, Mennonites, and Swedenborgians. In addition, there were 27 Roman Catholic churches, including the new cathedral on 18th and Race Streets, and 5 Jewish synagogues. The spring and summer of 1857 witnessed a large number of churches about to be opened or in the process of construction. There were among the clergy some well-known figures. Dr. Albert Barnes was the prominent pastor of the First Presbyterian Church on Washington Square. Phillips Brooks, a celebrated Episcopalian, was from 1859 to 1869 at the Church of the Advent and at Holy Trinity. Dr. W. H. Furness led the small but prominent group at the Unitarian Church at 19th and Locust Streets, the only Unitarian church in the city, which had a congregation of not more than 500. The Quaker city was dominated by Presbyterians, with large numbers of Episcopalians and Methodists, and with a growing Catholic presence.

In the waning months of 1857, Philadelphia citizens spoke of a government train destined for a battle with the Mormons destroyed near South Pass, the exposure of a shocking swindle in the Philadelphia Board of Health, confusion brought about by the Lecompton convention in Kansas, informal antislavery meetings taking place throughout the city. But the overriding concern of citizens in the autumn and winter of the year, the matter that eclipsed all others as the object of concern, was the economic panic and ensuing depression that had overcome not only Philadelphia, but the nation.

After a period of energetic growth and expansion from

the mid-40s through the mid-50s, a boom psychology infected the popular mind, buttressed by surging production, sales, and population.[9] Every economic indicator showed the optimism to be well-founded. Land values soared and purchasing on credit was common. Based on optimistic projections, railroads were constructed into a thinly settled West. While domestic overexpansion was a factor, world conditions also played a key role, for with the end of the Crimean War, Russian wheat returned to the world market and caused prices to fall. The American economy experienced once more one of its periodic collapses and depressions.

In the winter of 1856-57, stock in the new railway systems began to decline, banks began to contract loans, distrust seeped into the public mind. The suspension in August of the Ohio Life Insurance and Trust Company, considered a most stable institution, precipitated the crash. Early September brought the panic to the New York money market and by October there was no sale of any stocks and a general bank failure followed. Throughout the country stock exchanges and banks failed and leading railroads collapsed. Prices plummeted, small businesses failed, and factories closed, throwing thousands out of work. In all, a total of 6,000 firms failed. It was the northern states that felt the economic shock the hardest. In Philadelphia the shock came on September 25, 1857, when the Bank of Pennsylvania failed. Within the hour, the Girard and the commercial banks declared suspension of specie payments. Alarm spread through the city and businessmen were in a fever of excitement. Some banks were forced to call for police to protect them from clamorous creditors. Business was prostrated and people thrown out of work. The streets were filled with idle workmen and a call was issued for an extra session of the Pennsylvania legislature. Mass meetings were called, one on October 8th at Independence Square, seeking help from the General Assembly, and another on November 12, in which 10,000 workers met in Independence Square and demanded that the city give them work.[10] Week after week newspapers published news of business failures and suspensions, until at last *The Evening Bulletin* stopped this procedure, feeling that it exacerbated the situation. Distress became extreme through the early winter, overloading organized relief societies. Extra contributions were sought from public-spirited citizens.[11]

It is often noted that Americans perceive reality in moral terms. Certainly history provides us with abundant examples to buttress this hypothesis. The panic of 1857 is another such example. To many, the economic situation was seen, not in terms of a collapse of a complex business and industrial structure, but as the hand of God punishing men for unrepented sins. They viewed the disaster as a lesson that Providence had induced to teach the people.[12] *Harpers Magazine* perceived a relationship between the economic failure and moral shortcomings. Undue pursuit of wealth, said an editorial in May of 1858, took men's minds away from Christian activities. "The commercial losses of 1857 shocked people out of this attitude and forced a realization that their spiritual nature is above the animal."[13] Even the *Friends Intelligencer*, which saw the reasons for the depression as "too ready facilities for obtaining credit; the excessive bank loans encouraging unwise extension in business; the heavy foreign importations and demoralizing stock speculations, attended with corresponding extravagance in houses, equipage and furniture . . .," advised that the solution was "moderation in all things, whether in drinking, eating, dressing."[14]

If the disaster was the result of a neglect of religion, then a return to religion was the way out of this darkness. "God Himself would drive Mamon [sic] out that He Himself might reign."[15] Consequently evangelical Christians quietly began to move to respiritualize their brethren. The Revivals of 1858 were the fruit of this evangelical effort. The characteristic feature of these revivals was the noonday prayer meeting, in which thousands of people met for an hour of services and prayer in the midst of their workday. Where Finney's revivals had appealed largely to craftsmen and the uneducated working class, the noonday prayer meetings drew large numbers of businessmen and clerks, often new to the city. The noonday service was started in New York on September 23 in a third-floor meeting room at the rear of the Old Reformed Dutch Church on Fulton Street. As financial difficulties increased, so did attendance. The first meeting drew only three people, the next, six, and then twenty. Soon the noon-day prayer meetings caught on and attracted increasing numbers. At first weekly, they became daily, and soon hundreds were drawn to this hour of prayer and hymns.[16]

In Philadelphia, businessmen's prayer meetings were started by a young clerk not yet twenty-one years old, John C. Bliss. A native of Alabama, he had found employment in Philadelphia, and then in New York, where he had experienced religious conversion. The New York noonday services had impressed him, and upon his return to Philadelphia he suggested to members of the Young Men's Christian Association in Philadelphia that such a method be tried in this city.

The Young Men's Christian Association was intimately associated with the Revivals of 1858, and provided the extrainstitutional agency for sponsoring the various activities of the revivals. The YMCA was a product of evangelical Christianity and became the arm of the church in the cities. It was started in London in 1844 by George Williams, a farmer from Somerset who had apprenticed to a dry-goods merchant in Bridgewater at the age of sixteen, converted, and joined the Congregational church. In the glow of his new religious faith, he came upon the writings of the American evangelist Charles G. Finney, which were being read throughout the English-speaking world and in translation elsewhere.[17] He absorbed its practical gospel, its straight-laced morality, and its lack of denominational emphasis. The Young Men's Christian Association was conceived as an organization of Christians to counteract the evils of the city. London was then filled with young men from farms and small towns, seeking opportunity in the city. The YMCA attempted to take the young stranger by the hand, find him a quiet boardinghouse pervaded by Christian influences, introduce him to church and sabbath school, and thus keep him from the baleful influence of the city with its vice, alcohol, delinquency, and crime. Its program included prayer meetings, Bible classes, a reading room, an employment bureau, and a lodging-house register. It was an effort to counteract the appalling loneliness of the city and to lead young men into church membership.[18]

When George H. Stuart, a prosperous young Philadelphia linen merchant, visited London in 1851 at the time of the World's Fair at the Crystal Palace, he met George Williams and was impressed with his work. Stuart himself was the product of a rural Protestant home in Ireland. His parents, Scotch-Irish Presbyterians, were deeply religious people, the father an elder in the church, and the boy, born in 1816, was named after the pastor of their church, the Reverend George Hay. The boy had an early desire to be a minister, but his father's death when he was only ten diverted him from his ambition. When the family emigrated to Philadelphia to join the father's only brother, who had settled there in 1790, George Stuart started an importing house, Stuart and Brothers, at the southwest corner of Fourth and Arch streets. The business prospered and was later to have branches in New York and Manchester. Stuart retained the interest in religious affairs that stemmed from his rural evangelical background, and became active in church affairs and temperance reform. He was ordained as an elder in Dr. Wylie's First Reformed Presbyterian Church, and served as Sunday School Superintendent for twenty-five years.[19] When Stuart organized the Philadelphia Young Men's Christian Association on June 15, 1854, he was unaware that three such organizations had already been started on the continent, in Boston, Montreal, and

New York. He became president of the group, which contained 57 members, of whom 17 were vice-presidents, 33 managers, and only seven ordinary members. Its development was haphazard at first. Stuart realized the need for a full-time worker, and hired the first paid secretary of the YMCA, a nineteen-year-old clerk in a clothing store, John Wanamaker. There were no funds for his salary, so it was paid by Stuart. Wanamaker's extraordinary talent for organization put the YMCA on a businesslike basis. Within the first year of his secretaryship, Wanamaker reported 2,000 new members, tireless visitation of those who dropped in or were met by chance, the distribution of hundreds of Bibles, noon-day prayer meetings, and the placing of forty teachers in various Sunday schools.[20]

John Wanamaker was a remarkable young man by any standard. He was a man of exceptional organizational skill and forceful drive, the prototype of the self-made man so admired by generations of Americans. His maxims, which were used and quoted with some frequency, carry a Horatio Alger flavor:

> Almost every human being has some natural gift and is very much nearer than he thinks to the staircase of success, if he would only take the first step and keep on until he got to the top.

> To believe you cannot do a thing is a way to make it impossible.

> Most people who fail only work half-time, take too many holidays and are quitters.[21]

John Wanamaker was born at Buck Road and Long Lane, somewhat west of Broad and South Street. The area contained many truck farms and a number of ponds, and Wanamaker always referred to himself as a "country boy." His grandfather was a farmer, his father a bricklayer. The family had descended from Palatine stock that had immigrated from Germany in the 1730s. Young John Wanamaker was of pious background: his grandfather was a lay preacher in the Methodist church and his father taught Sunday School. His mother told him frequently that she hoped he would be called to the ministry. His relatives and friends, according to his memories of them, were all churchgoing people whose chief reading was the Bible.[22]

The boy had only a grade school education and started working at the age of fourteen, first as an office boy in a law office, then in a book store at $1.25 per week. His health faltered and he was sent West to Minnesota as a probable consumptive. Returning, he came under the influence of one of the most colorful ministers in Philadelphia, the Reverend John Chambers. Chambers was considered unorthodox, refusing to accept the dogmas of the Westminster Confession, and when he was refused ordination, he established the First Independent Church of Philadelphia. He was a fearless crusader against vice and one of the first Philadelphia preachers to make total abstinence a test of morals in spite of the fact that most of his church members enjoyed their whiskey, and many liberal supporters of the church were distillers. He was emotional and practical in his appeal; he "roared like the bull of Bashan."[23] Chambers is said to have been the first preacher in Philadelphia to use advertising space in newspapers. Young John Wanamaker came under the influence of this charismatic preacher and became, in 1856 at the age of eighteen, a Sunday-School teacher in the basement of John Chambers's church. He became involved in its missionary efforts. In later years he declared that he would have become a minister but for his poor health and the fact that he felt he could accomplish more in the domain of morals as a businessman influencing fellow merchants. In retrospect, it seems to have been his entrepreneurial drive that got in the way of his ministerial ambitions. In 1858, not ready to go back into business nor ready to enter the ministry, he embarked upon religious work and became the first full-time secretary of the YMCA in the United States, with a salary of $1,000—excellent pay at the time for a man of twenty. It was with the money he saved from three years of this service that the Wanamaker business was founded.[24]

Wanamaker's religious zeal, together with his great organizational ability, made the YMCA an association to be reckoned with. Its evangelistic emphasis expressed itself in various program activities. The YMCA sent men to preach on street corners, at wharves, in neighborhood fire houses, wherever they could gather an audience. They distributed tracts and established rescue missions. There were interdenominational revivals aimed at interesting those who would attend a meeting in a public hall but would not attend a church. The middle-class white-collar workers, clerks, and merchants who provided the membership for the YMCA sought to reach the young men who, like themselves, had moved from rural areas to the city, and to draw them into city congregations. The Philadelphia Association would circularize rural clergymen within fifty miles, requesting them to furnish letters of introduction to young men about to leave their congregations for the city.[25] Merchants encouraged their clerks to join the YMCA for those qualities of temperance, moderation, industry, and perseverence which they felt its influence would encourage. The clerks needed little encouragement, for the YMCA promulgated the creed of the age.

Yet the Young Men's Christian Association met with the hostility of the evangelical churches, whose goals it shared. The organization seemed to be diverting membership from the church. John Wanamaker told of the hostility he experienced as the paid secretary of the organization because the idea of anyone but a clergyman's accepting a salary for religious work, for "trying to make money out of religion," was new and startling, and was repugnant to many.[26] Nonetheless, the YMCA soon became the arm of the church in preaching the Gospel to the unchurched of the city, for while it appealed directly to young men fresh from the country, the whole city became its mission field. This was

the extra-institutional organ of the church which, because
of the crusading zeal of its membership and its nondenominational character, soon assumed leadership in the revivals
of 1858.

The mind-set of the YMCA and that of the "union meetings" and "prayer meetings" it sponsored were the same.
Neither considered the world its province but felt that the
ills of society were due to evil men under the Devil's control
and that conversion to Christ offered the only possibility of
social reform. Through the years, the YMCA remained
uninvolved in public affairs, oblivious to the rise of the
American labor movement or the Social Gospel movement
in the churches. Such reforming tendencies as appeared
were concerned with temperance, gambling, tobacco, and
other private vices consistent with the evangelical world
view. The Revival of 1858 reflected this individualistic and
inward-looking emphasis.

The noonday prayer meetings were the unique development of the revivals. The first one in Philadelphia was on
Monday, November 23, 1857, in the midst of the searing
panic and depression that were overcoming Philadelphians. It was held in the lecture room of the Methodist
Episcopal Union Church on Fourth Street below Arch, and
it was sponsored by the Philadelphia YMCA. For a long
time the response of businessmen was meager, 36 being the
highest number in attendance and the average at each
weekly meeting never exceeding twelve. A more central
location was sought and found in the anteroom of Jaynes
Hall on Chestnut Street, where meetings began on February 3, 1858. After a gradual increase, suddenly the noon-
day meetings caught on. On Monday, March 8, attendance
reached 300, and the next day many were turned away for
lack of space. By March 9 meetings had moved from the
anteroom to the large hall with seats for 2,500, and it was
filled. Galleries and platform soon were utilized and the
partition between smaller and larger rooms taken down to
open up the entire building. The sight was heartening to

participants. The hall was unusually high, with several tiers of elegantly ornamented boxes extending across the back. The entire hall held 3,000 when filled.[27]

There were no revivalist ministers leading these meetings. Although ministers were in attendance, the meetings were conducted by laymen. There was no noise of confusion, but a quiet, emotional fervor pervaded the meetings, and they were conducted with a businesslike efficiency. People would congregate starting at 11 o'clock and by noon the room would be fully occupied and awesomely silent. The meeting was kept moving—a hymn by a well-known merchant or unknown clerk, a prayer offered, a passage of Scripture read. A comment was added and the leader of the meeting invited any Christian man in the congregation either to pray or to exhort. Sometimes a minister, but usually laymen, would accept. Signs on the wall gave notice that such prayer and exhortation were not to exceed three minutes, nor were more than two consecutive offerings to be made. Furthermore, no controversial points were to be discussed. If remarks were not brought to a close within the limit, a bell would sound and the speaker was obliged to be seated. Eyewitnesses told of hardheaded businessmen rising to give testimony with tears streaming down their cheeks.[28] Those who could not stay for the full hour came and went at their own convenience. After the offerings of prayers and testimonials, a verse of hymn was sung standing, and the group was dismissed. Within a half hour they were completely dispersed.

While the noonday prayer meetings were the most characteristic feature of the revivals of 1857-58, they were accompanied by other kinds of services. There were prayer services at Handel and Haydn Hall and at the American Mechanics Auditorium. There were evening services in meeting halls sponsored by the YMCA for special groups of people. Firemen, students, and transient guests at the city's hotels were among those sought out by these meetings.[29] City churches of various denominations were opened daily in the mornings and many afternoons as well. All denominations participated.[30] There were revivals in Germantown and Manayunk under the Reverend Jacob Helffenstein.[31] The prominent Methodist revivalist and exhorter Alfred Cookman, was, during this revival, stationed at the Green Street Church in Philadelphia. The scenes of his preaching were blazing revivals and they counted many conversions. His pocket diary records religious services night after night, and participation in special services in the city as well as outside.[32] Cookman's extemporaneous and ringing style brought many tears, and many people sought out his services for their warmth and emotion. Two pious Quaker ladies long associated with Joseph John Gurney and Elizabeth Fry, the Quaker evangelicals, united with some of the young men of the Young Men's Christian Association and held meetings in the rural districts near the city. These meetings were crowded and emotionally charged, with much tear-shedding and weeping.[33]

When the revival seemed to be ebbing in the spring, the YMCA reactivated it with the Union Tabernacle, a movable tent set up in various parts of the city. It aimed at preaching the Gospel to masses who would not enter a church. "Wise fishermen use all the various kinds of means and appliances to catch the different kinds of fish," its leaders explained.[34] The tent was respectable, yet not so much so as to repel the humbler classes of society. It was an attempt to break down the social inequalities that were reflected in church membership and that were felt to be so inappropriate to religious life. Here all classes of society, rich and poor, were on equal footing. The tent, costing $2,000, accommodated 1,200 people yet was often insufficient to hold the crowds who attended.[35] Under the direction of George J. Mingus, appointed by the YMCA as Superintendent of the Union Tent, the services were started May 1, 1858 and had the support of almost all denominations: Lutherans, Episcopalians, German Reformed, Moravians, Presbyterians (Old and New Schools), Baptists, and Dutch Reformed.[36] It was moved during its four-and-a-half months in the city to four different stations. Its first was at Broad and Locust Streets, on the lot of ground adjoining the Academy of Music then being built. Other sites were Broad and Girard, 10th and Callowhill, and 4th and George Streets. The program consisted of prayer meetings and preaching several times on the Sabbath and sunrise prayer meetings daily. Preaching on weekday evenings was by ministers recruited from various denominations, and on Wednesday evenings was conducted by laymen. In addition, there were "special" meetings for the children and the "anxious."[37] At the end of its use in Philadelphia, the tent was removed to a rural district, Quakertown, where meetings of an intensely exciting character took place.[38]

According to the YMCA account, the Union Tabernacle produced gratifying results and before the year's end the services were attended by from 150,000 to 170,000 people.[39] In addition to the prayer meetings and other services, distribution of tracts was promoted, fast days selected, and new churches started. It was during the 1858 revivals that John Wanamaker founded the Bethany Sunday School, which became the Bethany Presbyterian Church in Philadelphia. The area to the south of his home in the southwestern part of the city had become a refuge for criminals and a notorious band of toughs known as the Schuylkill Rangers. They made life miserable for the families who lived there. Those who could moved away from the reign of terror produced by these gangs. On February 7, 1858, Wanamaker set up a Sunday School in a cobbler's shop, gathering together a group of a dozen or so South Street boys in a second-floor room over the shop. He enjoined the boys to attend, gave them a bit of candy, and then offered them prayers and a chapter of Scripture. The hoodlums invaded the school one Sunday afternoon and drove everyone out with their hooting and jeering. Undaunted, Wanamaker not only continued but enlarged his meetings, outstaying pelting with snowballs and rotten eggs, and damage done to property, not to mention hooting and threats. When volunteer firemen, admiring his persistence, let it be known that they would be on hand the next Sunday, the rowdyism came to an abrupt end. By July there were over 300 children present, and Wanamaker moved the Sunday School into a tent and, later, a building of its own.[40]

John Wanamaker was equally persistent with the Philadelphia firemen, long a trial to the community with their turbulence and profanity. The 92 companies enrolled thousands of members, principally young men. The Revival of 1858 sought to reach these young men to reform their character. Sermons delivered to them and prayer meetings held especially for them witnessed emotional testimonials and conversions.[41] They were encouraged to come in their firefighting outfits if they wished. Wanamaker took his services to the Phoenix Hose Company on Tuesday, March 30, and within three weeks there were 17 meetings among firemen, reported the *Philadelphia Inquirer*.[42]

The revival that stirred Philadelphia had its counterparts in large and small cities throughout the country. Chicago, Boston, New York, and Baltimore, as well as smaller cities like Wilmington, Buffalo, Milwaukee, and Cleveland felt its impact. Finney was in Boston and New York during this time, rejoicing, his qualms allayed by the apparent vindication of his life's work. He conducted noonday prayer meetings and conferences for anxious inquirers in the afternoon and preaching services in the evening, while Mrs. Finney held ladies' meetings daily to crowded rooms.[43]

A new aggressiveness was evident in the advertising procedures used. Notices for prayer meetings were distributed in banks and stores and printed announcements were displayed in public places. Tracts were distributed in street cars, omnibuses, and ferry boats, and many were simply dropped on pavements for passers-by to pick up and read.[44] Unlike earlier revivals, which were reported only by the religious press, the Revival of 1858 was reviewed by all the secular newspapers. But the newest device used in this revival was the telegraph. The newly completed electric telegraph, symbol of progress and technology, created a curious sense of community among participants in distant cities. It brought together the various threads of the revival into a consciously realized movement. It became the practice for businessmen in one city to wire businessmen in another, acquainting them with the progress of their prayer meetings. For this purpose, the telegraph company allowed messages to be sent free of charge at certain specified hours.[45] The following wire went out to the "Philadelphia Union Prayer-Meeting in Jaynes' Hall" from New York, March 12, 1858:

CHRISTIAN BRETHREN—The New York John Street Union Meeting sends you greetings in brotherly love: "And the inhabitants of one city shall go to another, saying, Let us go speedily to pray before the Lord, and to seek the Lord of Hosts—I will go also."

Praise the Lord—call upon his name—declare his doings among the people—make mention that his name is exalted.

Benj. F. Manierre
Cephas Brainard, Leaders

The response was read to the New York meeting in John Street:

To George P. Edgar, for John Street meeting, Philadelphia, March 13, 12-1/4 o'clock, p.m. Jaynes Hall Daily Prayer-Meeting is crowded; upward of 3000 present; with one mind and heart they glorify our Father in heaven for the mighty work He is doing in our city and country in the building up of saints and the conversion of sinners. The Lord hath done great things for us, whence joy to us is brought. May He who holds the seven stars in his right hand and who walks in the midst of the

churches, be with you by His Spirit, this day. Grace,
Mercy, and peace be with you.

George H. Stuart,
Chairman of Meeting[46]

In addition, messages spilled forth to all parts of the
country announcing conversions. "Dear Mother, the revival
continues and I, too, have been converted," or "My dear
parents, you will rejoice to hear that I have found peace
with God," or "Tell my sister that I have come to the cross of
Christ."[47] Many young men engaged in business in Eastern
cities sent such messages to loved ones at home, assuring
them that their childhood teachings were being pursued in
the city.

The new technology linked the nation as never before,
and news, whether of bankruptcy or of revivals, moved
rapidly, creating a sense of community never before possible in so large a geographic area. The revivals, born in rural
isolation, had entered the modern age.

The Revival of 1858, so widely accepted among Protestant denominations, met with the criticism of earlier oppo-
nents, the Unitarians and the Jews, and faced the articulate
opposition of a newly emerged presence in the city, the
Roman Catholics. Among dissident groups it was the
Roman Catholics who now became the most strenuous op-
ponents of revivals.

Catholics sensed among the evangelical groups a deep-
seated hostility, and they considered evangelical attempts
among their membership a clear threat. Furthermore, the
lay-led revivals were an affront to their hierarchical style of
organization. Consequently Catholic response to the revival
reflected these anxieties. The young men of the YMCA,
they felt, were more productive of harm than of good, and
they were ignorant or had crude and confused notions of
Christian truth.[48] Attempts to use public school buildings
for prayer meetings they felt to be reprehensible. They

cited with disapproval prayer meetings held three times a
week in the High School building:

> The lads are from parents of all religious de-
> nominations . . . and it would seem part of an implied, if
> not an expressed compact that no such thing should be
> done in such a mixed audience.

Since Catholics, Jews, and Unitarians had to pay their proportion of expenses to the schools, such public institutions
should not be used for sectarian purposes. "What a howl
would be raised by the No-Popery fanatics were a Catholic
priest to perform the solemn office of religion in one of the
rooms of Central High School!"[49]

The *Catholic Herald and Visitor* ran a continuous story on
the new revivalism. They criticized the American interest in
public gatherings and decried the Methodists, who with
their camp meetings sought to pervert this interest to their
own uses. These self-satisfied men, said the article, were
interested only in their own salvation, and believed that no
person could be saved unless he believed as they did. Of
current revivals in the city, the article went on,

> I am sincere in the opinion that all revivals, got up in a
> preconcerted way, are a kind of blasphemy. They act
> upon the physical nature alone . . . . Why is it that among
> the intelligent and enlightened we find so few con-
> verts . . .? Why is it that these men stand aloof from all
> show of religion beyond that of being good, moral men,
> except the ordinary ceremonies of the church. It is be-
> cause that [*sic*] we are disgusted with shallow artifice, and
> surface piety and find no sympathy and receive no bene-
> fit from a religion founded in ignorance and supported
> by blasphemy and misrepresentation.[50]

The Unitarians continued their withering blasts at revivals, the most famous attack being the widely read sermon
of Theodore Parker, "A False and True Revival of Reli-

gion," delivered on April 4, 1858. In a blast at John Wanamaker, who by now was building his clothing store—called "Oak Hall," the precursor to the Wanamaker Store—Parker derided revivals as an "ecclesiastical business operation." "Park Street Church," he said, "is the Oak Hall of slop clothing." They worked on men's fears, he went on, and attacked the small vices like gambling, drinking, and so on, while many men, well born and well educated, turn away in disgust from real religion. They would create church members, he conceded, but not good husbands, good wives, daughters . . . farmers, lawyers, mechanics, and the like. He predicted that, if all Boston were converted and admitted to the churches that were getting up this revival, it would not "add one ounce to the virtue of the city, not one cent's worth of charity to the whole town." He continued, "You weaken its intelligence, its enterprise, you deaden the piety and morality of the people."[51]

Along with the Catholics and the Unitarians, and in uneasy alliance with them, the Jewish community expressed similar criticism. Isaac Leeser wondered why the revived sinners were to be found in a few years among the backsliders? He saw nothing strange in the curious phenomenon of so many conversions coupled with so absolutely little religious progress. The imagination was heated by descriptions of the torture of the damned and the felicity of the blessed, and by the promise of purification by merely adopting some speculative views, a procedure that cost him no great trouble. Such a convert, he said, "has no duties to learn, no practices to acquire, he is merely told . . . to bathe in the Jordan and he will become clean. He acquires blessed relief." The conversion, Leeser continued, was accordingly but a form of selfishness, to acquire pardon in the cheapest manner, where the outlay was absolutely nothing and the expected benefit extremely large. No spiritual cure had been effected and a relapse into previous indulgences was apt to take place, when the excitement of the thing had worn away.[52] Leeser questioned the validity of counting numbers in religion. "Is heathendom in truth more power-ful because its followers outnumber all other persua-sions? . . . is the principle more enduring, more likely to outlive a contest with other systems?"[53]

Despite some Quaker evangelists, the Quakers as a whole demurred against either overwhelming acceptance or criti-cism. The *Friends Intelligencer* reported that in Philadelphia alone there were thousands of men and women who turned from the active duties of life of worship an hour each day. This was admirable, but the revival would be tested by its fruits, not by its present effect. The Society of Friends should not be consistently associated with the movement. But on the other hand, Friends should not condemn or ridicule the revival as they had been doing. They were urged to withhold judgment and refrain from attending Jaynes Hall out of curiosity.[54]

Indeed, many were drawn to the prayer meetings and the tent services out of idle curiosity. Others were scornful of the proceedings. *The New York Herald*, in a sharply critical editorial, felt that the revivals had little or no appeal to the poor, the industrious, the hard-working classes.

> It is evident from this state of things, that the revivalists have not, so far, brought to grace those persons who need it most. They have captured a few clerks, a broken-down stock broker or two, a repentent pugilist, etc . . . . of the more genteel and idle classes—of those who are, or pre-tend to be, above the common working classes.[55]

By the end of the summer of 1858, the movement, for all practical purposes, had come to an end.[56] Churches re-ported great accession in membership and increased num-bers of candidates for the ministry; according to the YMCA account of the revivals, the number added to the evangelical churches in the space of twelve months was estimated at 10,000.[57]

Despite these claims of great accessions, Philadelphia

church statistics show no dramatic rise in numbers of churches or in total number of communicants as a result of these revivals. The increase reflected in the following chart must be understood in the context of a continuing shift from rural to urban communities as well as immigration from abroad, and a continuing shift from inner-city areas to the new suburbs.

TABLE 10.1
Philadelphia Churches, 1857-1859[58]

Number of Churches

Denomination	1857	1858	1859
Presbyterian*	62	62	68
Protestant Episcopal	50	53	56
Methodist Episcopal	42	42	49
Baptist	31	29	30
Lutheran	15	13	15
Friends Meeting Houses	11	10	10
German Reformed	5	5	5
Dutch Reformed	4	4	4

Among the denominations, the Presbyterians, Episcopalians, and Methodists show a greater rise in the number of churches than the remaining denominations. But even though the number of churches rose, the evidence of intra-city mobility indicates that this is probably a contributory factor along with the revivals. As members moved away from old churches, they started new ones convenient to their new homes. The Revival of 1858 probably acted as a catalyst to this development.

Total church membership seems to have remained stable. While new members increased during and immediately after the Revival of 1858, they soon leveled off to earlier levels, and the total number of communicants remained essentially the same, indicating that there were probably

---

*This is a comprehensive number that includes unaffiliated churches falling into the Presbyterian category.

sufficient members dropping away to offset new members even in the revival year.

TABLE 10.2
Philadelphia Presbyterians (Old and New School),
1857-1860[59]

	1857	1858	1859	1860
Number of churches	43	42	47	47
Number added	737	1,080	988	969
Total Communicants	13,203	13,240	14,616	13,630

The statistics among Old and New School Presbyterians in Philadelphia illustrate this (Table 2). The number of churches rose in 1859 to 47. While 1858 saw the largest number of new members, 1,080, in 1859 they dropped off to 988, and in 1860 diminished further. But the total number of communicants remained stable, implying that since there were a considerable number of members added, there must also have been considerable attrition. When the evangelical activity died away in the summer of 1858, despite extravagant claims to the contrary, the Presbyterian, Methodist, and Episcopal churches had shown new churches added to their numbers, but total church membership, even among these denominations, remained stable.

The revivals, firmly fixed to their rural evangelical beginnings, were most effective with Philadelphians from evangelical homes, newly arrived in the city from rural areas or small towns. This transplanted rural-bred youth utilized the revival as a device to reaffirm his status and his values. For him the noonday prayer meetings and peripheral evangelical activities became a coping mechanism for dealing with the cold impersonality of the city. Through the revival he tried to counteract the searing anonymity of the city. In prayer meetings he could meet with his own kind and reaffirm his values and status. But the revival was not successful in reaching those whom it felt needed its message the most. It simply had little or no appeal to the poor, the immigrant, the laborer. It had little success in reaching these elements of the population because it spoke a kind of intellectual shorthand that had little meaning to those people. Revivals evoked mythical rural longings and images of the self-made man. They demanded rigidity of personal habits. Immigrants sensed that what was required of them was an "Anglo-conformity," a complete renunciation by immigrant groups of their ancestral heritage in an attempt to make the United States a harmonious and homogeneous people.[60]

The revivals reinforced and were in turn reinforced by the middle-class values that bolstered the American industrial system. The message was loud and clear: work hard, abstain from drink, go to church, be honest and pious, and you can achieve great success. This had relevance to the rural-bred Protestant youth who came to the city and entered the white-collar ranks. For the uncouth immigrant or the poor laborer in the city, such virtues were hardly a passport into the middle class. For them, the message was a hollow one indeed.

With the Revival of 1858, the church attempted to meet the new realities of American life. It sought to keep churches filled despite the constant outward growth of the city. It sought to reach the stream of young men new to the city and bind them into the texture of church life. The twin organs of the church and the YMCA were engaged in a fierce struggle to bring the city to its own understanding of Americanism.

There were no prominent revivalists in these urban revivals of 1858, no Finney or Moody to lead the way. Instead, the meetings were conducted by dozens of laymen, earnest young businessmen and clerks. These lay leaders of the revival had, almost to a man, a rural background and a middle-class orientation. As a class they understood themselves to be carriers of the heritage. There were other changes in revivals. Some tendencies had faded while others were confirmed and strengthened. The individualism inherent in revivals not only continued but was enhanced. Gone was the radicalism of earlier years; what remained of elements of reform narrowed into concern with individual vice and private sins of a pietistic sort. With the nation racked by economic disaster and torn by the agony of slavery, the revivalists of 1858 agonized over the state of their souls. This turning inward had always been a component of revivalism; now it became a central theme. By 1858 business efficiency and modern technology became handmaidens of religion. It was at this time that the congeniality between the business community and the religious establishment first became evident. This congruence of interest and attitude would become more intense in ensuing decades. The Revival of 1858 manifests the fusion of the American business culture with religion. Business efficiency and modern technology were put into the service of religion and found themselves marvelously congenial. In an earlier revival, Charles Finney would stop the machinery in a factory in order to hold a prayer meeting; by 1858 it was important to fit it into the business day at the noon hour. Religion must fit into the organization of the business day, not disrupt it. Where earlier revivals had depended upon word of mouth or religious periodicals to spread their message, by the end of the 1850s new methods, such as advertising, the use of secular newspapers and periodicals, and the fruit of American inventiveness, the telegraph, were put into use to bring religion to the American people. Instead of emotional ranting and confusion in revival meetings, orderly procedures made them consistent with modern life.

Other aspects of American life were in similar fashion being infected with the business world view. For example, nineteenth-century schools were obsessed with problems of punctual and regular attendance. It was not just that school attendance was so important, but that habits inculcated in school would be valuable in the world of business. System and order characterized industrial employment. Regularity must characterize the business-oriented community. These qualities must be instilled in the minds of pupils as a principle. Thus did the values of the business community became culturally assimilated. The school was meeting the problem of transforming agrarian habits into traits necessary to conduct city life and large-scale manufacturing. Without promptness, neither city nor factory (nor school) could function properly.[61]

The ecumenism of earlier revivals was continued and enlarged. Old and New School Presbyterians could participate along with Baptists, Methodists, Episcopalians, and even some Quakers. This was achieved through the careful avoidance of doctrinal matters. The result was a diminution of theology in favor of a broad, general religiosity. Not only were controversial religious isues avoided, but also troublesome social and political matters. Accounts of the revivals of 1858 are revealing, as much for what they ignore as for what they express. One can read contemporary accounts for hours without finding any mention of the burning social issues of the day. American churches sought to increase their numbers at the expense of theological purity and ethical forthrightness.

Employers, however, were under no illusions as to the conservative thrust of the revivals. Their clerks were urged to involve themselves in the prayer meetings in the hopes that, occupied with matters of the soul, they would not become embroiled in labor unrest or political disturbances. The gospel of success and the gospel of business supported each other. Clerks became convinced that piety and wealth went hand in hand; that, attending to matters of the soul, they would achieve success.[62]

Increased professionalization was the hallmark of the age. It manifested itself in various aspects of culture. In popular education, reforms started in a blaze of passionate optimism in the 1830s and 1840s, but by the 1860s they diminished into mere professionalization and bureaucratization. The roots shriveled, and educators, like revivalists, were talking in terms that bore little relevance to the earlier movement. Educators, responding to a perception of an unraveling social fabric compounded of increased industrialization and social stratification, sought reform by imposing upon the working class the ethic of the middle and upper classes in an effort to achieve social harmony, a truly unified society. To educational reformers, the public high school became a mechanism for social discipline. Middle-class families joined the socially and intellectually prominent in promoting public high schools to achieve a more cohesive society.[63]

The leaders of penal reform followed the same pattern of development, from evangelical reformers to professional penologists. The 1830s experienced fresh surges of humanitarianism. A band of energetic reformers under the leadership of men like Louis Dwight of Boston, a devout evangelical reformer, sought redemption of the criminal. They instituted better care of women in prisons, commutation of sentences for good behavior, and other reforms. The dominant reform influences were religious. But by the late 1870s, the reform movement faltered and a new rationalization set in. A class of men who regarded themselves as penologists took over. In an effort to avoid competing with outside industrial production, they became concerned with education and training. The self-supporting prison gave way to the pedagogical institution. With the maturity of the profession, early reforming wardens were displaced by social statesmen with a scientific turn of mind, but with less zeal for reform.[64]

Developments in medicine followed a similar pattern, although not so clearly defined. In the first half of the century, individual doctors practiced medicine in an unscientific way, with conflicting methods and ideologies and much controversy. One became a doctor through apprenticeship to a doctor who was called a preceptor. Soon apprenticeship became institutionalized, and medical societies developed rules to govern student and preceptor. The standard apprenticeship lasted three years, at a fee of $10 per year. When it was realized that apprentices could be taught more economically and efficiently in classes, medical training became professionalized. By the middle of the nineteenth century, with the founding of the American Medical Association, medicine was a profession.[65]

The efficiency and organization of business life came to dominate all institutions in American life. In revivals, rationalization created a new order—that of revivals without ministers or even revivalists, run in a businesslike manner with clockwork precision. Men like Wanamaker and Stuart, with their zest for business and their evangelical interests, had molded revivalism into a new form. It was to come increasingly under the aegis of American business culture.

11
Colossus in Philadelphia

The decades after the Civil War brought pervasive changes in American society. Urbanization and industrialization expanded at a rapid pace, accelerating social problems and economic conflict. The new technical advancements, heavy immigration, and social displacements that were inherent in America's industrialization process created a new mood in the land. The "Brown Decades" had begun—darker, sadder, and soberer than any America had yet experienced.[1] The characteristic response of evangelical Protestantism was to promote revivalism as the best means of revitalizing the faith and thereby solving the problems that beset the nation. Revivalism had become a fixture of evangelical churches, but it was a changing institution. The blazing intensity of Finney's urban revivals had softened into the quiet piety of the Revival of 1858. With the entrance of Dwight Lyman Moody into professional revivalism, new elements were brought into juxtaposition with the old. With Moody, revivals came to reflect the key American theme of the late nineteenth century—a celebration of American business values and techniques. Revivals became a well-oiled, businesslike enterprise.

200

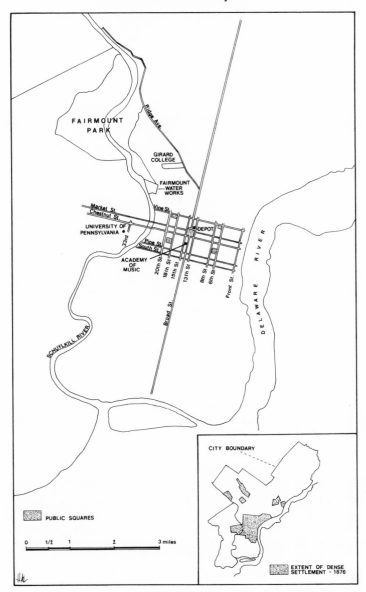

Philadelphia, 1876

Philadelphia in 1875 was the second largest city in the United States, with a population of about 794,000.[2] About 71% of the residents were native-born and 28% foreign-born, largely German and Irish.[3] Philadelphia was known as "the city of homes," for it boasted more homes than Brooklyn and New York together and had less than half as many people living in each home. Philadelphia proudly claimed that her working people lived better and were better fed than in any city in the world. The boundaries had been extended by the Consolidation Act of 1854 so that the distinction between the city and the adjoining districts was abolished. Thus the suburbs of Kensington, Germantown, West Philadelphia, Northern Liberties, Spring Garden, Richmond, Penn, Southwark, Moyamensing, and Passyunk were now parts of the city proper.[4]

The population was pushing outward from its earlier limits. West Philadelphia was filling up, and in the early seventies, the University of Pennsylvania moved to its present site. The no man's land between the central city and the districts like Germantown was being eradicated. The wealthy now lived south of Chestnut Street and west of Seventh, with Tenth and Walnut Streets the most desirable residential location in the city. Homes were typically brick with white marble steps and facings, and with wooden shutters. Pavements were brick, but streets were either unpaved, or paved with Belgian blocks—in either case filthy and muddy.[5] Although the city was large, it was not yet fully of age. Despite an ordinance forbidding it, goats ran wild at Eleventh and Passyunk Streets. Russell Conwell, Baptist clergyman and later the founder of Temple University, described the city in 1875 like this:

> In those days, Broad Street was more like a country "Main" or "High Street" than a city thorofare. To be sure, the Academy of Music and the LaPierre House [a prominent hotel] gave a metropolitan air to the immediate

surroundings; but the street generally was straggling, unkempt, and truly rural in appearance. South of Washington Avenue or Prime Street and north of Columbia Avenue it lapsed into a country road. There was no City Hall as yet; old Penn Square had not made way for the vast marble pile from whose towers William Penn surveys the growing city of his foundation. There were practically no retail stores west of Twelfth or Thirteenth on Chestnut. The greater part of Walnut Street between Seventh and Broad Streets was given over to aristocratic-looking residences of a colonial type. Arch Street had likewise an air of refined ease, as if it said to the merchant, "You may live here, but you must have your place of business elsewhere." Well-to-do people were beginning to build houses west of Broad Street, but when they moved into them, they felt as if they were living in the country.[6]

The city had matured enough to have a paid fire department and police protection. The police force was a sophisticated system of 1,200 patrolmen, 25 turnkeys, 8 detectives, 50 sergeants, 27 lieutenants, 4 captains, a fire marshall, and a chief of police, all under control of the mayor. Economically, Philadelphia was an important manufacturing center, excelled by New York only in value of manufactured products.[7] There were over 8,000 manufacturing plants in the city, employing over 150,000, about 26% of them women over 15 and about 6% young people under 15.[8] They produced molasses and sugar, woolen goods, clothing, hosiery, carpets, boots and shoes, machinery and locomotives.

Transportation was provided by street railroads, charging seven cents for adults and four cents for children, and often offering an exchange ticket to a crossroad. There were carriages and hackneys as well. This public transportation helped to bridge the greater separation between residence and place of work. Ferries and steamboats operated on the Delaware River to New Jersey and other points. The streets were well lighted with gas, and modern technology was making communication more rapid: the local telegraph company would send a ten-word message to any part of the city for twenty cents, and Western Union and Atlantic and Pacific Company to points outside the city for equivalent rates. But the effects of technology were uneven; not everyone had a bathroom, and a bathhouse in every ward with proper accommodation for both sexes was still an unreached goal.[9] The open air markets had gradually been torn down, to be replaced by large separate buildings for markets. They were well ventilated, costly, and owned by individual companies. Farmers brought their wares in to display and sell them, paying a small charge for use of the space.

Culturally, the Academy of Music, a structure of Byzantine elegance, vied with some half-dozen theaters and various concert halls to bring music and theater to the Quaker City. But pride in the city was severely undercut by dirt, provinciality, and political corruption. Like the rest of the state, Philadelphia operated under the new constitution of 1874. Controlled by a Republican ring, public life attracted chiefly men of limited intelligence and demagogues. City Hall, begun in 1871, was not yet completed by the Centennial of 1876, but taxpayers already dubbed it "The Temple of Philadelphia's Folly."[10] This, then, was Philadelphia in 1875 on the eve of the Moody campaign. It was an industrializing city, replete with residential areas separate from occupational areas. It was growing in size and complexity and losing its sense of community.

The revivalist who sought to evangelize the city was a man whose talents were well suited to the task. Dwight Lyman Moody was born in the small town of Northfield, Massachusetts, on February 5, 1837, the sixth child and the fifth son of Betsey and Edwin Moody. The Moodys had broken away from Puritan orthodoxy into Unitarianism.[11] Betsey

Moody was a woman of unusual piety, who impressed upon her family habits of thrift and economy as a matter of virtue, not need. But need soon arose, for the death of the senior Moody in 1841, when Dwight was four, left the young widow with seven children, all under thirteen, and twins to be born a month later. The family struggled to stay together. Young Dwight had the equivalent of a fifth-grade education, and in 1854, seeking the economic opportunity that the city offered, he left Northfield for Boston. Unsuccessful in obtaining a job elsewhere, he went to work for an uncle who owned a retail shoe store. The cities of America were inundated with youths from farms and small towns, seeking their fortune. It was a lonely life and Moody wrote home frequently. He sought church membership, perhaps as much to ease the pangs of separation he was experiencing as for purely spiritual reasons. Moody underwent a religious conversion experience and attempted to join the Mt. Vernon Congregational Church, where he had been impressed by the minister, the Reverend Edward Kirk, and a teacher, Edward Kimball. He was, however, unsuccessful in his first attempt to join. When questioned by the committee on admissions, he displayed a remarkable ignorance of religious matters. A year later, on March 12, 1856, however, Moody was accepted into the church. In addition to joining the church, he became a member of the young YMCA, which was attempting to meet the needs of young men like Moody, new to the city. Moody was impressed by the group's nondenominational emphasis and warm fellowship. It was a group of young men determined to get ahead. But Boston proved a disappointment to Moody, for his relationship with his uncle had soured and he felt that opportunity for advancement was lacking in the East. He decided to go West to Chicago, where he had an uncle engaged in farming outside the city.

Chicago in the 1850s was a boisterous, rapidly growing city, with mushrooming factories and business establishments, drawing young people from rural areas by the thousands. Using his previous experience, Moody got a job as a shoe salesman, earning thirty dollars a week. His aggressiveness and application brought him success almost immediately. Instead of reading or chatting when finished with a customer, as the other clerks did, he would go out on the sidewalk seeking new customers.[12] Barely five months after he arrived, he was investing in land in the Des Plaines area near his uncle's farm, and lending money in small amounts at the rate of 17% a day.[13] Privately, he set a goal of $100,000 as the size of the fortune he would eventually accumulate. Moody reveled in the competitive world of business and soon began traveling as representative for the shoe concern to the retailers in the Mississippi Valley. He relished the contacts he made and the excitement of traveling.

In addition to his business concerns, Moody continued with his religious interests. He joined the Congregational Church in Chicago as well as the YMCA, and he became caught up in the revival excitement of 1858. He participated in noon-day prayer meetings and Scripture study classes. In addition, he was involved in evangelical work on his own. He organized a mission Sunday School on Chicago's north side; in the summer he addressed groups in open-air talks. Every night during the summer he could be found on the steps of Court House Square, seeking converts. He sought out everyone he could reach—chance acquaintances, people on the street. There was frequently opposition in the form of heckling and throwing of objects. His evangelical zeal won him the title of "Crazy Moody."[14]

While Moody did not allow his religious interests to interfere with his dedication to his job, conflict was developing. By 1860 he realized that he was at a crucial point in his life. Torn by indecision he finally, after a struggle of three months, decided to give up business and concentrate his efforts on religious work. It was an enormously hard decision. "The greatest struggle I ever had," he reported in later years, "was when I gave up business."[15] He had been earning $5,000 a year in addition to special commissions, an unusually large salary for a young man under twenty-four. He had saved $7,000 and had made close connections in the business community that he felt would be helpful in his religious work. Eventually Moody was aided regularly by John Farwell, a prominent Chicago merchant, and by other businessmen connected with the Young Men's Christian Association.[16] Quitting his job, he became librarian for the Association at no salary. He left his boardinghouse and began to sleep in the prayer-meeting rooms of the YMCA in order to economize. Moody had now committed himself completely to evangelical work. His strong entrepreneurial spirit was put into the service of religious goals.

With the coming of the Civil War, Moody continued his labors, serving as the first representative of the YMCA to soldiers. Out of the uncoordinated work of the Association in the war grew the Christian Commission, the forerunner of the Red Cross. Moody worked with the Commission, making friendships with business leaders in various cities. In addition, he kept up with his religious work in Chicago, founding the Illinois Street Church in 1864. In the late 1860s and early 1870s, Moody again began to experience personal distress and uncertainty. Another crisis ensued, with prolonged weeping and attacks of anxiety. He was overworked and exhausted, it was true, but it was the question of where to move professionally that was the primary concern. He longed for a new direction.[17] It was perhaps another manifestation of the conflict between his drive for success and the striving for Christian humility. Finally he decided to leave Chicago and embark upon a career as a traveling evangelist. This decision enabled him to work his way out of the conflict that plagued him: through his evangelical work and dedication to Christ he would achieve the success his personality demanded. He decided that an evangelical tour in England would establish him as a professional revivalist.

With him went his new evangelical companion, Ira David Sankey. Sankey had come to Moody's attention in 1870 at the YMCA convention. Moody was tone deaf and unable to sing a note, but he realized the importance of music in revivalism. Ira Sankey met his needs perfectly. Born in western Pennsylvania and converted at sixteen, Sankey had long been active in church work, partly because of a genuine religious interest and partly because the choir provided exercise of his musical interests. His father had been a licensed Methodist exhorter before becoming president of a local bank, so Sankey's early life had been drenched in the warm emotionalism of small-town Methodism. He became active in the YMCA and participated in Sabbath School meetings and YMCA conventions, where he met Moody. Sankey had a suave manner and a polished look, with large expressive eyes, smoothed-back hair, and mutton-chop whiskers.[18] He had had no vocal training, but possessed a clear and forceful baritone. More important, his distinct enunciation made the lyrics of his music easily understood. They were sentimental songs, delivered with deep feeling, and he himself was often reduced to tears by their effect. He would introduce a hymn with a small talk concerning its origins or its message, then sing the simple song, loudly and clearly. Many of his songs were indistinguishable from the ordinary secular songs of the day. Sankey's solos, however, were not the only music in Moody's meetings. There were ensembles by the choir and congregational singing by the audience, since most of Sankey's songs had a simple refrain that the congregation could pick up quickly. Sankey became an important component of the Moody campaigns, and few evangelists since have dispensed with a musical companion.

A series of successful revivals in England in 1870-1873 was the "trial flight" for Moody's new itinerant evangelism. He returned to America in 1875, flushed with success from his English tour. He had been well received there and sought to continue his work in American cities, for he knew that "Water runs downhill and the highest hills are the great cities . . . ." He felt that if he could move the cities, he could stir the whole country.[19] But he was unsure where to start his American campaign. While still in England he had been urged by a petition from the Philadelphia branch of the Young Men's Christian Association to come to that city for an evangelical campaign.[20] When he returned home on August 14, 1875, he was met by George H. Stuart and others of the Philadelphia group, renewing the invitation. Moody placed two conditions upon the city he would choose: the promise of united support from the evangelical denominations of that city, and a guarantee of adequate physical facilities. Later, another was added—that no activities of a competitive nature be scheduled by churches while the revivals were in progress, no church fairs or festivals, nor evangelical activities of any sort. Moody invited a conference of a few representatives from the five cities that had invited him. The Philadelphia delegation urged him to come to Philadelphia in the autumn of 1875, for postponement would mean the failure of the revival because the Centennial Exposition was scheduled to begin in January, 1876, and would provide too great a counterattraction.[21] Furthermore, Philadelphia had already lined up 200 ministers behind the movement and had a tabernacle ready for him. Convinced, Moody agreed to shorten his revival in the Brooklyn skating rink to three weeks, and to come to Philadelphia on November 21, 1875. It was a revival the like of which Philadelphia had never before witnessed.

Philadelphia in 1875 had 526 religious congregations. Although it did not dominate the social structure, religion was still important to many people, and the minister was still a voice of authority to his congregants. A few of the congregations were small and met in halls or meeting rooms, but over 500 of them owned their own church buildings, some plain, others costly. By 1875, the largest in number were the Methodists, who had 101 churches, among them seven African churches and one free Methodist church. Close in number and equally important in power were the Presbyterians, with 98 churches of various shades of Presbyterian doctrine.[22] Protestant Episcopalians counted 97 churches; Reformed German, now known as the Reformed Church of the United States, numbered 17. The Roman Catholic Church was still growing at a rapid rate, and 1876 witnessed the appointment of the first Roman Catholic Archbishop of Philadelphia, James Frederic Wood.[23] There were 42 Roman Catholic churches, all large in size. Smaller in number, but active nonetheless, were the 32 Lutheran churches, 17 of them holding services in English, the remainder still in German or Swedish. The orthodox branch of the Society of Friends had nine meeting houses in the city, the Hicksites seven. The oldest of these meeting houses at 4th and Arch streets no longer held Sunday services because so few Quakers still resided in the neighborhood. Philadelphia Jews counted 10 synagogues. The oldest, Mikveh Israel, was now in the Seventh and Arch Street building dedicated in 1860. The new German-Jewish congregation, Rodeph Shalom, had in 1870 dedicated their new building at Broad and Mt. Vernon Streets. In addition to the churches, Bible, Tract, and Mission societies continued their efforts to bring Philadelphians the Word of God.

Revivals had never completely left Philadelphia. The popular Methodist revivalist, the Reverend James Caughey, preached in Philadelphia regularly. John Newland Maffitt and Mrs. Maggie Van Cott, both Methodist itinerants, were warmly received in Philadelphia. Jacob Knapp, the Baptist revivalist whose career and character were so clouded with dispute because of his tendency to character defamation, worked in Philadelphia in 1865 for extended periods. While he was never satisfied with the response in Philadelphia, he nevertheless spoke to crowded churches. Quaker revivalists Eliza Paul Gurney and Sarah Smiley were active in the Philadelphia area and in the surrounding countryside through the middle decades of the nineteenth century. During the Revival of 1858, George Stuart's attention was called to a young evangelist, Henry Grattan Guinness, and he was invited to visit Philadelphia. This eloquent and fervent evangelist came to the city in 1859 and remained for several months, speaking every night of the week but Saturday to huge throngs at Jaynes Hall or at Dr. Wylie's Presbyterian Church.[24] George Stuart was also instrumental in bringing Edward Payson Hammond, known as the Children's Evangelist, to Philadelphia as well as to other cities, where he conducted large-scale meetings in the 1860s and 1870s.[25] Hammond was an ordained Presbyterian minister, a graduate of Williams College and the Union Theological Seminary in New York. With the campaigns of Dwight L. Moody, however, Philadelphia revivalism assumed a new intensity and a special flavor.

Philadelphians had known of Moody even before 1875. George Stuart was among the fourteen Philadelphians who had served with the Christian Commission during the Civil War. He had come to know the ebullient evangelist in that connection. He brought a relatively unknown Moody to Philadelphia in 1866, and had difficulty obtaining a church for him. He was finally able to obtain the Central Presbyterian Church, of which Dr. Alexander Reed was pastor, and Moody spoke to large crowds. Some complained to Stuart that it was a mistake to have in the pulpit a man of so little education and with such bad grammar. Stuart, however, responded that he cared little or nothing about his grammar so long as he brought sinners to Christ.[26] When the great Chicago fire in 1871 left more than a hundred thousand homeless, Stuart was one of the relief committee from Philadelphia sent to visit the desolated city. Moody was among the homeless; his house and furniture had been destroyed along with his church. Stuart insisted on rebuilding the church and was designated treasurer in seeking the contributions of the Christian public.[27] Thus George Stuart had a long-time friendship with Dwight L. Moody.

The enterprising young merchant John Wanamaker, then building his department store, was also interested in Dwight L. Moody. Wanamaker had been involved in the religious affairs of Philadelphia since youth, and he was particularly interested in evangelism, remaining so until the end of his life. In his thirties he supported Dwight Moody and in his seventies, Billy Sunday. In 1868 he succeeded Stuart as president of the Philadelphia YMCA. He held open-air religious meetings, initiated evangelical work in colleges, and in 1870 rented a house on Lombard Street for a Negro branch of the Association. He had heard Moody in the pulpit of an Albany church at a YMCA convention years earlier and written home commenting on Moody's poor grammar. But by 1871, when Moody came to Philadelphia again, he was a guest in Wanamaker's home. By this time Wanamaker had come to agree with Stuart that Moody's poor grammar was inconsequential when compared to his great religious work.[28]

Wanamaker's religious interests had been of inestimable value in building his commercial empire. Through the YMCA he had met many influential bankers and businessmen. Furthermore, it was with money saved from his three years as secretary of the organization that the Wanamaker business was founded.[29] Wanamaker was a man of strong determination and good business judgment. In March 1861 he and his brother-in-law, Nathan Brown, with a joint capital of $3,500, went into the clothing business, "Oak Hall," in a six-story building at the southeast corner of Sixth and Market Streets. Before the end of the week, Fort Sumter was fired on and the Civil War had begun, but John Wanamaker had started his department store operation.

His new store had many innovative features. He was selling three-dollar suits at a fixed price, a novelty at the time. He had to reeducate the public to this concept, for they had difficulty understanding that the price would not be reduced by shrewd bargaining. In addition, the customer could return the purchased article and get his money back, another innovation in retailing. Business throve, and in the 1870s, Wanamaker sought to expand. But property on Market Street below Sixth was costly, and furthermore, he perceived the city was moving westward. In 1875 he went to Thomas A. Scott, president of the Pennsylvania Railroad, for a piece of property he wanted. A year earlier the company had abandoned its dilapidated depot at Thirteenth and Market streets when the decision had been made to put a new city hall at the intersection of Broad and Market streets, cutting off the railroad's right of way. Wanamaker secured an option on the property for a half million dollars. When word got around that John Wanamaker was purchasing property at Thirteenth and Market streets, "the consensus was that John Wanamaker was crazy; he would ruin himself."[30] The location was considered too far away from the business center of the city; who would come to such an out-of-the-way location? Nevertheless, Wanamaker finished the transaction and left for a trip abroad. When in 1875 a committee of Philadelphia businessmen headed by George Stuart decided to invite Moody and Sankey to conduct a revival in Philadelphia, they thought of the old depot across from which the city had started to build a city hall.[31] When they approached the Pennsylvania Railroad, they discovered to their astonishment that John Wanamaker had the option on the property. Cabling him in London, they soon received his enthusiastic invitation to use the depot. He returned home, eager to help with the meetings. Completing the purchase, he turned the depot over to the committee, rent free.[32]

The old freight depot, 1875-1876.

Theo. R. Davis's 1875 sketch of the depot crowded by people braving the storm to hear Moody and Sankey. (From Herbert A. Gibbons, *John Wanamaker* [New York: Harper & Bros., 1926].)

The Moody-Sankey Philadelphia revivals were the most meticulously planned and efficiently executed revival meetings the city had ever seen. Nothing was left to chance. The preparations for the visit of the evangelists were handled by two committees. A committee of fifteen ministers was selected, representing all the evangelical denominations of the city, to handle the spiritual aspect of the revival. A committee of thirteen laymen arranged details and cared for the business management.[33] George H. Stuart was elected chairman, Thomas K. Cree secretary. They appointed chairmen for various subcommittees, each charged with a specific task. There was a finance committee to raise and expend funds, a home visitation committee, a committee to select and train ushers and choir members, and committees for charitable work, temperance, Bible study, ticket arrangements, and publicity. Immediately the depot was fitted out for its new use. A prominent architect, Addison Hutton, designer of the Ridgeway branch of the Library Company, worked free of charge to design the changes.[34] Some 200 workmen were set to work. Within three weeks, the old depot had been transformed. It was a large building, extending from Market to Kelly Street and from thirteenth to Juniper Street. Tracks had been taken up and wooden floor put down. The main auditorium was fitted with over 10,000 chairs, purchased from a Connecticut firm for 28 cents per chair. It was believed to be the largest lot of chairs ever purchased in this country.[35] John Wanamaker insisted on publicizing all these details, feeling that the huge numbers would make the revival more memorable. At the front end was the speaker's platform and behind it, some 1,000 of the chairs were arranged in tiers for honored guests, ministers, and their wives. The floor sloped to the front, giving the entire audience an excellent view. The room was lighted at night by a thousand gas jets, and was pleasantly heated during even the coldest days.

In addition to the main auditorium, there were three large inquiry rooms, and a committee room fitted with 752 more chairs. A 33-foot-wide vestibule went around three sides of the building and ten large wide doors opened out onto Market, Filbert, and Thirteenth streets. Large cross-aisles ran the length of the building. In addition, a neatly furnished room adjoining the platform and connected with it by a private stairway was provided for Moody, Sankey, and their direct assistants. There were speaking tubes connecting all parts of the hall and telegraphic communication with the central police station in the city.

The carefully trained choir numbered 500 singers from all the churches. It was directed by a local man, William F. Fischer, a piano dealer and composer, but under the overall direction of Sankey. Rehearsals were held at the YMCA at 1210 Chestnut Street.[36] In addition, 300 Christian men acted as ushers, having been carefully instructed on procedures to be followed in seating the congregation, and in handling illness in the crowd, or possible disorders. Another 300 Christian men and women, selected by local pastors, were trained for work in the inquiry rooms. A corps of ladies was charged with giving out tickets, writing the name of each person on the ticket. The task force was completed by a large band of janitors, ticket-takers, and the like, as well as a strong force of city police, often numbering as many as 180 to handle the large crowds.[37]

Complete arrangements were made for the accommodation of the press, and many leading journals of major cities were represented. An extensive and painstaking advertising program was instituted, under the direction of Thomas K. Cree. Daily notices to the local newspapers and regular reports to the religious press of the country poured out of Cree's office. Three large sheet posters were used to advertise the event, as well as small circulars, of which 50,000 or more were issued each week.[38] On one Saturday alone, 162,000 circulars were distributed.[39] Moody insisted that advertisements for his meetings be placed on the amusement pages of the newspaper, finding nothing incongruous about such advertisement. "Some ministers think it undignified to advertise their services.... It's a good deal more undignified to preach to empty pews, I think."[40] In addition to local advertising, recruits were sent to congregations for fifty miles outside the city, seeking support for the Moody campaign.[41]

Never before had Philadelphia witnessed a revival on such an impressive scale. Earlier revivals had been organized by a specific church or a small group of laymen. This campaign utilized literally thousands of people in a well-orchestrated program to evangelize the city. It used technological and organizational skills never before available to itinerant evangelists. Authority was delegated in a manner that had previously been peculiar to the business world. Some days before the opening of the campaign, Moody arrived to check the accoustical properties of the hall and to oversee the final arrangements. He was the house guest for the duration of his stay in Philadelphia of John Wanamaker at his Twentieth and Locust Street home. Sankey found accommodations at the home of another businessman, John F. Keene. They were agreed that Philadelphia was ready for the beginning of a massive evangelical campaign.

Sunday, November 21, the opening day of Moody's Philadelphia revival, produced a deluge of freezing rain that lasted most of the day. Advance publicity had been effective, however, and by 7 A.M., an hour before the first meeting was to begin, 10,000 faithful stood and shivered on Market Street, waiting to be admitted. Thousands came by various railway lines running by or near the building, and others walked. At 7:30 the doors opened and people streamed into the newly decorated depot under the direc-

tion of carefully trained workers. The hall was quickly filled. Banners decorated the room announcing "God is
Love" and "Now is the Appointed Time."[42]

In the center of the platform a small projection with a low
railing served as Moody's lectern. Nearby was the cabinet
organ for Sankey to accompany his own solos and the choir.
On the platform sat prominent clergymen and their wives,
and important businessmen, including George Stuart and
John Wanamaker. Precisely at 8 A.M. Moody appeared.

He was of medium height and stocky, in later years becoming very massive in physique. He wore a tightly fitting,
black frock-coat buttoned across his expansive chest. His
large head and full, dark beard above a short neck gave him
a curious neckless appearance. His mouth was concealed in
his heavy black mustache and his cheeks shone with ruddy
health.[43] Moody stepped into the enclosure that served as a
pulpit and began the service. Moody meetings always followed a rigid schedule. Morning and afternoon services
would follow the same format: a hymn was sung, then a
benediction by a local minister, a sermon of approximately
one half hour, then the closing benediction. At the end of
this benediction, a gong sounded, the doors opened, and in
less than ten minutes the hall emptied. The noon-day
prayer meetings begun in the 1858 revivals were reinstated.
In his noon-day prayer meetings Moody would include a
hymn, a brief Bible reading and exposition, then a series of
prayer requests and letters received in advance from the
platform.[44]

The main attraction, however, was the evening service.
The ambience at this meeting was warmly anticipatory. A
general hubbub and excitement filled the air. Throngs of
people bustled about, some purchasing hymnbooks or
photographs of Moody and Sankey. The warming singing
and the lively anecdotes created an evening of pleasure
bordering on the secular but with an aura of piety. In
addition to the major evening meeting, however, was a

nightly meeting at some church near the tabernacle. Nightly John Wanamaker conducted meetings for young men at the Methodist Church at Broad and Arch streets, while John Feld, the Philadelphia postmaster, conducted meetings for parents in the Baptist Church on the opposite corner.[45] Moody would frequently address one of these meetings after his regular evening service. There were also special meetings of all sorts—some only for men, others just for women, some for reformed men, for young men, for Christian workers, for temperance.[46] In urban revivals, the camp meeting that lasted for days was replaced by a congeries of meetings, many of them quite protracted, and often running over into each other. While the tabernacle meetings were short, an inquiry meeting in one church was six hours long, at the end of which it was time for the evening meeting.[47] At a meeting of January 10, 1876, Moody, Sankey, and Wanamaker presided while 206 converts, nearly all young people, assembled to speak of their experiences. "From 1 P.M. to 8 P.M., with continual ingress and egress . . . everyone [was] making known his weaknesses to somebody else."[48]

The Moody meetings were a paradigm of efficiency in religion. Services began promptly and anyone who came after the doors were closed was denied entrance. A gong signaled the end of the meeting. Workers were carefully trained to handle the meetings efficiently. The Reverend John A. Broadus, a visiting minister commented, "He makes men feel that religion is business. . . . He applies practical sense and business-like skill and tact to the management of religious services . . . it is pleasant to see a number of leading businessmen bringing to bear their native and practical administrative powers . . . he is a thorough businessman in matters of religion."[49]

Ushers were clean-cut young men who had eagerly sought the privilege of wearing the red or blue ribbon and carrying the tall wooden pole, called a "wand," which was their badge of office. John Wanamaker required all the salesmen in his store to act as ushers. Not only were the ushers carefully trained, but also the personal workers in the inquiry rooms, usually deacons, elders, and Sunday School teachers. They had been advised against telling their own experience, but instead were to listen to the words of the anxious and gently lead them to conversion.[50]

Absolute stillness was required. No interruptions, no ejaculations were allowed. Early in Moody's Philadelphia campaign, on November 24, a black woman could no longer restrain her emotions and hallelujahs. He quietly stopped preaching, announced a hymn, and the offending woman was taken out of the auditorium. Moody would not tolerate the slightest disturbance or emotional display at his meetings.

Moody sought to construct a broad religious umbrella that would be acceptable to all Christians, whatever their denomination. His opposition to sectarianism stemmed from early association with the YMCA, and he attempted always to avoid matters of controversial nature, seeking instead to emphasize matters that could be universally accepted among his listeners. Asked one day what he would do if he were a pastor in a town where there were five churches and room for only one, he replied,

> Get out mighty quick. No power on earth can make me believe it is God's will that a Methodist and a Baptist and a Congregation and a Presbyterian and an Episcopalian church should be in one town where there is not room for more than one or two. There is scarcely any difference in their creeds and it is a waste of time to be preaching in such a town. I believe that sort of thing is the work of the devil.[51]

In a modification of Finney's revivalism, Moody abandoned the anxious bench as overly connected with Methodism and inclined to offend Presbyterians and Episcopalians. Instead, he asked the anxious to retire to an adjacent room and talk to attendants there. The personal workers in the inquiry rooms realized that their ministrations were of utmost importance, for most conversions were not in the tabernacle, although that experience prepared them, but in the inquiry room afterwards.[52] In addition to abolishing the anxious bench, Moody's revivals differed from Finney's in the inclusion of music. Charles G. Finney had rejected singing at revivals. "I never knew a singing revival [to] amount to much," he said. He felt that when people were in agony of soul, "supplicating and pleading with God with strong cryings and groanings that cannot be uttered," singing was injurious to the mood.[53] Dwight Moody, however, understood the usefulness of music in revivals, and used choirs and solos by Sankey as an important adjunct to his preaching. The swelling sounds of the favorite hymn of the Philadelphia revival frequently brought tears to the eyes of listeners. It was about a sheep who resisted the Savior:

> There were ninety and nine that safely lay
> Within the Savior's breast
> But one was lost and far away . . . .

When this hundredth sheep could stand it no longer, the hymn beseeches him,

> For you I am praying,
> For you I am praying,
> I'm pra-ay-aying for you.

Audiences could not be asked to sing "The Ninety and Nine" too often for their taste.

But the most noticeable difference between Moody and Finney was in the realm of style. Gone were the harsh denunciations that brought listeners to an agony of anxiety. Moody's style was informal, full of anecdotes, and designed to bathe the listener in a glow of warmth and acceptance. Moody was an easy man to like, a man whose forcefulness was immediately felt. His manner was informal and hearty, his handshake firm. His sermons were colloquial and full of homely illustrations. Sometimes two thirds of an entire sermon consisted of illustrations, many drawn from his own experience in the Civil War, or from prison visits, and some drawn from the experience of friends. Many portrayed poignantly sentimental scenes, invariably bringing tears to the eyes of the audience. Deathbed scenes, stories of prodigal sons come home, of dying children and old mothers with dimming eyes, exhausted soldiers found asleep on duty—these were the gist of Moody's sermons.[54] When he told the pathetic story of a dying soldier who expired during the Civil War on a government transport floating down the Tennessee River, "a thousand women put their handkerchiefs to their eyes to dry the tears that fell thick and fast," reported the Inquirer.[55]

He was a superb storyteller, jerking his audiences from tears to laughter, and providing a welcome change from the dull and stylized church service. His grammar was faulty, a fact noted by all, but soon disregarded as inconsequential by admirers.[56] In contrast to Sankey's careful enunciation, Moody's pronunciation was haphazard. It was said that Dwight L. Moody was the only man living who could say "Jerusalem" in two syllables![57] His vocabulary was limited to words of three or four syllables and his sentences were short. The combination of short sentences and simplicity of language gave flow and smoothness to his style that listeners found very appealing.

He would start to speak in a conversational manner. His voice would change as he continued until his ringing voice reached a shout. Words poured out in a torrent, his eyes were aglow. "His voice achieved a heart reaching quality commonly known as magnetism," commented a reporter for the Philadelphia Inquirer.[58]

Moody preached a simple gospel with one center—God's saving act in Jesus Christ. With conversion came salvation. The new birth was not a gradual development, he insisted, but a gift, to be accepted or rejected. He cited biblical conversions as examples of this point. Just as before the Civil War, he said, the slave was instantly free once on Canadian soil, so was Christ the lifeboat—a leap into the lifeboat brought salvation. A man could come into the Tabernacle a sinner and go out a saved man. "Conversion is instantaneous, one minute you may be outside, and the next minute you are inside."[59]

Instant salvation had a powerful appeal for its simplicity and lack of ambiguity. Plain people could understand it. The concept offered an island of certainty in the transience and confusion of modern life. Theologically, however, it was a curiously passive Arminianism that Moody offered. One did not need to be troubled about morality, personal or otherwise. "Morality will not save," he said in speaking of Nicodemus, a highly moral ruler of the Jews, a doctor of divinity, and a man of spotless character. This was not enough.

> You cannot do anything toward saving yourself, you cannot work towards salvation . . . God does not require one to do anything, for Jesus Christ has done it all. When He said 'It is finished!' He meant what He said. It is finished, it is completed, and all that poor mortals have to do is to accept it.[60]

Thus it mattered not at all whether one was baptized or not, or lived a righteous life. "To take substitution out of this Bible you take all that is in it."[61] Where Finney had earlier demanded, "Religion is something to do, not something to wait for,"[62] Moody instead urged, "He will save you if you trust in Him . . . . Just stop trying, that is a lesson that God wants you to learn."[63]

Moody's lack of activism represents, perhaps, a loss of heart, a withdrawal from the optimism that had characterized earlier American thought. Charles G. Finney and other pre-Civil War revivalists had been postmillennialists. For them, life on earth would grow better and better until the millennium arrived. The last judgment would occur after Christ had reigned on earth for a thousand years. Consequently, it was important to improve the world to hasten the coming of the millennium. With Dwight L. Moody, revivalism turned to a more pessimistic view of life and man. Moody believed that the world was growing more corrupt and evil, and that the millennium would come only after the present world had been destroyed by the avenging hosts of Christ. Premillennialism reflected the disillusion many felt in the latter half of the nineteenth century, with its rapid and unprecedented social and economic change. It expressed a withdrawal from the unpleasant realities of industrial strife, class struggles, and urban blight. In certain fashionable churches, the doctrine of premillennialism proved unpopular, for it was inconceivable to the affluent that the world was growing worse. But often these church-goers would pay lip service to the doctrine. For the less affluent who followed Moody, the message of premillennialism had real meaning and reflected their deepest anxieties. After Moody, premillennial pessimism was the characteristic stance of revivalism. But Moody was aware that gloom does not draw audiences. Furthermore, he knew that many of the well-to-do businessmen who supported him were contented with the changes that were adding to their material well-being. Moody could ill afford to alienate such patrons. Consquently, he muted his premillennial views. Although he believed the world doomed, he preached the love of God and the salvation of men.

Like earlier revivalists, Moody emphasized a literal acceptance of the Bible as the principal authority. Moody followers read their Bibles constantly, the books becoming well-thumbed and marked. "It is divine authority and vindicates its own claims," he said of the Bible.[64] Consequently he rejected the higher criticism developing in the last decades of the nineteenth century as tampering with the Scriptures, and this remained essentially his view to death. He rejected Darwinism as completely atheistic, but refused to reject some influential colleagues who believed in it.[65] Moody preferred to ignore evolution as a divisive force, and this refusal to deal with modern science alienated revivalism from contemporary intellectual currents of thought and ultimately estranged it from the mainstream of society. Henry Ward Beecher, son of Lyman Beecher and a leading spokesman for Protestantism in mid-nineteenth-century America, was able to incorporate Darwinism into his thought in an attempt to adjust the conflict between science and religion. For him, science conformed to moral truth because God created both.[66] Moody and his followers, however, thoroughly rejected the scientific developments of the time. Indeed, Moody's distrust of reason itself symptomized the inability of revivalism to deal with the complexity of human thought, and its retreat into one aspect of that thought. "The voice of reason," he would say, "is the voice of the devil . . . ." God must be sought "with your heart, not with your head."[67]

There were inconsistencies in Moody's thought that were never reconciled. Men must simply accept, they must stop trying; yet, they must work. It was not secular work that Moody demanded but work of a special sort. In the evangelical vocabulary, *work* meant to evangelize, to seek new converts, to distribute tracts, to speak to sinners, But it was a word that had grown comfortable to Americans through long tradition, and the word *work* came to have a double image, both aspects sanctified. "Let Christians wake up and go to work. More conversions may be made in the next three months than in the last three, if you Christians would do your duty."[68]

For two months the meetings continued daily. Moody and Sankey took Saturday as a day of rest, but meetings were held without them. Interest flagged somewhat during the middle weeks, with newspapers reporting the tabernacle only half filled, but it picked up again near the end, many having postponed attendance and now wanting to see the revivalist before he left the city. December 19, 1875, was an important day, for on that day President Ulysses Grant, visiting the city to inspect preparations for the Centennial Exposition being planned, honored the revival by attending, along with most of his Cabinet and many judges of the Supreme Court.[69]

Sometimes Moody was plagued by derision, people hooting at him in the streets, making fun of his evangelical meetings.[70] He responded by warnings in his sermons to those who made light of the revival. Noah had drawn jeers when he warned of the coming flood, said Moody, admonishing those who ridiculed the meetings to "escape the damnation of hell."[71] His message, however, was unchanging—the necessity of accepting Christ as a condition of Salvation, avoidance of controversial doctrine, the Bible as the highest authority. He emphasized the importance of owning a Bible, the most valuable one a person could afford. "It is the only news book in the wide, wide world. The newspapers can only tell you what has taken place. This tells you about what is to take place."[72] Religion must be a cheerful thing, he impressed upon his listeners, for cross, crabby Christians were the great hindrance of the Church of God. Revivals were a necessity: "There is not a church on earth that does not owe its existence to revivals."[73]

The campaign in Philadelphia lasted for eight weeks, from Sunday, November 21, 1875, to January 16, 1876. Directly afterwards, on January 19 and 20, 1876, Moody and Sankey held a Christian Convention, to advise Christian workers on methods of evangelization. They invited evangelical ministers, editors of religious papers, professors at theological seminaries, and delegates from Young Men's Christian Associations within a hundred-mile radius of Philadelphia. The remainder of the auditorium was open to the public. Topics included "How to Conduct Prayer Meetings," "How Shall the Music be Conducted in the Lord's Work," and "How to Get Hold of the Non-Church Goer." Arrangements were made to sell railroad tickets at reduced rates, and it was asked that private homes be opened to house ministers from outside the city.[74] About 5,000 people were present at the noon meeting on the first day and about 12,000 on the same evening. Moody advised them on every aspect of revival meetings, from his growing experience as an evangelist. There was little of theological nature in his advice; he spoke almost entirely of the mechanics of the meetings. He was the purveyor of salvation, giving others the secrets of his success. "Keep the meetings short," he urged. "Let the people go away hungry—do not wear them out. Let the people say at its close. 'Why the service ain't over, is it? I thought it had just begun.' None of our meetings have gone over one hour and ten minutes and herein lies one secret of our success."[75] Moody advised that the air must be kept fresh through proper ventilation in order that people be comfortable. Good singing was important, for nothing works upon the feelings as good music—preferably old, familiar tunes. He cautioned against offending any denominations: "Do not have any 'isms.' Let the meetings be purely union and devoted wholly to preaching salvation . . . . We must all make concessions. Here are my Quaker friends who have given up their ideas and attended these meetings, and our Methodist friends have given up their feeling. Why they have not shouted once since they have been here."[76] Preaching should not be overly long: "When you see that you have properly worked on the feelings of your hearers, stop right there, and let the feelings and the imagination do the balance." At prayer meetings, the man in charge should get to the point: "... do not let your preachers occupy minutes saying what could be said with profit in 3 minutes.... If a person were in your employ and talked so much he was likely to injure your business, you would be likely to bring him down. So with your cold, lengthy preacher."[77] While verbosity disturbed Moody, excessive zeal did not. When questioned about this, Moody commented that he would rather have zeal without knowledge than knowledge without zeal.[78]

On the last night of the Christian Convention, Moody collected funds for the new YMCA building in the process of being built at Fifteenth and Chestnut streets. The Association had a large debt and was unable to complete the building. Moody made some statements concerning the Association, and announced that he was seeking $280,000, an amount that created a sensation among the audience. The collection was spirited. Ushers, supplied with red bags attached to long poles, circulated among the congregation for cash or for pledge cards previously distributed. A young women sent up a diamond ring that brought $1,000 in bids. Three men pledged $70,000 among them.[79] In addition, furniture and fittings were auctioned off. The sum of $3,100 was realized from the sale of the furniture used in the revival. The chair used by President Grant went to John Wanamaker for $25, Moody's chair went to Stuart for $55. The platform and Bible rest were auctioned; even the towel used by Moody went for $5. By the end of the meeting, $100,000 had been raised for the YMCA.[80] The revivalist returned to the city on Friday evening, February 4, for a farewell meeting specifically for young converts. At this time additional money was raised for the organization that had brought the revival to Philadelphia.[81]

The cost of the revival campaign was estimated at $29,538.[82] It was raised by private contributions from among Moody's admirers in Philadelphia. In addition to contributions in money, there were contributions in the form of services or materials. The heating, for example, was put in and rented for the term of the meeting by a generous J. P. Wood and Company. Gas pipes and fixtures were installed by the same arrangement. The architect, Addison Hutton, donated his services. John Wanamaker generously donated the building, as well as the living quarters for Moody during his Philadelphia visit. It is probable that Moody and Sankey received an honorarium privately from generous patrons. Sums were not disclosed, but Moody's style of life implies an adequate income.[83]

The meetings over, Moody and Sankey slipped quietly away from Philadelphia. No sooner had the hymns died when carpenters started making the depot-tabernacle into a store for John Wanamaker. Actually, the revivals had delayed the starting of the store, for Wanamaker had wanted it ready before the Centennial visitors began flocking to the city. After the first month of their occupancy, the Committee had come to him to request the use of the depot until after the holidays. Wanamaker assented, in spite of his wishes to ready the building for its new purpose.[84] Now he pushed the construction to completion. While the site of Wanamaker's new store had been ridiculed earlier as being too far from the shopping habits of the city, by now Philadelphia had grown accustomed to the Thirteenth and Market Street location. Wanamaker has been accused of bringing Moody and Sankey to Philadelphia to advertise the location of his new venture, but to imply a cynical motive is to deny the authentic evangelical impulse manifested by John Wanamaker all his life. On May 6, 1876, on the site of the Moody-Sankey revivals, he opened America's first department store. The juxtaposition of events, however, is not without symbolic significance. Business and religion had been mutually useful to each other.

Finney's revivals had been a divisive force in Philadelphia church life and left in their wake institutional and personal debris. With institutionalization, however, the divisiveness faded. Adjustments made revivals acceptable to almost all Protestant denominations in spite of their theological and historic differences. But the process of changing from new measures to accepted measures required changes. The rich, emotional tone of the Finney revivals softened into the sentimental loam of the Moody meetings. The thundering invective and guilt-producing pronouncements from Finney's pulpit changed to the melodrama of Moody's stories. Revivals lost their spontaneity; they became less informal and better organized.

They were attended primarily by middle-class Philadelphians of a rural evangelical background, who found them a pleasant diversion from increasingly ritualized church services and from the monotony of daily life. In spite of massive expenditures in money and energy, the revivals added relatively few new converts to church rolls. In spite of Moody's entreaties the same people attended meeting after meeting. Consequently, the Moody revivals, although they caused much comment and excitement, were of limited value to city churches.

Among the various denominations, the Methodists were probably the most active, but the revivals were enthusiastically endorsed by Presbyterians, Episcopalians, Baptists, and Lutherans, and they won qualified assent from Quakers and Unitarians.[85] At a regular meeting of the Philadelphia Conference of Baptist Ministers, the question of revivalism came up. The Reverend Ray W. H. Conard expressed the majority view that revivalists like Moody were doing the same work as the pastor, just as everyone who had the ability to preach should do.[86] The *Presbyterian Quarterly* approved: "The teaching and tone of Mr. Moody have been singularly scriptural and sound, and his attitude toward the stated ministry, always brotherly and helpful, never harsh or injurious; his measures and methods, with rare exceptions, judicious and safe."[87] Even the Episcopalians found little fault. The famed Philadelphia Episcopalian Phillips Brooks, the rector of Trinity Church, joined in the accolade to Moody. Later, during the Boston campaign when Moody was unable to attend a meeting, Brooks took his place. It was an interesting spectacle to many: the eminent upper-class Episcopalian clergyman who had hitherto shown little sympathy with revivals taking the place of the uneducated, sometimes crude Mr. Moody. With earnestness and eloquence, he expounded the principle of conversion as he experienced it.[88] "There is a good healthy religious influence, I think, and underneath our little work, the deep thunder of the Moody movement is rolling all the time."[89]

The Quakers gave qualified approval of Moody's work. While the "voice that speaks to the soul" was the more excellent way, "let us not forget that we need, notwithstanding, often to be 'aroused' and 'stirred up.' The unavoidably engrossing concerns of this life have a tendency to absorb us, and to disturb that balance of the mind upon which true serenity depends."[90] The Reformed Church accepted the revivals as a measure pursued by the greater part of American Christians, but could not in good conscience promote them. While, admittedly, they were not a sham or a delusion, yet they were responsible for underemphasis of doctrine and education as well as casual language and irreverent attitudes.[91]

Even the Unitarians, traditionally hostile to revivals, found much to admire in Moody's work. The editor of the *Unitarian Review* admired Moody's "business-like directness and vigor," the planning and advertising the Moody campaign utilized, and felt that "we Unitarians especially need to be taught that the kingdom of heaven is to be advanced by the same energy, activity, and enterprise that are effective in all efforts." He was profoundly impressed by the vitality and Christian love in the Moody movement. While Moody's was a "coarse and commercial conception of

Christianity," yet, "liberal Christianity can generously recognize the purpose of his work, if they cannot join."[92]
    Clearly by 1875 mainstream Protestantism had accepted
revivalism. Some thoughtful people, however, questioned
the permanence of Moody's work. "A common com-
plaint... is that Mr. Moody's sermons have no direct
application to the relations and duties of everyday life, that
they do not aim to make men less selfish and cold-hearted
and more charitable, genial, generous and kind, and that
their sole purpose is to induce people to accept a certain
form of faith and to lead devoutly religious rather than
moral lives."[93] This criticism, however, was met by Moody's
followers, who asked, "Why should he try to tell people how
to live when the important thing is to prepare them for
death and the last judgement?"[94]
    The Roman Catholics, however, were still openly hostile
to Moody and revivalism. To them, the anti-Catholic
currents inherent in the revival movement were clearly
evident. They considered him vulgar and blasphemous.
Using the most cutting weapon of all, wit, the *Catholic World*
lampooned him. In an article entitled "A Revival at Frogtown," an imaginary Rev. Eliphalet Notext, the "great
Revivalist who made more converts than any other man in
England, Ireland, Scotland, Wales, the United States and
Territories, and the British Provinces of North America"
opened a three-week campaign. Brother Notext was not a
theological scholar, nor a preacher; "in truth he was almost
illiterate." His exhortations were "vulgar and often unin-
tentionally blasphemous." But he understood the business
of getting up revivals. He had something about him and his
work in every issue of the newspaper. He cared little
whether the report was favorable or unfavorable; abuse
made friends for him. The *Catholic World* criticized his
methods as contrary to the spirit of religion. He was,
however, an excellent organizer, having originally been the
business manager of a circus. His advertising, posters, and

handbills showed that he had not forgotten his old profession! The Catholic press continued its caustic comments, satirizing his side-shows and music by a melodeon and the "hymns by Rev. Mr. Notext, sermons by Rev. Mr. Notext, tales by Rev. Mr. Notext, appeals by Rev. Mr. Notext, photographs of Rev. Mr. Notext." They described him tellingly as stout, not ascetic, and "gifted with no inconsiderable share of physical energy and magnetism." Meetings were replete with sentimental tears, and friendly newspapers gave the number of converts as miraculously large. When all was over, and "the great tidal wave of the revival had disappeared, the youthful converts had gone back to their peg-tops, their kites and their china alleys and Alderman Charley Biggs was again taking his whiskey-toddies in the time-honored way."[95]

Catholics opposed revivals for reasons on various levels. Lay-led revivals were alien to the Catholic tradition of a carefully controlled institution, with authority emanating from upper echelons. But at a more intuitive level, they understood that revivals expressed the style and values of middle-class Protestantism, a class that was often hostile to Catholic immigrants. Catholics resented the equation of Americanism with Protestantism, the shibboleth of revivalists. They resented attempts to use prayers in school, or to evangelize school children. Consequently, the Catholic establishment could find no redeeming qualities in Dwight L. Moody.

During his Philadelphia revival, Moody became involved in an imbroglio with the Jews of Philadelphia. During a morning service in December, he presented a vivid word painting of Christ's crucifixion that was so eloquent it brought tears to the eyes of many listeners. He condemned the Jews for the crucifixion, and told an apocryphal story of Jews in Paris applauding a speaker who claimed as a Jew to be proud of this accomplishment. Moody concluded with a diatribe against Jews: "What are Jews today but a people

without a kingdom, without a leader, without a home,
wanderers up and down the earth!'"[96]

Jews considered his remarks inflammatory, if not incen-
diary. Moody received much outraged mail from Jews and
Christians alike, but refused to withdraw his comments.
When asked about the reported incident in Paris, he
blandly commented that he had merely plucked the incident from an article in a London paper.[97] The original
report was never validated. The *Philadelphia Times* rejected
Moody's response, feeling that severe attacks on other
religions based on hearsay and made by one who professed
to be working outside sectarian limits was excessively
careless.[98] Rabbi Gottheil of Temple Emmanuel on Fifth
Avenue, when asked if he or any other Jews intended to
respond to Moody's comments, sharply criticized Moody
for using a hearsay article without bothering to check its
veracity.

> What else can you expect of a man who reads his Bible in
> the same offhand way without the will or capacity to
> examine the true bearing of its contents? Whatever is
> printed it would seem is true, provided it fits in with his
> narrow views and is calculated to serve an oratorical
> effect. I am aware that calumnies are a very dangerous
> weapon in the hands of a man whose forte is simply to
> fanaticize mobs of the vulgar or the educated kind. Yet
> nothing could induce me or any of my brothers to take up
> the cudgels with Mr. Moody.[99]

While Catholics and Jews dissented, and some small
Protestant groups had reservations, by the 1870s the
consensus of organized Protestantism was approval of
Moody's revivalism. It was considered a viable means of
enlarging church membership and respiritualizing Christians. Some, undoubtedly, came to the depot meetings as a
lark. A woman reporter for the *Sunday Times* commented on
December 19, 1875, that she had no objection to the

meetings for they were a delightful entertainment and kept many people out of mischief.[100] As in other cities, Moody was often ridiculed on the streets. On December 26, he mentioned this and, as reported above, reminded those who hooted at him that Noah too had been jeered at when he warned of the coming flood.[101] But institutional Protestantism, with few exceptions, endorsed Moody's work as ancillary to their own.

The rural evangelical basis of urban revivals is illuminated by the Philadelphia Moody campaign. It was the rural-born-or-bred from evangelical homes who provided the foundation of Moody's urban audiences and his patrons. In addition, Moody's Philadelphia campaign would not have been possible without the thousands of people from outlying towns and villages. For weeks before the campaign, small towns around the city were recruited for delegations. Newspapers and other accounts during the eight-week revival were constantly reporting on groups from towns along the Pennsylvania Railroad line who came to Philadelphia expressly for the meetings. While some of the incoming groups were from good-sized cities, they were more often from small towns. The *Inquirer* on December 16, 1875, for example, told of a large delegation from Trenton, and another from elsewhere along the railroad line. An excursion party from Chester, Pennsylvania, and another from Wilmington, Delaware, were present praying for a Sunday School at Rahway, New Jersey, and for churches at Newark, Perth Amboy, and Pottstown.[103] On December 2, the newspaper reported that a large proportion of those present indicated that they were from surrounding suburbs. On the same day a special train brought 6,000 excursionists from Harrisburg and Lancaster.[104] On December 7, 1875, Moody read a note from a manufacturer with a factory about forty miles from the city who asked for a special train to be arranged and seats in the tabernacle set aside for the 500 who would come to the city if such arrangements could be made.[105] This large influx of people from the suburbs and small towns around Philadelphia forced Moody to discontinue his early-morning meetings and substitute 12 noon to 1 P.M. meetings to accommodate the small-town residents who found it inconvenient to attend either early morning or evening services.[106]

Small-town evangelical church members found the Philadelphia meetings a pleasant outing, a diversion from their quiet, often austere lives. Moody understood the small-town basis of his support in the city. From his YMCA days, he understood that many of the backsliders, "those who dropped away from church affiliations in the cities were new residents of the cities who failed to find the cordiality they wanted in city churches, and consequently, stayed away."[107] He understood from personal experience the intense need for fellowship among new arrivals in the city, their desire to recapture the sense of community they had known. He knew their need for the religion of their youth. "The people who come to pray and worship God do not come there to be pleased or hear operatic music," he advised the Christian Convention in Philadelphia. "The old tunes should be used . . . . I would also introduce into the prayer meeting an occasional Sunday school hymn—those good old hymns we all heard in our youthful days."[108] It was those of rural orientation, then, who were the major participants in Moody's meetings. Furthermore, in spite of Moody's desire to reach the backslider or the infidel, most of his audiences were already churchgoers. Cree estimated that a total of 869,000 people attended the meetings, besides an additional 31,000 who attended the two-day Christian Convention, bringing the numbers to a total of 900,000. But probably half of each audience, and perhaps more, was made up of substantially the same people.[109] Accounts of the meetings frequently reported the audience as churchgoers, since they were familiar with the hymns sung. Furthermore, they had brought along their Bibles, for when Moody mentioned a chapter in the Scriptures, the leafing of pages was heard.[110] Moody tried to discourage Christians from attending with such regularity. To this end, he tried to use a system of distributing tickets, but to no avail. On November 30 he announced that the meetings were not for Christians, but for those "out of Christ," and he hoped that Christians would not crowd the latter out. On another evening he asked of a standing audience that those who were not Christian should take a seat; very few sat down. By his last week in Philadelphia he expressed some annoyance at this state of affairs. He announced that he had grown familiar with the faces that surrounded the pulpit and that he wanted these Christians to attend churches where they belonged, rather than the meetings.[111] The problem had got so bad in his Brooklyn revivals that people lied and even stole tickets to get into the Rink.[112]

Since the major support for the revivals was among church members, and the new converts were usually people who had had earlier conversions, the incidence of youth among converts was not noticeable. During the Philadelphia campaign, a number of Princeton students attended and invited Moody back to their college, where he subsequently spoke to an audience of college boys and townspeople. In spite of this, there is no evidence that the Moody revivals attracted young people in the way that the Finney revivals had done. One might speculate that the absence of emotionalism was in part responsible. In addition, revivals had become institutionalized and had accepted the dominant American values. This made revivalism less attractive and less psychologically useful to youth.

Moody's work would not have been possible without support from rich patrons. In every major city Moody was supported by rich and powerful bankers, merchants, and businessmen. In New York, J. P. Morgan, the banker, served as treasurer, and Cornelius Vanderbilt, Jr., guaranteed expenses. Another New York backer was William E. Dodge, the country's leading copper manufacturer. Chicago supporters included Cyrus H. McCormick, John V. Farwell, and J. F. Armour.[113]

In Philadelphia patrons fell into two major categories. The first group was a wealthy elite, well educated and often with interests beyond the Quaker City. They were often members of the evangelical branch of the Episcopal Church. The second group, and the most numerous, was composed of local businessmen, often merchants in dry goods, notions, or some consumer product. These were men who had emerged from obscurity as self-made men. The former group gave its official sanction to the meetings, and sometimes sat on the platform during an evening service. But it was the latter, the self-made merchants, who manned the committees, handled the business, and fully participated in the Moody meetings.

An example of the first group was Jay Cooke, the wealthy railroad manipulator and investment banker. Born in Sandusky, Ohio, in 1821, of a father who was a leading lawyer and for some years a member of Congress, Cooke entered the banking house of E. W. Clark and Company in Philadelphia at the age of eighteen and quickly became the firm's confidential clerk. On reaching age twenty-one, he was made a partner and remained in that position until 1858, when he left to pursue broader interests. In Philadelphia, he supported the Academy of Natural Sciences, the Historical Society of Pennsylvania, the Union League, and the Home Labor League, a high tariff group. He was also active in his support of the YMCA and the American Sunday School Union.[114] Cooke was an usher for a time at the Moody revivals in Philadelphia.[115] Anthony J. Drexel was another son of wealth. His father had founded the banking house of Drexel and Company, one of the largest in the United States. Anthony entered the banking house in 1839, at the age of thirteen. He was a lover of art and music,

and spent much money and time as an active philanthropist, founding Drexel Institute in 1890.[116] Drexel too
lent his name to the Moody revivals.

Alexander Brown also lent his support to Moody's
campaign. He had been born to wealth and station in a
family well known in banking. A grandfather had come
from Ireland to Baltimore, where he founded the banking
firm of Alexander Brown and Sons. The four sons of the
founder all went into the banking business, one of them
founding the Philadelphia house after the war of 1812. His
son, young Alexander Brown, was born near Baltimore,
Maryland, in 1815, was educated at Northampton, Massachusetts, at the famour Round Hill School, where one of
his precepters was the historian George Bancroft. He
graduated from Rutgers in 1836. Brown never actively
engaged in the family business, preferring to devote his
time and means to philanthropy. He was a liberal patron of
the Protestant Episcopal Hospital and the Sunday School
Union (he was for a time an official of both these organizations) and a generous contributor to the Young Men's
Christian Association.[117] Alexander Brown was on the
committee that invited Moody to Philadelphia, lending his
name to that cause.

In spite of these prominent men of great means who lent
their names to the revival, it was the local businessmen of
more modest wealth who played the most active role in the
Moody revivals. They were more likely to be merchants
than bankers, and often self-made men of obscure origins.
It was noted that many of Philadelphia's business firms
were headed by men who were country born-and-bred. "A
majority of the leading business firms in Philadelphia, for
example, are constituted on the whole, or in part, of those
who came from the country. On Market Street, in Philadelphia, for example, in the business district of the city, ¾ of
the firms are in whole, or part, from the country. Many of
these people came to the city as clerks, salesmen, laborers,"

commented the Reverend George H. Johnston in *The Mercersberg Review*.[118] These businessmen shared the rural evangelical outlook because they shared its roots. They understood the American success story in personal terms. The old, simple virtues of evangelical religion that Moody emphasized had enabled them, they felt, to climb the economic and social ladder. Therefore they felt that everyone who subscribed to these virtues would experience a similar rise to wealth. John Wanamaker was one of these men. He called himself a country boy, came of simple pious parents, and was the paradigm of the self-made man. He was involved in revivals all his life. He evangelized with the YMCA in his twenties and he never missed a service during the two months of the Moody meetings. Wanamaker's businesslike efficiency showed a mind-set that was characteristic of these businessmen and of the revivals they supported. In an article entitled "Bringing Business Efficiency into Christian Service," Wanamaker advised as follows on church affairs: Pay off debts and don't incur any others, even if it stops the organs and keeps coal bins empty; don't spend money on any kind of work unless the money is in hand, except for missionary work, which can be paid for in installments; settle on a permanent system of collections for church support. Wanamaker suggested that each member sign a paper stating the free-will offering he would make for the year, and that he be reminded of this pledge if necessary. "Be sure to follow up and follow up and keep on following up immediately those who do not pay, for their sakes, as well as for the sake of the church." In conclusion, he recommended: "Like the United States Government, constitute a Banking Board or Pastor's Aid . . . to be selected by the pastor, who will be watchmen and lamplighters for the church . . . . They shall see that there is business efficiency in their church as well as their other businesses."[119]

George H. Stuart, another Philadelphia merchant who worked with Moody in Philadelphia, shared the rural evangelical mold; he was another example of a man grown rich through his own efforts. He had started his business in a small store at Fourth and Arch streets, to have it grow to a large importing house with branches in New York and Manchester, England. Stuart, the son of deeply pious Scotch-Irish Presbyterians, was the product of rural Protestantism in Ireland. Also on the committee to bring the itinerant evangelist to Philadelphia was Alexander Whilldin. Whilldin was a commission merchant in wool and yarns. He too was a self-made man. Born on a farm in Cape May County, New Jersey, he had lost his father in a shipwreck and came to Philadelphia as a boy to work on the wharf, rising from his humble beginning to head what was considered the most reliable firm of its kind in the city.[120] John Field, another member of the committee, who held a parents' meeting nightly at a neighboring church, was a Market Street merchant in wholesale notions and a well-known Methodist. Born of Protestant parents in County Derry, Ireland, in 1834, the had set out for this country with his parents at the age of fourteen. The father died on the voyage, leaving the mother with eight children and in very bad straits. Landing at Philadelphia, she put her older sons to work. Young John became an office boy and, being bright and industrious, gradually worked his way up in the same business, from office boy to stockkeeper, then buyer, bookkeeper, and finally partner in the firm. He was a longtime friend of John Wanamaker, and gave wholehearted support to the religious revivals of 1875.[121]

Thomas Potter, the prominent manufacturer of oilcloth and linoleum, was yet another rural boy who made good in the city. Born in County Tyrone, Ireland, he was brought to America in 1828 at the age of nine. The elder Potter died shortly after arrival, leaving the family to make their way in the strange city. Thomas had wanted to enter the ministry, but his father's death caused him to forgo this aspiration. At nineteen, the boy founded the company that brought him his wealth. He married a socially prominent young woman, became involved in the municipal government, and was instrumental in organizing the paid fire department. In 1868 Potter was made president of the City National Bank of Philadelphia.[122] Joshua Baily, a dry goods merchant, was also active in Moody's Philadelphia campaign. He had entered the dry goods business at sixteen and remained in it for seventy years. His firm grew to have branches in several other cities, retaining its headquarters in Philadelphia.[123]

These prominent Philadelphians, products of rural Protestantism, were self-made men, working their way to wealth from clerks, salesmen, errand boys. They shared the attitudes and habits of mind of the typical Moody follower—belief in the simple virtues and a confidence that all who pursued these virtues would achieve wealth and position, or at least comfort. The values and style of revivals had meaning for them in an intensely personal way. Yet they must have understood that the revivals provided a sort of social control. Moody's revivals were essentially conservative, and his distaste for social engineering endeared him to business magnates.[124]

Critics noted Moody's failure to reach the unchurched and the industrial workers in American cities. Newspapers often expressed the view that Moody and Sankey should work more among the poorer classes.[125] *The Nation* in 1875 commented on the inability of Moody and Sankey to attract the poor. The churches in all American cities were failing to bring the consolations of religion to those who most needed consoling. Except for the Catholic Church, the church had lost its original character as the religion of the lowly and miserable and had become the religion of the comfortable and the well-to-do. Moody and Sankey, charged *The Nation*, had not changed this, for

9/10 of their hearers, at least are persons already connected with religious organizations, or the near relatives of such persons, or members of the well-to-do classes attracted by curiosity. Mr. Moody's discourses are plainly, in their very method and phraseology, addressed to persons who are already familiar with both, and indeed, with the whole mechanism of revivals.[126]

Revivals were more successful, it appears, in boosting the morale of the regular, middle-class churchgoer of rural orientation, than in drawing the urban poor into the fold.

Assessments of the actual results of the meetings vary widely, for no two reporters had the same count and Moody kept no statistical records. After the first three weeks of the Philadelphia revival, the *Philadelphia Times* reported that Moody took a counting of his converts and they totaled 134 persons, or an average of 44⅔ a week.[127] Cree's evaluation was that the number of professed converts was 206 out of an aggregate number of 869,000 attending the meetings, or 1 convert to every 4,218 persons attending.[128] After the meetings in Philadelphia, the names were tabulated of 17,000 persons who had given their names and addresses and who had listed themselves as inquirers and not Christians. A book on regeneration with a few words of counsel and a facsimile signature of Dwight Moody was sent by mail to each.[129] Later, when they could be found, they were visited and consulted with by local pastors in an attempt to bring them into church life. Many, however, had given the address of an empty lot or a saloon.[130] None of the available statistics can show whether new members represent new converts or people returning to the fold of the church. It seems clear, however, that enthusiastic reports of large numbers converted by Moody in his Philadelphia campaign must be discounted. If Cree's estimate of 206 converts is taken as accurate, then the 3,000 "converts" who met at a special meeting in Philadelphia at the end of the campaign were not new converts at all, but Christians seeking to hear Moody before he left the city.

The effect of the Moody revivals on Philadelphia church life was short-lived. While churches received an immediate boost in membership, the numbers soon dropped back to earlier levels. Lefferts A. Loetscher, in his study of Philadelphia Presbyterianism, concludes that while Presbyterian churches in the city received more members (either returning or joining for the first time) than in any other year in their history, the effects soon wore off. In the five years before the Moody revivals, Philadelphia Presbyterians averaged 678.8 new members per year; in 1876 the number jumped to 1,492; in 1877 it was down to 709; and it dropped every year afterwards to a low in 1881 of a scant 396.[131]

Philadelphia Methodism showed a similar short-term leap and subsequent reversion to normal numbers. Statistics show, then, that Loetscher's conclusions regarding the Presbyterians held also for the Methodists: Moody's work caused an immediate spurt of new members, then a drop to previous levels.

TABLE 11.1
Membership in Philadelphia Conference
of the Methodist Episcopal Church[132]

Year	Members	New Accessions
1870	33,370	1,199
1871	34,003	976
1872	35,582	1,225
1873	34,880	1,116
1874	35,978	1,370
1875	38,830	1,330
1876	39,841	1,646
1877	41,959	1,487
1878	40,660	1,175
1879	41,010	1,110
1880	43,816	1,191

What the revivals did most effectively, however, was to serve as a diversion for churchgoers from Philadelphia and the surrounding towns. It was a welcome change from the routine of regular sermons and services. The charismatic revivalist with his melodramatic stories that they loved and the music that they remembered provided a warm, social evening. It was an exercise in nostalgia. But in the end, the revival added very little to the numbers in Philadelphia churches or to the quality of church life.

Moody himself was never satisfied with the results of his revivals in the large Eastern cities. A month before he died, while on his way to Kansas City, he stopped to see Wanamaker in Philadelphia. "My great longing," he said, "has been to get a good hold upon one of the cities on the Atlantic Coast. If I could just get under New York or Philadelphia and lift them to God, I believe I could sweep the country to the Pacific."[133] Although he continued to hold revival meetings until his death, he increasingly realized the inadequacy of evangelism in cities and grew to favor religious education. After 1878 he changed his operations and worked in each city for six months or more, working in several churches during that time instead of in a tabernacle. But the lack of a central tabernacle diffused interest, and none of his campaigns was particularly successful. After 1880 he concentrated on Northfield Seminary for Girls (founded in 1879) and in 1881 he founded Mount Hermon School for Boys. The Chicago Evangelization Society founded in the 1880s became in 1900 the thriving Moody Bible Institute, with a continued emphasis on education. Moody's evangelical campaigns were over.

12

The Social Message

While the social views of Charles G. Finney had been essentially conservative, there was an element of radicalism in his challenge to the religious establishment as well as in his opposition to slavery.[1] But pietism is, ultimately, neutral, and can be a force against the values of society or a support to the status quo.

With Dwight L. Moody, the radicalism had disappeared, and his pietism joined with an acceptance of the late-nineteenth-century laissez-faire capitalism. With Moody, revivalism accommodated itself to the society around it. With no solid theological base, it was quick to accept the secular values of the day. Moody's views on poverty are an example of this stance. For him, poverty was a badge of failure, and he blamed it on lack of thrift, laziness, or idleness. If a man lost his job, it was God judging him for his sins. Poverty would disappear, he felt, if all men would accept Christ. "It is a wonderful fact that men and women saved by the blood of Jesus rarely remain the subjects of charity, but rise at once to comfort and respectability," he commented. "I don't see how a man can follow Christ and not be successful."[2] Yet, while poverty was connected with sin, on the other hand, for those who followed Christ and were still afflicted by misfortunes, he offered platitudes. For them poverty became the sign of God's love.

> O ye children of poverty and toil, of misfortune and sorrow! God is better to you than ye know. Ye see but one side of the veil now; and that is fretted with troubles, and dark with adversity. But it has another side.... Your worldly plans are thwarted and you are tempted to think the Lord unkind. Your business becomes entangled in events, which shift ye see not how.... O weeping followers of Jesus, look! Your crowns are gathering lustre. Your harps are being attuned to sweeter notes and deeper melodies of joy. Your trials project their shadows upon the walls of your heavenly mansion; and lo! they are transformed into images of seraphic loveliness that shall gleam in beauty there forever.[3]

It was rough work, he felt, that polishes. "It is rough treatment that givss souls as well as stones their lustre; the more the diamond is cut the brighter it sparkles." In what seems to be hard dealing, God has no end in view but to perfect his people's graces. "He sends tribulations ... [that] worketh patience, patience experience, experience hope."[4]

The inconsistency in Moody's views on poverty is evident: poverty is at one time a mark of failure and, at another, a sign of God's grace. He probably never thought his views through to a logical conclusion. But the rich could accept his former premise and draw satisfaction from that view, while the poor could draw whatever comfort they could from the latter view. His analysis, however, had no place for a rich man who was not converted. Clearly, his riches were not a mark of God's grace. Such a man, said Moody, would undoubtedly soon suffer some misfortune. Furthermore, if a man converted and still did not rise to comfort and prosperity, it was a sign that he had not truly converted![5]

The rich had an obligation, however, to be generous in their support of religious activities. Like Finney, he reminded them of this duty. Moody did so by pointing out to the rich that, despite their wealth, they too were but mortal and would one day have to account for their actions. "You may buy grain, you may buy land, you are not sure whether the value will go up or down, but there is one thing you are sure of, and that is death."[6] Consequently the rich must prepare for their ultimate demise by giving generously to religious work. Such stewardship was the only justification for wealth. It is true that Moody needed men of means for his work. But aside from his need for them, he truly admired them, and identified with their bold inventiveness and unbounding energy. It was often a mutual admiration, for such men as John D. Rockefeller, William E. Dodge, John V. Farwell, George and J. F. Armour, and Cyrus H. McCormick were benefactors to Moody's activities. Astute Philadelphia businessmen George H. Stuart and John Wanamaker supported him with unfailing generosity. It was a matter of congeniality of spirit. "How is it," a prominent financier was asked, "that while you and other like men are all but inaccessible, fenced in by closed doors and guarded by polite but immovable private secretaries, Dwight Lyman Moody sees you at any time?" "He is one of us," was the reply.[7]

Indeed, to many, Moody epitomized the self-made man. "If I were called upon to name the two most thoroughly typical Americans," said Dr. Theodore Cuyler, a famous Presbyterian, "men who had fought from obscurity to wide influence, the men whom our American boys should be taught to study as the model patriot and the preacher of righteousness, I should not hesitate to name Abraham Lincoln and Dwight Lyman Moody."[8] John Wanamaker recalled Moody thus in later years: "I can call to mind many who, during these forty years, have been distinguished in the business world, in railroad enterprises and in public life. He has done the best business of us all."[9]

The wholehearted approval given Moody by his moneyed businessmen was due not only to their acceptance of him as a fellow entrepreneur, but because they perceived that the Moody revivalism was to their interest. His message of pietistic individualism buttressed the laissez-faire economic system that had enabled them to enrich themselves. Moody did not advocate reforms that would give them trouble. Since all sin was personal, according to Moody, all reform must be personal as well. He was opposed to card playing, dancing, drinking. He would not even read a Sunday newspaper. He had no use for signing temperance pledges, insisting that only conversion could save a man. Regeneration, not legislation, changed the human heart. He had little to offer the working class in the way of concrete or realistic proposals, advising them to utilize prayer, patience, Bible reading, witnessing, and attending religious services as the route to a better world.[10] As the gulf between big business and labor grew, Moody's advice became increasingly irrelevant to workers and increasingly useful to employers. He had no use for labor unions and their strikes. He felt union activity to be so dangerous as to threaten the well-being of the nation. He predicted that in the labor struggle, if evangelism failed, an apocalyptic struggle would ensue:

> Either these people are to be evangelized or the leaven of communism and infidelity will assume such enormous proportions that it will break out in a reign of terror such as this country has never known. It don't take a prophet or a son of a prophet to see these things. You can hear the muttering of the coming convulsion even now, if you open your ears and eyes.[11]

Not only was evangelism the way to avoid labor strife, but it was the way to make good Americans out of the foreign-born element of the masses, "the dangerous classes," which were corrupting public morals in the cities, and would ultimately, if not stopped, overthrow American political institutions.[12] Revivalism became the solution for all the troublesome problems that were afflicting American society.

Timothy Smith in his *Revivalism and Social Reform* traces the Social Gospel movement to its roots in evangelical revivalism. Certainly it is possible to see similarities between the two. Antebellum revivals with their optimistic, activist philosophy engaged in many activities aimed at improving man and thus hastening the millennium. Societies of various sorts proliferated and although they were religiously motivated, they soon became sensitized to the plight of the poor and moved into meliorative activity.[13] But such organizations were never aimed at reforming society; rather, they wanted to reform the individual. They never questioned the rules of the society that permitted such human problems. This reform impulse is only superficially similar to the thrust of the Social Gospel. In world view, in methods, in the men and women involved, in all important particulars, the two were different.[14] Mainstream revivalism's individualistic and pietistic stance led it to distrust organized charity and political reform. Finney, we recall, opposed poor relief, limitation of child labor, the eight-hour work law, labor unions, and strikes. Even his opposition to slavery was on the basis of concern for the soul of the slave owner. To Finney, anti-slavery was always secondary to soul winning. Similarly, Dwight Moody distrusted charity and reform. In his early years he hoped that through charity he could achieve conversions, but subsequent experience showed that such conversions, when they did occur, were superficial.

> My idea was that I could open a poor man's heart by giving him a load of wood or a ton of coal when the winter was coming on, but I soon found that he wasn't any more interested in the Gospel on that account. Instead of thinking how he could come to Christ, he was thinking

how long it would be before he got another load of wood.
If I had a Bible in one hand and a loaf in the other, the
people always looked first at the loaf, and that was just
contrary to the order laid down in the Gospel.[15]

Moody came to view charity with some reservation. "There
is a good deal that we think is charity that is really doing a
great deal of mischief," he said, explaining that it encouraged people to expect doles instead of working for a
living.[16] Eight months before he died, Moody stated his
lifelong position on reform:

> For forty years I have heard in every city along about
> election time, the cry, "Reform! Reform!" But things go
> on in about the same old way. You can't reform govern-
> ment without men who have been themselves reformed
> and that reformation must be a regeneration through the
> power of the Holy Ghost.... Human nature has not
> changed in the last 1900 years. Preach a different gospel
> from that which was successful in the apostolic days? Oh,
> bosh![17]

His attitude toward reform was succinct: "Whitewashing
the pump won't make the water pure."[18]

Historians are generally in agreement on the conservative thrust of late-nineteenth- and twentieth- century revivalism. On the earlier period, the revivals of the Second
Great Awakening, there is no consensus. Bernard Weisberger interprets the earlier revivals as part of the reform
movement, but concludes that once they were emptied of
their reforms, they continued on barren and empty. Gilbert
H. Barnes, in *The Antislavery Impulse, 1830-1844*, interprets
Charles Finney as the moving force of abolitionism and
reform in the antebellum years. Timothy Smith, in his
*Revivalism and Social Reform in Mid-Nineteenth-Century
America*, sees in midcentury revivalism the roots of the later
Social Gospel movement. These historians have all over-
stated the case for reform. Barnes uses abolitionism as the

litmus paper to identify a liberal reformer. Smith reads twentieth-century liberal values back into revivalist thought. True, the antebellum revivalists were avidly involved in improving man for the coming millennium, but they were just as interested in the minor vices like smoking tobacco, Sabbath-breaking, and reading novels, as in abolition. They were consistently opposed to poor laws, unions, and any changes in the status quo. Revivalists touched upon social reform issues like abolition at various points, for the line between moral reform and social reform is a fine one, but their major concern was always in the realm of personal virtue and salvation. Social reform as we understand it today was beyond their scope or understanding. Evidence in Philadelphia suggests that the revivalists were not a mighty social force at all. They were usually narrow, anti-intellectual, abstemious individuals who were concerned with petty vice at the expense of a broader ethical morality. Had they been more successful, they would have crippled American science, literature, and the arts. In spite of their differences, Finney as well as Moody shared this world view.

With Dwight L. Moody, the social conservatism of Charles J. Finney flowered into a wholehearted celebration of the status quo in American life. Moody represents the fusion of American pietism with the American business ethic. He blended the inward-looking individualism, the anti-intellectualism, and the simplistic world view of the earlier revivalists with new elements. He talked like a businessman, he was a skillful organizer, he embraced the values of the popular culture.

By the 1880s and 1890s, severely undercut by the new scientific currents and new waves of thought in the church, revivalism waned among mainline Protestants, who were opting for education, training, and new social attitudes. It was taken over by Pentecostal and Holiness sects—the churches of the disinherited, the uneducated, the unsophisticated. Revivalism in these sects still paid its homage to Charles G. Finney.[19] But it had left upon generations of Americans a residue that was essentially anti-intellectual, apocalyptic, and simplistic. Its sense of certitude of its own values made it insensitive to the needs and expressions of other religious traditions. If, as Judge Learned Hand once observed, liberty is that spirit which is not too sure it is right, revivalists were incapable of this spirit.

APPENDIX

TABLE A.1
Growth of Philadelphia Churches
According to Denomination

Denomination	1828	1857	1875
Presbyterian	12	62	98
Episcopalian	6	50	97
Baptist	5	31	70
Methodist	6	42	101
Lutheran	3	15	32
German Reformed	2	5	17
Dutch Reformed	2	4	3
Roman Catholic	4	27	42
Universalist	1	3	3
Unitarian	1	1	2
Jewish	2	5	10
Quaker	5	13	16*
Moravian	1	not avail.	4
Congregationalist	0	0	2
Mennonite	1	not avail.	3
Swedenborgian	2(congs.)	not avail.	3

*9 Orthodox, 7 Hicksite.

Sources: For the 1828 period: Robert De Silver, *Philadelphia Directory and Strangers Guide for 1828* (Philadelphia: James Maxwell, 1828); supplemented by *Philadelphia*

254

in 1824; or a Brief Account of the Various Institutions and Public Objects in This
Metropolis. . . . (Philadelphia: Carey and Lea, 1824) and James Mease, *Picture of
Philadelphia for 1824, Containing the "Picture of Philadelphia for 1811"* (Philadelphia:
Thomas Town, 1823). Figures for 1857 came from *McElroy's Philadelphia Directory
for 1857* Philadelphia: Edward C. and John Biddle, 1857). Figures for 1875 were
derived from Thompson Westcott, *Official Guide Book to Philadelphia* (Philadelphia, 1857) and *Gopsill's Street Index and City Guide of the City of Philadelphia*, 1875.

Notes

Introduction

1. Frances Trollope, *Domestic Manners of the Americans* (New York, 1832) p. 75.
2. Anthony Trollope, *North America* (New York, 1862), p. 281.
3. Philip Schaff, *America, A Sketch of its Political, Social, and Religious Character* (New York: Scribner, 1855), p. 76.
4. Franklin H. Littell, *From State Church to Pluralism* (New York: Doubleday, 1962), p. 32. Daniel Dorchester, *The Problem of Religious Progress* (New York: Hunt, 1881), p. 545, analyzed it in different terms: in 1800, 1 in 14.5 inhabitants of the U. S. were church members; in 1850, 1 in 6.57; in 1870, 1 in 5.78 were church members.
5. Winthrop S. Hudson, *American Protestantism* (Chicago: University of Chicago Press, 1961), p. 78.
6. See accounts of Francis Lieber, *Stranger in America* (Philadelphia: Carey, Lea and Blanchard, 1835), and the Rev. G. Lewis, *Impressions of America and the American Churches* (Edinburgh: W. P. Kennedy, 1845), and Trollope, *Domestic Manners*, as well as Charles A. Johnson, *The Frontier Camp Meeting* (Dallas, Texas: Southern Methodist University Press, 1955).
7. William G. McLoughlin, Jr., *Modern Revivalism, Charles Grandison Finney to Billy Graham* (New York: Ronald Press, 1959); Bernard Weisberger, *They Gathered at the River* (Boston: Little, Brown, 1958); William Warren Sweet, *Revivalism in America* (New York: Abingdon Press, 1944); Perry Miller, *The Life of the Mind in America, Revolution to Civil War* (New York: Harcourt, Brace, 1965); Russell E. Francis, "Pentecost: 1858, A Study in Religious Revivalism" Ph.D. dissertation, University of Pennsylvania, 1948; or Russell E. Francis, "Religious Revivalism in 1858 in Philadelphia," *Pennsylvania Magazine of History and Biography* 70, no. 1 (January 1946): 52-77; Lefferts A. Loetscher,

"Presbyterianism and Revivalism in Philadelphia Since 1875," *Pennsylvania Magazine of History and Biography* 68 (January 1944): 54-92; Timothy L. Smith, *Revivalism and Social Reform in Mid-Nineteenth-Century America* (New York: Abingdon Press, 1957).

8. Edward Digby Baltzell, *The Philadelphia Gentlemen: The Making of a National Upper Class* (New York: Free Press, 1958); Nathaniel Burt, *The Perennial Philadelphian: The Anatomy of an American Aristocracy* (Boston: Little, Brown, 1963).

9. William E. B. DuBois, *The Philadelphia Negro* (New York: Benjamin Bloom, 1899); Sam Bass Warner Jr., *The Private City: Philadelphia in Three Periods of its Growth* (Philadelphia: 1968); Allen F. Davis and Mark H. Haller, eds., *The Peoples of Philadelphia: A History of Ethnic Groups and Lower Class Life, 1790-1940* (Philadelphia: Temple University Press, 1973).

10. See Arthur M. Schlesinger, *The Rise of the City* (New York: Macmillan, 1933); Oscar Handlin, *Boston's Immigrants* (Boston: Belknap Press of Harvard University Press, 1941); Michael Feldberg, "Urbanization as a Cause of Violence: Philadelphia as a Test Case," in Davis and Haller, *Peoples of Philadelphia*, pp. 53-69.

11. Davis and Haller, *Peoples of Philadelphia*, p. 7.

12. John F. Sutherland, "Housing the Poor in the City of Homes: Philadelphia at the Turn of the Century," in Davis and Haller, *Peoples of Philadelphia*, pp. 175-201.

1. A Fire and a Hammer

1. McLoughlin, *Modern Revivalism*, p. 17.

2. Charles G. Finney, *Memoirs* (New York: Barnes, 1876), written when Finney was in his eighties. Often inaccurate on details, it contains much information on his childhood and life. See also George F. Wright, *Charles Grandison Finney* (New York, 1891).

3. Fawn M. Brodie, *No Man Knows My History* (New York: Knopf, 1963); Whitney R. Cross, *The Burned-Over District, The Social and Intellectual History of Enthusiastic Religion in Western New York, 1800-1850* (Ithaca, N.Y.: Cornell University Press, 1950).

4. Finney, *Memoirs*, p. 5.

5. Ibid., pp. 34-35, 381.

6. Ibid., p. 25.

7. Cross, *Burned-Over District*, p. 7.

8. Charles G. Finney, *Lectures on Revivals of Religion*, ed. William G. McLoughlin (Cambridge, Mass.: Harvard University Press, 1960; first published 1835), pp. 379-80. See also pp. 203, 214, 227 for expressions of Finney's activism.

9. Ibid., p. 413.
10. Ibid., p. 404.
11. Ibid., p. 429.
12. Ibid., pp. 41ff.
13. Ibid., Lecture 15. Finney shared, however, the distaste of other abolitionists for social equality with the Negro. See Bartram Wyatt-Brown, *Lewis Tappan and the Evangelical War Against Slavery* (New York: Atheneum, 1971), p. 177.
14. Theodore Weld to Lewis Tappan, Nov. 17, 1835 in Gilbert H. Barnes and Dwight L. Dumond, eds. *Letters of Theodore Dwight Weld, Angelina Grimké Weld and Sarah Grimké, 1822-1844*, 2 vols., (New York: Appleton-Century, 1934), 1: 242-43.
15. James A. Thome to Theodore Weld, August 9, 1836(?), in Barnes and Dumond, eds., *Letters*, 1: 327-28.
16. Charles G. Finney to Theodore Weld, July 21, 1836, in Barnes and Dumond, eds., *Letters* 1: 318-19.
17. Finney, *Lectures on Revivals*, p. 22.
18. Ibid., pp. 252, 184.
19. Finney, *Memoirs*, p. 84.
20. Johnson, *Frontier Camp Meeting*, pp. 132-42.
21. Finney, *Lectures on Revivals*, p. 267.
22. See above for Finney's identification of sin.
23. Finney, *Lectures on Revivals*, p. 359.
24. Finney, *Memoirs*, p. 255.
25. Ibid., p. 218.

2. Philadelphia—the Sacred and the Profane

1. Ellis Paxson Oberholtzer, *Philadelphia: A History of the City and its People*, 4 vols. (Philadelphia: S. J. Clarke, 1912), 2: 79.
2. Descriptions of Philadelphia appear in Trollope, *Domestic Manners*, and the Rev. G. Lewis, *Impressions of America*.
3. Sam Bass Warner, Jr., *The Private City* (Philadelphia: University of Pennsylvania Press, 1968), pp. 50-53.
4. Oberholtzer, *Philadelphia*, 2: 144.
5. Ibid., pp. 144-45.
6. Warner, *Private City*, pp. 50-56.
7. Anne Royall, *Sketches of History, Life and Manners in the United States* (New Haven, Conn., 1826), p. 202.
8. Oberholtzer, *Philadelphia*, pp. 89-91.
9. Warner, *Private City*, pp. 50-56.
10. James Hosmer Penniman, *Philadelphia in the Early 1800's* (Philadelphia: St. Stephens Church, 1923), pp. 6, 107; Oberholtzer, *Philadelphia*, 2: 101.

11. Charles Dickens, *American Notes* (Gloucester, Mass.: Peter Smith, 1842), p. 119.
12. Trollope, *Domestic Manners*, p. 271.
13. Descriptions of Lafayette's visit to Philadelphia are in Penniman, *Philadelphia*, pp. 41ff. and Oberholtzer, *Philadelphia*, 2: 132-48.
14. For an analysis of this problem, see Littell, *From State Church to Pluralism*, pp. 47-52.
15. Winthrop S. Hudson, *Religion in America* (New York: Charles Scribner's Sons, 1965), pp. 116-17.
16. There are no statistics on numbers in each denomination, so I have relied on numbers of churches. The problem of numbers is complicated, since some directories count churches and some count congregations, which sometimes met in school buildings or in private homes. In addition, while most numbers include black churches, they may not all do so. However imprecise, these statistics can tell us something of the religious structure of the city. Robert De Silver, *Philadelphia Directory and Strangers Guide for 1828* (Philadelphia: James Maxwell printer, 1828); where De Silver was inadequate, I used *Philadelphia in 1824; or a Brief Account of the Various Institutions and Public Objects in This Metropolis . . .* (Philadelphia: Carey and Lea, 1824) and James Mease, *Picture of Philadelphia for 1824, Containing the "Picture of Philadelphia for 1811"* (Philadelphia: Thomas Town, 1823).
17. A detailed discussion of theological aspects and the Philadelphia development of each of these denominations is contained in subsequent chapters.
18. Quoted in Othniel A. Pendleton, "The Influence of the Evangelical Churches upon Humanitarian Reform," Ph.D. dissertation, University of Pennsylvania, 1945, p. 48.
19. For a chart showing relative growth of denominations in Philadelphia, see Appendix.
20. Sweet, *Revivalism in America*, p. 164. For a theoretical analysis of how denominationalism developed out of class differences, see H. Richard Niebuhr, *The Social Sources of Denominationalism* (New York: Holt, 1929). Niebuhr used the classical sociology theory of Troeltsch, Weber, and Tawney.
21. Robert G. Torbet, *A History of the Baptists* (Valley Forge, Pa.: Judson Press, 1950), p. 30.
22. Winthrop S. Hudson, *Religion in America*, p. 129.
23. Penniman, *Philadelphia*, p. 34.

3. They See the Light

1. Albert Barnes, *Revivals of Religion in Cities and Large Towns* (New York: John S. Taylor, 1841), p. 154.
2. Ibid., p. 162.

3. Ibid., p. 97.
4. See Morton and Lucia White, *The Intellectual Versus the City* (Cambridge, Mass.: Harvard University Press, 1962).
5. Barnes, *Revivals*, p. 15.
6. Ibid., pp. 168ff.
7. D. L. Dodge, New York to Charles G. Finney, Philadelphia, Feb. 25, 1828, Finney Papers (original papers in the Oberlin College Library, Oberlin, Ohio; microfilm copy in Presbyterian Historical Society, Reel I, #236).
8. Robert Adair, *Memoir of Rev. James Patterson* (Philadelphia: Perkins, 1840), p. 312.
9. Thomas James Shepherd, *History of the First Presbyterian Church of Northern Liberties* (Philadelphia: Privately printed, 1882), p. 55. (Cited hereafter as *History of FPCNL*.)
10. See chapter 5 for revivalism in other denominations.
11. *Christian Advocate*, April 1823, p. 184.
12. Charles G. Finney, *Can Two Walk Together Except They Be Agreed?* (Philadelphia: William F. Geddes, 1827). Sermon given at Troy, N.Y., March 4, 1827.
13. Ibid., p. 10.
14. *Christian Advocate*, June 1827, pp. 245ff.
15. Testimonial of the Rev. Thomas Brainerd, August 6, 1857, in William B. Sprague, *Annals of the American Pulpit*, 9 vols. (New York: Robert Carter, 1859), 4: 427.
16. In May 1819 he speaks in his diary of rupturing a blood vessel during a sermon, and often mentions the "weakness" of his body, and chastens himself to be short in his sermons, but, once engrossed, he would forget and preach longer. Adair, *Memoir of Patterson*, pp. 81-82.
17. Sprague, *Annals of American Pulpit*, 4: 427; Alfred Nevin, *History of the Presbytery of Philadelphia* (Philadelphia: W. S. Fortescue, 1888), p. 188.
18. Adair, *Memoir of Patterson, p.* 27.
19. Shepherd, *History of FPCNL*, p. 36.
20. Adair, *Memoir of Patterson*, p. 45.
21. Nevin, *History of Presbytery of Phila.*, p. 188.
22. Adair, *Memoir of Patterson*, p. 49.
23. Ibid., pp. 94, 221.
24. Accounts of this revival in Shepherd, *History of FPCNL*, pp. 55ff. and Adair, *Memoir of Patterson*, p. 312.
25. Adair, *Memoir of Patterson*, p. 67. There were, however, as many as 180 converts joining churches as a result of this revival, according to Patterson, 70 of them joining the Northern Liberties church.
26. Ibid., p. 82.
27. Many of his sermons are at the Presbyterian Historical Society in Philadelphia. See particularly sermon of Feb. 25, 1837.

28. Adair, *Memoir of Patterson*, p. 174.
29. L. Brainerd, Trenton, to Charles G. Finney, Lancaster, Penna., May 16, 1829, Finney, Papers, Reel I, #395.
30. Adair, *Memoir of Patterson*, p. 190.
31. Chart and text, ibid., p. 185.
32. James Patterson, Sermon, Nov. 21, 1827, p. 11. Presbyterian Historical Society, Philadelphia.
33. Ibid., p. 20.
34. Adair, *Memoir of Patterson*, pp. 152-53.
35. James Patterson, Philadelphia, to Charles G. Finney, Troy, N.Y., April 20, 1827, Finney, Papers, Reel I, #93.
36. James Patterson, Phila., to Charles G. Finney, Wilmington, Del., Dec. 14, 1827, Finney, Papers, Reel I, #194.
37. John P. Cushman, Z. R. Shipperd, N. S. S. Beman, Troy, N. Y., to Charles G. Finney, New Lebanon, Penna., May 8, 1827, Finney Papers, Reel I, #110.
38. Finney's *Memoirs*, written when he was an old man, are often inaccurate on details; according to his letters, he came sometime around January 17, 1828.
39. Ibid., p. 255.
40. Nevin, *History of Presbytery of Phila.*, p. 830.
41. Charles G. Finney, Philadelphia, to Theodore Weld, Mar. 27, 1828, Barnes and Dumond, *Letters of Weld*, 1: 10-14.
42. First Presbyterian Church of Northern Liberties, Philadelphia, to Charles G. Finney, Whitesboro, N. Y., July 14, 1828, Finney, Papers, Reel I, #306.
43. David Van Horne, *A History of the Reformed Church in Philadelphia* (Philadelphia: Reformed Church Publication Board, 1876), p. 15.
44. The doctoral dissertation of John B. Frantz, "Revivalism in the German Reformed Church in America to 1850, with Emphasis on the Eastern Synod" (Ph. D. dissertation, University of Pennsylvania, 1961) was enormously helpful on revivalism within this denomination, and I lean upon it heavily in this section of my work.
45. Ibid., p. 75.
46. H. Harbaugh (the Rev.), *The Fathers of the German Reformed Church in Europe and America* (Lancaster, Pa.: J. M. Westhoeffer, 1872), 4: 39.
47. Members of the Congregation of the German Reformed Church, undated, #101, Old First Reformed Church (United Church of Christ), Philadelphia, Pa. (Hereafter referred to as OFRC.) This communication describes the complaints brought on Sept. 3, 1816, against the Reverend Helffenstein by the Board.
48. Resolution, German Reformed Church, 1819, #104, OFRC.
49. Accounts of these problems in the church are given in Van Horne, *History of Reformed Church*, pp. 64ff.
50. Caspar Schaeffer, Philadelphia, to Finney, Whitesboro, New York, Aug. 4,

1828, Finney, Papers, Reel I, #310.

51. These dates may be somewhat inaccurate. They must be drawn from Finney's letters, since his *Memoirs* are vague on the subject.

52. Caspar Schaeffer, Philadelphia, to Finney, Reading, Pa., April 24, 1829, Finney, Papers, Reel I, #387.

53. Mary C. Knowles, Philadelphia, to Mr. and Mrs. Finney, New York, May 28, 1830, Finney, Papers, Reel I, #486.

54. His son, Jacob Helffenstein, was convinced that it was the contrast between "the preaching of the powerful revivalist [Finney] and the plain presentation of the Gospel truth" by his father, that brought about the difficulty. Van Horne, *History of Reformed Church*, pp. 64ff.

55. Samuel Helffenstein to the German Reformed Church, March 19, 1830, #109, OFRC.

56. Samuel Helffenstein to the German Reformed Church, January 4, 1830, #111, OFRC.

57. Two members of the congregation to the Corporation of the German Reformed Church, January 4, 1830, #108, OFRC.

58. Samuel Helffenstein to the Corporation of German Reformed Church, May 31, 1831, #114, OFRC.

59. Van Horne, *History of Reformed Church*, pp. 70-72.

60. Caspar Schaeffer, Philadelphia, to Finney, New York, Aug. 31, 1830, Finney, Papers, Reel I, #501.

61. Finney, Boston to George Troutman, Phila., Sept. 22, 1831, Finney, Papers, Reel I, #118.

62. Finney, *Memoirs*, p. 245.

63. Van Horne, *History of Reformed Church*, p. 79.

64. See Frantz, "Revivalism in German Reformed Church," for a detailed examination of these developments.

65. John W. Nevin, *The Anxious Bench: A Tract for the Times* (Chambersburg, Pa., 1843).

66. Albert Barnes, *Life at Three Score* (Philadelphia: Parry & McMillan, 1859), pp. 60-65.

67. George M. Marsden, *The Evangelical Mind and the New School Presbyterian Experience* (New Haven, Conn.: Yale University Press, 1970), pp. 53-54.

68. Quoted in ibid., p. 54.

69. *Funeral services held* [for Albert Barnes] *in the First Presbyterian Church*, Philadelphia, Dec. 28, 1870 (Philadelphia: James B. Rodgers, 1871), p. 3.

70. Ibid., pp. 4-5.

71. William Williams Keen, *The Bi-Centennial Celebration of the Founding of the First Baptist Church of the City of Philadelphia* (Philadelphia: American Baptist Publication Society, 1899), pp. 87ff.

72. Robert Torbet, "A Social History of the Philadelphia Baptist Association, 1707-1940" (Ph. D. Dissertation, University of Pennsylvania, 1944), p. 262.

73. Ibid., p. 10.
74. Henry C. Vedder, *A History of the Baptists in the Middle States* (Philadelphia: American Baptist Publication Society, 1898), p. 1503.
75. J. L. Rhees, *Error Refuted or a Brief Exposition of the Leading Features of the Baptist Controversy in Philadelphia and its Vicinity* (Philadelphia: Wm. Stavely, 1827).
76. *Our Jubilee*, Souvenir Program of 150th Anniversary of Spruce St. Baptist Church, Phila., May 10-17, 1896 (Philadelphia: 1896), pp. 14-15.
77. *Confession of Faith*, adopted by the Philadelphia Baptist Association (Philadelphia: Published by the Church, 1825), p. 19.
78. Keen, *Bi-Centennial Celebration*, pp. 91ff., describes the problems at the First Baptist Church of Philadelphia.
79. Torbet, *A History of the Baptists* (1950), pp. 30-34. The slow growth of the Baptists in the ante-bellum period in Pennsylvania is also noted by Vedder, *History of the Baptists*, p. 160.
80. See Table 3.1.
81. See Table 3.2.
82. A resolution of May 28, 1828, reported a great number of vacant churches due to the number of people moving to the western part of the city, and suggests evangelism among the heathen as a cure. Presbyterian Church, *Minutes of the General Assembly*, 1828, p. 242.
83. Sweet, *Revivalism in America*, xiii. The fifties and sixties witnessed a general decline. However, the census of 1960 reported voluntary church membership at 70% and popular identification even higher.
84. D. McClure, Philadelphia, to Finney, Reading, Jan. 22, 1829, Finney, Papers, Reel I, #349.
85. O. Hoover, Philadelphia, to Finney, Reading, Feb. 5, 1829, Finney, Papers, Reel I, #355, and D. McClure, Phila., to Finney, Reading, Feb. 21, 1829, Finney, Papers, Reel I, #358.
86. Thomas Elmes, Philadelphia, to Finney, Reading, April 7, 1829, Finney, Papers, Reel I, #375.

4. Crisis at Noon

1. Erik H. Erikson, *Young Man Luther* (New York: Norton, 1958); *Identity: Youth and Crisis* (New York: New York, 1968); *Gandhi's Truth on the Origins of Militant Nonviolence* (New York: Norton, 1969); "Youth: Fidelity and Diversity," *Daedalus* 91, no. (Winter 1962): 5-27; "The Problem of Ego Identity," *Identity and the Life Cycle* (New York: International Universities Press, 1959), pp. 101-64; "Growth and Crisis of the Healthy Personality," *Identity and the Life Cycle*, pp. 50-100.
2. Erikson, *Young Man Luther*, p. 254. See also Kenneth Kenniston, *Young Radicals* (New York: Harcourt Brace and World, 1968), and idem, "Social Change

and Youth in America," *Daedalus* 91, no. 1 (Winter 1962): 145-71.

3. Kenneth Kenniston, "Youth, a New Stage of Life," *American Scholar* (Autumn 1970), pp. 631-53.

4. Lois W. Banner uses Kenniston's concept of youth and suggests the role of youth in reform in "Religion and Reform in the Early Republic: The Role of Youth," *American Quarterly* 23 (Dec. 1971): 677-95.

5. See Erikson, "Youth: Fidelity and Diversity," pp. 5-27; S. N. Eisenstadt, "Archetypal Patterns of Youth," *Daedalus* 91, no. 1 (Winter 1962): 28-46; Bruno Bettelheim, "The Problem of Generations," *Daedalus* 91, no. 1 (Winter 1962): 68-96; Talcott Parsons, "Youth in the Context of American Society," *Daedalus* 91, no. 1 (Winter 1962): 97-123; Anna Freud, "Adolescence," *Psychoanalytic Study of the Child* (New York: International Universities Press, 1958), 13: 255-76.

6. John and Virginia Demos, "Adolescence in Historical Perspective," *Journal of Marriage and the Family* 21 (1969: 632-38.

7. [Juvenis], "Considerations Addressed by Youth," *The Magazine of the German Reformed Church*, Sept. 1829, pp. 276-78.

8. Barnes, *Revivals of Religion in Cities and Large Towns*, p. 176.

9. Finney, *Memoirs*, p. 247.

10. Adair, *Memoir of Rev. James Patterson*, p. 77.

11. Finney, *Memoirs*, p. 250.

12. Adair, *Memoir of Patterson*, p. 67.

13. Lieber, *Stranger in America*, p. 318.

14. Trollope, *Domestic Manners of the Americans*, p. 143.

15. *The Messenger*, April 1830, p. 128.

16. *The Magazine of the German Reformed Church* 2 (1829): p. 158.

17. "Religious Intelligence," *The Messenger*, April 1830, p. 128.

18. Ibid., April 1831, pp. 76-77.

19. James Porter (Rev.), *Revivals of Religion; Their Theory, Means, Obstructions, Uses and Importance* (Boston: James H. Earle, 1849), pp. 5-6.

20. Henry C. Fish, *Handbook of Revivals* (Boston: James H. Earle, 1887), chapter 7.

21. Edwin D. Starbuck's *The Psychology of Religion* (New York: Scribner's 1904) remains an authoritative work. All succeeding writers, even James and Erikson, have relied on Starbuck's work. See also Elmer T. Clark, *The Psychology of Religious Awakening* (New York: Macmillan, 1929).

22. Starbuck, *Psychology of Religion*, pp. 28, 392.

23. See also Frederick Morgan Davenport, *Primitive Traits in Religious Revivals* (New York: Macmillan, 1910). This book viewed revivals as caused by psychic processes, and predicted, with the glowing naiveté of 1910, that with man growing progressively more rational, revivals would come to an end.

24. Kenniston, *Young Radicals*, pp. 79-82.

25. Starbuck, *Psychology of Religion*, p. 53.

26. George Godwin, *The Great Revivalists* (Boston: Beacon, 1950).

27. Starbuck, *Psychology of Religion*, pp. 230, 284, 395.
28. Erikson, *Young Man Luther*, p. 14.
29. Richard L. Rubenstein, *After Auschwitz* (New York: Bobbs Merrill, 1966), pp. 146, 234-35.
30. Quoted from his Scrapbook, in C. Vann Woodward, *Tom Watson, Agrarian Rebel* (New York: Oxford University Press, 1963), p. 33.
31. Quoted from his Journal, Woodward, *Tom Watson*, p. 35.
32. Ibid., p. 37.
33. Ibid., p. 41.
34. Starbuck, *Psychology of Religion*, p. 53.
35. Cross, *The Burned-Over District*, pp. 177-78.
36. Lieber, *Stranger in America*, p. 318.
37. For this information on woman's place in society, I lean heavily on Eleanor Flexner, *Century of Struggle* (Cambridge, Mass.: Belknap Press of Harvard University Press, 1959).
38. Ibid., p. 42.
39. Pastoral letter from Council of Congregational Ministers of Massachusetts, ibid., p. 46.
40. Flexner, *Century of Struggle*, p. 52.
41. Elisha Bates, *The Doctrine of Friends* (Mountpleasant, Pa.: Printed by the Author, 1825), p. 210.
42. F. B. Noble, *A Century of Gospel-Work* (Philadelphia: Watts, 1876), p. 448. For more information on these women revivalists, see chapter 6.
43. Edward P. Thompson, *The Making of the English Working Class* (New York: Vintage Books, 1963), p. 368.
44. Finney, *Lectures on Revivals*, pp. 41ff.
45. Trollope, *Domestic Manners*, pp. 79, 49-80, 143, 221.

5. From Ecstasy to Form

1. Although the use of organic analogy has come under criticism, the zonal model, with qualifications, has never been adequately replaced as a matrix for urban growth.
2. E. Porter, *Letters on Revivals* (Andover, Mass.: Revival Association of Theological Seminary, 1832), p. 2.
3. A. V. Griswold, *Discourses on the Most Important Doctrines and Duties of the Christian Religion* (Philadelphia, 1830).
4. Charles Grandison Finney, *Lectures on Revivals of Religion*, ed. William G. McLoughlin (Cambridge, Mass.: Harvard University Press, 1960). Originally published in 1835.
5. Finney, *Lectures on Revivals*, introduction by Wm. G. McLoughlin, pp. lviiff.

6. Ibid., pp. 184, 196, 204, 252-53, 267, 359.
7. Thomas H. Skinner, *Thoughts on Evangelizing the World* (New York: John S. Taylor, 1836).
8. Alfred Nevin, *History of the Presbytery of Philadelphia* (Philadelphia: W. S. Fortescue, 1888), p. 830.
9. Skinner, *Thoughts on Evangelizing the World*, pp. 80-82.
10. For Skinner's later views see Thomas H. Skinner, *Lay Evangelism* (Cincinnati, Ohio, 1875).
11. James Porter, *Revivals of Religion: Their Theory, Means, Obstructions, Uses, and Importance* (Boston: Charles H. Peirce, 1849), p. 15.
12. See ibid., pp. 68, 80, 117, 124, 130.
13. Ibid., p. 170.
14. Ibid., p. 226.
15. Actually, there were small local societies earlier. The Reverend James Patterson had started the Union Sabbath School Association of Northern Liberties in 1815.
16. *The Saturday Evening Post*, March 22, 1828.
17. J. Thomas Scharf and Thompson Westcott, *History of Philadelphia, 1609-1884*, 3 vols. (Philadelphia: Everts, 1884), 2: 1471.
18. See chapter 8.
19. Pendleton, "Influence of Evangelical Churches Upon Humanitarian Reform," pp. 261ff.
20. Barnes, *Life at Three Score*, p. 36.
21. Ibid., p. 47.
22. Pendleton, "Influence of Evangelical Churches Upon Humanitarian Reform," p. 102.
23. John Wanamaker attended the Reverend Chambers's prayer meetings as a boy and became a lifelong evangelical worker.
24. Pendleton, "Influence of Evangelical Churches Upon Humanitarian Reform," p. 76.
25. Irwin G. Wyllie, *The Self-Made Man in America* (New Brunswick, N. J.: Rutgers University Press, 1954), p. 69.
26. Wyatt-Brown, *Lewis Tappan and the Evangelical War Against Slavery*, p. 66.
27. Scharf and Westcott, *History of Philadelphia*, 3: 380ff.
28. Pendleton, "Influence of Evangelical Churches Upon Humanitarian Reform," p. 146.
29. Ibid.
30. Finney, *Lectures on Revivals*, p. 300.
31. See chapter 1.
32. Charles C. Cole, Jr., *The Social Ideas of the Northern Evangelists, 1826-1860* (New York: Columbia University Press, 1954).
33. Finney, *Lectures on Revivals*, p. 297.
34. Ibid.

35. Charles G. Finney, *Lectures on Systematic Theology* (Grand Rapids, Mich.: Eerdmans, 1951), p. 297. (Revised edition of work originally published in 1851.)

36. Cole, *Social Ideas of Northern Evangelists*, p. 188.

6. The Sectarian Response

1. Francis H. Tees, *History of Old St. George's Methodist Episcopal Church* (Philadelphia: Privately printed, 1934), p. 10.

2. Finney, *Memoirs*, p. 90.

3. W. P. Strickland, *The Life of Jacob Gruber* (New York: Carlton & Porter, 1860), pp. 291-92.

4. James Caughey, *Helps to a Life of Holiness and Usefullness, or Revival Miscellanies* (Boston: James P. Magee, 1856), p. 424.

5. Emma Maffitt, *Life and Services of John Newland Maffitt* [by his widow] (New York: Neale Publishing Co., 1906), p. 42. Grover Cleveland Loud, *Evangelized America* (New York: Lincoln McVeagh, 1928), pp. 210-12.

6. Jacob Knapp, *Autobiography of Elder Jacob Knapp* (New York: Sheldon and Co., 1868), p. ix.

7. Jabez Smith Swan, *The Evangelist: Or, Life and Labors of Rev. Jabez S. Swan* (Waterford, Conn.: W. L. Pekcham, 1873), pp. 101, 181. See also Knapp, *Autobiography*, pp. 38-39, 62.

8. Knapp, *Autobiography*, pp. 40-41.

9. Ibid., p. 41.

10. Vedder, *History of the Baptists*, p. 154.

11. Knapp, *Autobiography*, p. xil.

12. Ibid., p. 226.

13. Ibid., pp. 226-27.

14. Ibid., p. 255.

15. Ibid., pp. 94-99.

16. Ibid., p. 182.

17. Ibid., p. 183.

18. Ibid., p. 184.

19. Ibid., p. ix.

20. Swan, *The Evangelist*, p. 4.

21. Loud, *Evangelized America*, p. 190.

22. William Wilson Manross, *A History of the American Episcopal Church* (New York: Morehouse-Gorham Co., 1950), p. 105.

23. "Forms of Prayer," in *The Protestant Episcopalian and Church Register* 1, no. 8 (August 1830).

24. Walter Herbert Stowe, ed., *Life and Letters of Bishop William White* (New York: Morehouse Publishing Co., 1937), pp. 134ff.

25. *The Protestant Episcopalian and Church Register* 1 no. 11 (Nov. 1830), pp. 453-54.
26. Ibid.
27. Manross, *History of American Episcopal Church*, p. 18.
28. Stowe, *Life of Bishop White*, p. 136.
29. Pendleton, "Influence of Evangelical Churches Upon Humanitarian Reform," p. 46.
30. Manross, *History of American Episcopal Church*, p. 238.
31. Frederick B. Tolles, *Quietism Versus Enthusiasm: The Philadelphia Quakers and the Great Awakening* (offprint from *Pennsylvania Magazine of History and Biography*, Jan. 1945), p. 33.
32. Ibid.
33. For a perceptive analysis of the separation, see Rufus M. Jones, *The Later Periods of Quakerism*, 2 vols. (London: Macmillan, 1921), 1: 435ff.
34. Ibid., p. 446.
35. Robert W. Doherty, *The Hicksite Separation* (New Brunswick, N. J.: Rutgers University Press, 1967).
36. For the theoretical foundation of my analysis, see Niebuhr, *Social Sources of Denominationalism*. Niebuhr uses the classical sociological theory of Tawney, Troeltsch, and Weber to describe the development of a sect into a church.
37. Elizabeth May Geffen, *Philadelphia Unitarianism, 1796-1861* (Philadelphia: University of Pennsylvania Press, 1961), p. 162.
38. Joseph John Gurney, *Observations on the Distinguishing Views and Practices of the Society of Friends* (New York: Mahlon Day, 1840), p. 182.
39. Ibid., p. 181.
40. *Quaker Biographies*, 5 vols. (Philadelphia: Philadelphia Yearly Meeting of Friends, 1926), Series 2, 2: 118.
41. Richard F. Mott, *Memoir and Correspondence of Eliza P. Gurney* (Philadelphia: Lippincott, 1884), p. 371.
42. Ibid., pp. 368-69.
43. "A Woman in the Pulpit," *Harper's Weekly* 16, no. 792 (March 2, 1872): 1.
44. Noble, *Century of Gospel-Work*, p. 426.
45. Edwin Scott Gaustad, *A Religious History of America* (New York: Harper and Row, 1966), p. 95.
46. Edmund Jacob Wolf, *The Lutherans in America* (New York: Hill and Co., 1889), p. 292.
47. Abdel Ross Wentz, *A Basic History of Lutheranism in America* (Philadelphia: Fortress Press, 1964), p. 73.
48. Ibid., pp. 133-37.
49. Wolf, *Lutherans in America*, p. 354.
50. Wentz, *Basic History of Lutheranism*, pp. 133-37.

7. Black Revivalism

1. DuBois, *Philadelphia Negro*, p. 206. For a superb analysis of the position of the church in Negro life, see E. Franklin Frazier, *The Negro Church in America* (New York: Schocken, 1964).
2. DuBois, *Philadelphia Negro*, pp. 25-45.
3. Ibid.
4. Leon Litwak, *North of Slavery, The Negro in the Free States, 1790-1860* (Chicago: University of Chicago Press, 1961).
5. DuBois, *Philadelphia Negro*, p. 143.
6. This is possibly due to the inability to locate black males for purposes of compilation. In addition, there were more occupational opportunities for females in the city, and perhaps for this reason more females migrated to the city. See ibid., p. 46.
7. Melville J. Herskovits, *The Myth of the Negro Past* (New York: Harper and Row, 1941).
8. Wesley, *Richard Allen*, pp. 71-72.
9. DuBois, *Philadelphia Negro*, p. 199.
10. William T. Catto, *A Semi-Centenary Discourse Delivered in the First African Presbyterian Church* (Philadelphia: Joseph M. Wilson, 1857), p. 82, and DuBois, *Philadelphia Negro*, p. 198.
11. Catto, *Semi-Centenary Discourse*, p. 27.
12. Ibid., pp. 86ff.
13. Charles H. Wesley, *Richard Allen: Apostle of Freedom* (Washington, D.C.: Associated Publishers, 1935), p. 190.
14. DuBois, *Philadelphia Negro*, p. 199.
15. Ibid., p. 205.
16. W. E. Burghardt DuBois, "Of the Faith of the Fathers," in *Black Church in America*, ed. Hart M. Nelson and Raytha L. Yokley (New York: Basic Books, 1971), pp. 30-31.
17. Wesley, *Richard Allen*, p. 21.
18. Ibid., p. 214.
19. Ibid., p. 89.
20. Catto, *Semi-Centenary Discourse*, p. 34.
21. Ibid., pp. 28-29.
22. Lieber, *Stranger in America*, p. 328.
23. Jarena Lee, *Religious Experience and Journal giving Account of her Call to Preach the Gospel* (Philadelphia: Published by the Author, 1849), p. 5.
24. Ibid., p. 18.
25. Ibid., p. 81.

26. Wesley, *Richard Allen*, pp. 196-97.
27. DuBois, *Philadelphia Negro*, p. 112.
28. See his essay "The Religious Life of the Negro," in Nelson and Yokley, *Black Church in America*.

8. The Outsiders

1. Robert Kelley, *The Transatlantic Persuasion* (New York: Knopf, 1969).
2. Trollope, *Domestic Manners*, p. 79.
3. G. Lewis, *Impressions of America and the American Churches: From the Journal of . . .* (Edinburgh: W. P. Kennedy, 1845), p. 407.
4. See Charles Grandison Finney, *Sermons on Important Subjects* (New York: John S. Taylor, 1836), p. 369.
5. Robert Baird, *Religion in America* (New York: Harper, 1856), p. 264.
6. Geffen, *Philadelphia Unitarianism*, p. 239.
7. Ibid., p. 188.
8. William H. Furness, *A Discourse Delivered Mar. 17, 1844 in the First Congregational Unitarian Church* (Philadelphia: J. Cressy, 1844).
9. Rebecca Gratz, Philadelphia, to Maria Gist Gratz, Lexington, Feb. 19, 1837 in *Letters of Rebecca Gratz*, ed. David Philipson (Philadelphia: Jewish Publication Society of America, 1929), p. 233.
10. Rebecca Gratz, Philadelphia, to Maria Gist Gratz, Lexington, undated, *Letters*, pp. 145-46.
11. Geffen, *Philadelphia Unitarianism*, p. 208.
12. Abraham K. Karp, *The Jewish Experience in America* (Waltham, Mass.: American Jewish Historical Society, 1969), p. 18.
13. Edwin Wolf, 2nd, and Maxwell Whiteman, *The History of the Jews of Philadelphia* (Philadelphia: Jewish Publication Society, 1956), p. 371.
14. Ibid., p. 242.
15. The first convert recorded in America, Judah Monis of Boston, was baptized in the city in 1730, and afterwards became professor of Hebrew at Harvard. His baptismal address, "The Truth, the Whole Truth and Nothing But the Truth," was published in tract form, with a preface written by Increase Mather. Albert Edward Thompson, *A Century of Jewish Missions* (Chicago: Fleming H. Revell, 1902), p. 227. Although Thompson identifies him as a rabbi and spells his name Morris, Jewish sources spell his name Monis and reveal that he was probably not an ordained rabbi.
16. Lee M. Friedman, *The American Society for Meliorating the Condition of the Jews, and Joseph S. C. F. Frey, its Missionary* (Boston, 1925), pp. 3-4.
17. Ibid., pp. 6-7.
18. See the excellent article by Lorman Ratner, "Conversion of the Jews and Pre-Civil War Reform," *American Quarterly* 13 (1961): 43-54.

19. Joseph L. Blau and Salo W. Baron, eds., *The Jews of the United States, 1790-1840, a Documentary History*, 3 vols. (New York: Columbia University Press, 1963), 3: 714.
20. "Jadownicky's Address," in *ibid.*, p. 730. Bernard J. Jadownicky was a converted Polish Jew sent to America to seek new Jewish converts.
21. American Society for Meliorating the Conditions of the Jews, *First Annual Report* (New York: American Society for Meliorating the Condition of the Jews, 1823). (Hereafter cited as ASMCJ.)
22. *Philadelphia Gazette*, January 8, 1823.
23. R. B. Van Kleek in Sprague, *Annals of the American Pulpit*, 5: 572-75.
24. *Christian Advocate* 2 (1824): 238.
25. Sprague, *Annals of the American Pulpit*, 9: 105.
26. Corwin, Edward T., *A Manual of the German Reformed Church in America* (New York: Reformed Church in America, 1902), p. 628.
27. Henry Boardman, April 9, 1855, in Sprague, *Annals of American Pulpit*, 3: 619-22.
28. William Edward Schenck, April 6, 1857, in *Annals*, pp. 622-626.
29. Letter of protest, #255, May 21, 1825, signed by four prominent converts: Bernard J. Jadownicky, Erasmus H. Simon, Wolf, and Jacobi. The last two were induced to withdraw their signatures. Blau and Baron, *Jews of the United States*, 3: 745.
30. Undated letter in *Magazine of the Reformed Dutch Church*, 1826; John H. Livingston to Peter Wilson in Blau and Baron, *Jews of the United States*, 3: 755.
31. *The Messenger* 1 (1828): 242.
32. Quoted from 13th report of ASMCJ, 1836, in Friedman, *American Society for Meliorating the Condition of the Jews*, p. 12.
33. ASMCJ, *22nd Annual Report*, 1845, p. 13.
34. ASMCJ, *21st Report*, 1844, p. 14.
35. Edward Dorr Griffin, *An Address Delivered at the Anniversary of the American Society for Meliorating the Condition of the Jews, May 11, 1824* (New York: D. Fanshaw, 1824), pp. 4-5. Dr. Griffin was president of Williams College in Massachusetts.
36. Ibid., p. 7.
37. Reports of missions to the Jews (in manuscript form) from 1833 to 1863 are at the Presbyterian Historical Society in Philadelphia.
38. See *Methodist Review* 4 (October 1821): 378-80; *Magazine of the Reformed German Church* 3 (December 1828): 262-64; *The Friend*, 1, no. 12 (January 1828): 3; "Religious Intelligence" of the *Christian Advocate* contains frequent articles on conversion of Jews.
39. Sprague, *Annals*, 6: 761.
40. *Jewish Chronicle* (1849), quoted by Ratner, "Conversion of the Jews and Pre-Civil War Reform," *American Quarterly* 13 (1961): 51.
41. Blau and Baron, *Jews of U. S.*, 3: 971.

42. From the first issue of *The Jew*, printed in Blau and Baron, *Jews of U. S.*, 3: 767-69.
43. [George Houston], *Israel Vindicated, Being a Refutation of the Calumnies Propagated Respecting the Jewish Nation* (New York: Collins, 1820).
44. Ibid., Letter #27, pp. 86-88.
45. Ibid.
46. Ibid., Letter #28, pp. 93-94.
47. Isaac Leeser to *U. S. Gazette*, 1836, in Karp, *Jewish Experience in America*, p. xv.
48. Rebecca Gratz, Philadelphia, to Miriam Cohen, Savannah, Ga., Aug. 29, 1842. Photostatic copy in American Jewish Archives, Box 370. Original in American Jewish Historical Society, Waltham, Mass.
49. Bertram Wallace Korn, "Isaac Leeser: Centennial Reflections," *American Jewish Archives* 19, no. 2 (November 1967): 127-41.
50. *The Occident* 2 (1845): 561.
51. ASMCJ, *21st Report*, 1844, p. 8.
52. *The Occident* 15 (June 1857): 123.
53. Ibid., 2 (1845): 605.
54. Ibid.
55. Robert Baird, *Religion in America* (New York: Harper, 1856), p. 268.
56. Quoted in Friedman, *American Society for Meliorating the Condition of the Jews*, p. 13.
57. Ibid., p. 17.
58. James Caughey, *Glimpses of Life in Soul-Saving, Selections from the Journal and Other Writings* (New York: Palmer, 1868), p. 134.

9. The Smoldering Fire

1. Presbyterian Church, General Assembly, *Minutes* (1835), p. 492.
2. *New York Evangelist*, Jan. 5, 1833.
3. Schaff, *America*, p. 144.
4. Ibid., p. 138.
5. Finney, *Lectures on Revivals*, p. 22.
6. Quoted in McLoughlin, Jr., *Modern Revivalism*, p. 147.
7. *Oberlin Evangelist*, April 23, 1845, p. 69.
8. Ibid., December 17, 1845, p. 205.
9. Ibid., Feb. 12, 1845, p. 27.
10. Quoted in Cross, *Burned-Over District*, p. 167.
11. Baird, *Religion in America*, pp. 200-202.
12. Franklin H. Littell speaks of the mass evangelism of the nineteenth century as being accompanied by a steady deterioration of the standards of membership. See Littell, *State Church to Pluralism*, pp. 51, 80-81.

13. H. Richard Niebuhr and D. D. Williams, "The Ministry in Historical Perspective," *The Rise of the Evangelical Conception of the Ministry, 1607-1850*, ed. Sidney E. Mead (New York: Harper, 1956).
14. Finney, *Lectures on Revivals*, p. 387.

10. Businessmen's Revivals

1. U. S. Census Office, *Seventh Census of the United States, 1850*, pp. 200-205; Ivan D. Steen, "Philadelphia in the 1850's as Described by British Travelers," *Pennsylvania History* 33 (January 1966): 38.
2. Steen, "Philadelphia in the 1850s," p. 49.
3. Ibid., p. 48. See also Theodore Hershberg, "Free Blacks in Antebellum Philadelphia" and Dennis Clark, "The Philadelphia Irish: Persistent Presence," in Davis and Haller, *Peoples of Philadelphia*. *the Peoples of Philadelphia* (Philadelphia: Temple University, 1971).
4. Warner, *Private City*, p. 65.
5. Ibid., p. 64.
6. R. A. Smith, *Philadelphia as it is in 1852* (Philadelphia: Lindsay & Blakiston, 1852), pp. 367ff.
7. Oberholtzer, *Philadelphia*, 2: 304.
8. Ibid., p. 346.
9. See George W. Van Vleck, *The Panic of 1857* (New York: Columbia University Press, 1943).
10. *The Evening Bulletin*, December 31, 1857, recounts the unfolding of the crisis of the past year in Philadelphia. See also Oberholtzer, *Philadelphia* 2: 332.
11. Editorial, *Eveing Bulletin*, November 27, 1857, p. 2.
12. John Jenkins, *Plain Thoughts on the Present Great Awakening* (Philadelphia: Presbyterian Book Store, 1858), p. 5. John Jenkins was the minister of the Calvary Church on Locust Street in Philadelphia.
13. "Editor's Table," *Harper's Magazine* 16, (May 1858): 838.
14. *Friends Intelligencer*, January 9, 1858, p. 680.
15. Jenkins, *Plain Thoughts*, p. 6.
16. William C. Conant, *Narratives of Remarkable Conversions and Revival Incidents* (New York: Derby and Jackson, 1858), pp. 357-58.
17. Charles Howard Hopkins, *History of the Young Men's Christian Association in North America* (New York: Association Press, 1951), p. 4.
18. Ibid., pp. 24-26.
19. George H. Stuart, *The Life of George H. Stuart* (Philadelphia, 1890), pp. 29-32.
20. Hopkins, *History of YMCA*, p. 44.
21. John Wanamaker, *Maxims of Life and Business*, with an Introduction by Russell H. Conwell (New York: Harper, 1923), pp. 7, 8, 16.

22. Herbert Adams Gibbons, *John Wanamaker*, 2 vols. (New York and London: Harper, 1926), 1: 7, 30-31.
23. Ibid., p. 32.
24. Ibid., p. 45.
25. Hopkins, *History of YMCA*, pp. 40-41.
26. Gibbons, *John Wanamaker*, pp. 41-44.
27. Noble, *A Century of Gospel-Work*, p. 421.
28. Jenkins, *Plain Thoughts*, p. 17; Conant, *Narratives of Remarkable Conversions*, p. 368; Noble, *Century of Gospel-Work*, pp. 420-21.
29. Young Men's Christian Association, *Fourth Annual Report*, 1858, p. 3.
30. Jenkins, *Plain Thoughts*, p. 20.
31. *Philadelphia Evening Bulletin*, January 23, 1858.
32. Henry Ridgeway, *Life of Rev. Alfred Cookman* (New York: 1874), pp. 200-201.
33. Noble, *Century of Gospel-Work*, p. 426.
34. Edwin M. Long, *The Union-Tabernacle; or Movable Tent-Church* (Philadelphia: Parry, 1859), p. 217.
35. *Philadelphia Press*, May 3, 1858.
36. Long, *Union-Tabernacle, pp. 28, 97-98*.
37. *For details on the tent meetings, see Gibbons, John Wanamaker*, pp. 43-45, and Long, *Union-Tabernacle*. In addition, an 80-page account of these revivals was published by the Philadelphia YMCA, *Pentecost or the Work of God in Philadelphia, A. D., 1858* (Philadelphia, 1858). The first edition was 10,000 copies and was prepared by a group of 15, representing each evangelical denomination.
38. Philadelphia YMCA, *Pentecost*, p. xii.
39. Conant, *Narratives of Remarkable Conversions*, p. 413.
40. Gibbons, *John Wanamaker*, p. 54.
41. Noble, *Century of Gospel-Work*, pp. 433-34.
42. *Philadelphia Inquirer*, April 19, 1858.
43. Noble, *Century of Gospel-Work*, p. 443.
44. Conant, *Narratives of Remarkable Conversions*, p. 413.
45. Ibid., p. 395; Henry C. Fish, *Handbook of Revivals* (Boston: James H. Earle, 1887), p. 70.
46. Conant, *Narratives of Remarkable Conversions*, p. 395.
47. Ibid., pp. 111ff., 396.
48. *Catholic Herald and Visitor*, June 12, 1858, p. 188.
49. Ibid., May 15, 1858, p. 156 and May 22, 1858, p. 164.
50. Ibid., March 27, 1858, p. 98.
51. Quoted in Grover Cleveland Loud, *Evangelized America* (New York: Lincoln MacVeagh, 1928), pp. 225-30.
52. *The Occident and American Jewish Advocate* 15, no. 3 (June 1857): 170-72.
53. Ibid., p. 171.
54. *Friends Intelligencer*, May 10, 1858.
55. *New York Herald*, March 26 and 28, 1858.

56. *The Presbyterian*, July 31, 1858.
57. Philadelphia YMCA, *Pentecost*, p. xix.
58. *McElroy's Philadelphia Directory for 1857*, pp. 902-6; *McElroy's Philadelphia Directory for 1858*, pp. 912-15; *McElroy's Philadelphia Directory for 1859*, pp. 916-20.
59. These statistics are of Old and New School combined but do not include unaffiliated Presbyterian churches, for which statistics were not available. Presbyterian Church, General Assembly, *Minutes* (New School), *1857*, pp. 493-95; *1858*, 684-868; *1859*, pp. 149-51. Presbyterian Church, General Assembly, *Minutes* (Old School), *1857*, pp. 108-10; *1858*, pp. 331-33; *1859*, pp. 630-31; *1860*, pp. 139-42.
60. Eric Foner, *Free Soil, Free Labor, Free Men* (New York: Oxford University Press, 1970), p. 229.
61. Michael B. Katz, *The Irony of Early School Reform* (Cambridge, Mass.: Harvard University Press, 1968), pp. 87-88.
62. Wyllie, *Self-Made Man in America*, pp. 64ff.
63. See Michael B. Katz, *The Irony of Early School Reform* (Cambridge, Mass.: Harvard University Press, 1968).
64. Blake McKelvey, *American Prisons; a Study in American Social History Prior to 1915* (Chicago: University of Chicago Press, 1936).
65. See William G. Rothstein, *American Physicians in the Nineteenth Century* (Baltimore and London: Johns Hopkins University Press, 1972).

11. Colossus in Philadelphia

1. See Lewis Mumford, *The Brown Decades* (New York: Harcourt, Brace and Co., 1959).
2. Thompson Westcott, *Official Guidebook to Philadelphia* (Philadelphia: Porter and Coates, 1876), p. 46.
3. U. S. Census Office, *Ninth Census of the United States, 1879*. Vol. 1 lists 490,308 native-born to 183,624 foreign-born.
4. Dorothy Elizabeth Caroline Ditter, "The Cultural Climate of the Centennial City: Philadelphia 1875-76" (Ph.D. dissertation, University of Pennsylvania, 1947), p. 7.
5. Ibid., pp. 9-10.
6. Arthur Emerson Harris, *Personal Glimpses of Russell H. Conwell* (Philadelphia: Baptist Temple, 1926), p. 53.
7. Westcott, *Official Guidebook*, pp. 151-52.
8. Ditter, "Cultural Climate of Centennial City," p. 22.
9. Ibid., p. 15.
10. Ibid., pp. 10-12.
11. Biographical information is from Moody's biography by his son: William R.

Moody, *The Life of D. L. Moody* (New York: Fleming H. Revell Co., 1900). See bibliographical essay for notes on other Moody biographies.

12. *Moody Joines the YMCA*, p. 2. In the files at the Moody Bible Institute, Chicago.

13. James F. Findlay, Jr., *Dwight L. Moody, American Evangelist, 1837-1899* (Chicago: University of Chicago Press, 1969), p. 29.

14. Moody, *Life of Moody*, pp. 75, 94.

15. Ibid., p. 63.

16. Findlay, *Moody*, p. 100.

17. Ibid., p. 132.

18. Noble, *A Century of Gospel-Work*, p. 472.

19. Moody, *Life of Moody*, p. 249.

20. Philadelphia, Young Men's Christian Association, *Annual Report*, January 20, 1876, p. 23.

21. Ibid., p. 24.

22. This number includes 11 United Presbyterian, 8 Presbyterian General Synod, 3 Presbyterian Synod, and 1 Presbyterian Reformed.

23. Ditter, "Cultural Climate of Centennial City," p. 44.

24. Stuart, *Life of Stuart*, p. 112.

25. McLoughlin, *Modern Revivalism*, p. 154.

26. Stuart, *Life of Stuart*, p. 272.

27. Ibid., p. 258.

28. Gibbons, *John Wanamaker*, p. 134.

29. Ibid., pp. 45-47.

30. Harris, *Personal Glimpses of Conwell*, p. 54.

31. The committee included Alexander Whilldin, Joshua L. Bailey, John R. Whitney, James Long, John Field, Alexander Brown, Thomas Potter, Thomas H. Powers, Leon E. Graeff, William M. Shoemaker, Nelson F. Evans, and William Levering. Philadelphia, Young Men's Christian Association, *Annual Report*, 1876, p. 11.

32. Actually rent was $1, and with repossession on thirty days notice. Gibbons, *John Wanamaker*, p. 134.

33. For an account of this Philadelphia revival see the manuscript report by Thomas K. Cree, "Mr. Moody as Evangelist," 34 pages, in the library of the Young Men's Christian Association, New York.

34. *Philadelphia Inquirer*, November 20, 1875.

35. Stuart, *Life of Stuart*, p. 278.

36. See announcement by John Field and L. P. Rowland of the Committee of Music, October 28, 1875 at Presbyterian Historical Society in Philadelphia.

37. Cree, "Mr. Moody as Evangelist," p. 9.

38. Copies of these circulars are in the files of the Presbyterian Historical Society in Philadelphia. See figure below.

39. Cree, "Mr. Moody as Evangelist," p. 9.

40. Moody, *Life of Moody*, p. 426.

41. Harris, *Personal Glimpses of Conwell*, p. 55.

42. *Philadelphia Inquirer*, Nov. 22, 1875.

43. McLoughlin, *Modern Revivalism*, p. 175; *Philadelphia Inquirer*, Nov. 22, 1875.

44. On January 7, 1876, the *Philadelphia Inquirer* reported these prayers read:

    30 requests from Christian mothers for 45 sons,

    10 requests from widows for prodigal sons,

      7 requests for 24 brothers away from the church,

    10 requests for 14 brothers away from the church,

    12 requests from mothers for their worldly daughters,

    14 requests from daughters for their worldly mothers and fathers,

    20 requests from wives or husbands for mates,

    12 requests for sons in law,

      6 requests for persons feeling the need of the Savior,

    10 from persons interested in their salvation,

    10 from unbelievers,

    14 from backsliders,

      6 from infidels,

and requests for 30 unconverted young men.

45. Stuart, *Life of Stuart*, p. 281.

46. *Philadelphia Times*, December 6, 1876, Jan. 7, 1876, and Jan. 10, 1876; *Philadelphia Inquirer*, Nov. 27, 1876. See also (the Rev.) Edgar Johnson Goodspeed, *A Full History of the Wonderful Career of Moody and Sankey in Great Britain and America* (New York: Goodspeed, 1876), p. 375.

47. *Philadelphia Times*, Dec. 14, 1876.

48. Ibid., Jan. 11, 1876.

49. Goodspeed, *A Full History of the Career of Moody and Sankey*, pp. 40-43.

50. Moody, *Life of Moody*, pp. 256ff.

51. Moody, *Life of Moody*, p. 246.

52. Simons M. Laird, *Evenings with Moody and Sankey: Comprising Sermons and Addresses at Their Great Revival Meetings* (Philadelphia: Porter and Coates, 1877), p. 240.

53. Finney, *Lectures on Revivals*, p. 133.

54. Wilbur M. Smith, ed., *The Best of D. L. Moody* (Chicago: Moody Press, 1971), p. 17.

55. *Philadelphia Inquirer*, Jan. 17, 1876.

56. Gibbons, *Wanamaker*, p. 133; Stuart, *Life of Stuart*, p. 272.

57. Smith, *Best of Moody*, p. 20.

58. *Philadelphia Inquirer*, Nov. 22, 1875.

59. Dwight L. Moody, *New Sermons, Addresses and Prayers* (Chicago: Goodspeed, 1877), pp. 263-362.

60. Dwight L. Moody, *Fifty Sermons and Evangelistic Talks* (New York: Barton, 1899), pp. 94, 297.

61. *Philadelphia Inquirer*, January 5, 1876.

62. Finney, *Lectures on Revivals*, p. 379.

63. Moody, *Fifty Sermons*, p. 95.

64. *Moody Bible Institute Charter*, 1887. On display at the Moody Bible Institute, Chicago.

65. Myron Raymond Chartier, *The Social Views of Dwight L. Moody and their Relation to the Working Man of 1860-1900* (Hays, Kansas: Fort Hays Kansas State College, 1969, Fort Hays Studies #), p. 31.

66. William G. McLoughlin, Jr., *The Meaning of Henry Ward Beecher* (New York: Knopf, 1970), p. 5.

67. Quoted in McLoughlin, *Modern Revivalism*, p. 260.

68. See sermon entitled "Work" in Moody, *Fifty Sermons*, pp. 545-53.

69. Ibid., Dec. 20, 1875.

70. Laird, *Evenings with Moody*, pp. 69, 73.

71. Ibid., Sermon "The Wicked After Death," pp. 66-73.

72. *Philadelphia Inquirer*, Dec. 26, 1875.

73. *Philadelphia Press*, Jan. 15, 1876.

74. Letters to ministers from George Stuart, Jan. 1 and Jan. 14, 1876, Presbyterian Historical Society in Philadelphia.

75. *Philadelphia Inquirer*, Jan. 20, 1876.

76. Ibid.

77. Ibid.

78. Ibid.

79. *Philadelphia Times*, Jan. 21, 1876.

80. Goodspeed, *Full History of Moody*, p. 405.

81. Cree tells us that, some years later, he, Moody, and Wanamaker secured an additional sum to remove the existing debts in connection with the YMCA building. Cree, "Mr. Moody as Evangelist," p. 18.

82. Statement of the committee to *Philadelphia Times*, Jan. 17, 1876. Other estimates run to 436,000. See *Philadelphia Inquirer*, Jan. 18, 1876.

83. McLoughlin, *Modern Revivalism*, p. 230.

84. Gibbons, *John Wanamaker*, pp. 140-42.

85. Goodspeed, *Full History of Moody*, p. 275; Vedder, *History of Baptists*, p. 157; concluded by McLoughlin, *Modern Revivalism*, p. 220.

86. *Philadelphia Inquirer*, Jan. 4, 1876.

87. *Presbyterian Quarterly and Princeton Review*, n. s. 20 (October 1876): 719.

88. Alexander V. G. Allen, *Life and Letters of Phillips Brooks*, 2 vols. (New York: Dutton, 1900), 2: 149.

89. Letter of March 5, 1877, in ibid., 2: 148.

90. *Friends Intelligencer* 32 (Dec. 25, 1875): 696.

91. The Rev. E. V. Gerhart, "Modern Revivals," *The Weekly Messenger*, pp. 34-52.

92. Editors Notebook, "Mr. Moody at the Tabernacle," *Unitarian Review* 7 (March 1877): 317.

93. Goodspeed, *Full History of Moody*, p. 274.

94. Ibid.

95. "A Revival at Frogtown," *Catholic World* 22, no. 131 (Feb. 1876): 699-707.

96. *Philadelphia Inquirer*, Dec. 30, 1875.

97. Ibid., Jan. 14, 1876.
98. *Philadelphia Times*, Jan. 16, 1876.
99. *New York Sun*, undated article in the files of Moody Bible Institute.
100. Eliza S. Bladen, in Ditter, "Cultural Climate of Centennial City," p. 42.
101. *Philadelphia Inquirer*, Dec. 26, 1875.
102. Goodspeed, *Full History of Moody*, p. 391.
103. *Philadelphia Inquirer*, Dec. 9, 1875.
104. Ibid., Dec. 3, 1875; see also Nov. 27, 1875.
105. Ibid., Dec. 8, 1875.
106. Ibid., Dec. 3, 1875.
107. See sermon "Where Art Thou" in L. T. Palmer, ed., *The Gospel Awakening, Comprising the Sermons and Addresses, Prayer-Meeting Talks and Bible Readings at the Great Revival Meetings Conducted by Moody and Sankey* (Chicago: Fleming H. Revell, 1883), p. 398.
108. *Philadelphia Times*, Jan. 20, 1876.
109. Goodspeed, *Full History of Moody*, p. 308; Noble, *Century of Gospel-Work*, p. 469.
110. *Philadelphia Inquirer*, Dec. 26, 1875; Jan. 10, 1876.
111. Ibid., Jan. 10, 1876.
112. Goodspeed, *Full History of Moody*, p. 263.
113. Findlay, *Dwight Moody*, p. 202.
114. Charles Morris, ed., *Makers of Philadelphia* (Philadelphia: Hammersly, 1894), p. 57; Warner, *Private City*, p. 86.
115. Loetscher, "Presbyterianism and Revivalism," pp. 54-92.
116. Morris, *Makers of Philadelphia*, p. 79.
117. E. C. Savidge, ed., *A Gallery of Eminent Men of Philadelphia* (Philadelphia: Henry L. Everett, 1887), unpaged.
118. The Rev. George H. Johnston, "The Gospel in the Cities," *The Mercersberg Review* (1875), pp. 365-368.
119. John Wanamaker, "Bringing Business Efficiency into Christian Service," *Sunday School Times*, undated clipping in the files of Moody Bible Institute.
120. *Industries of Philadelphia* (Philadelphia: Richard Edwards, 1881), p. 171.
121. Morris, *Makers of Philadelphia*, p. 291.
122. *Philadelphia, Pictorial and Biographical* (Philadelphia: Clarke, 1911), p. 104.
123. Charles F. Warwick, *Warwick's Keystone Commonwealth* (Philadelphia, 1913), p. 384.
124. See Clifford S. Griffin, "Religious Benevolence as a Social Control, 1815-1860," *Mississippi Valley Historical Review* 44 (1957-58): 423-44.
125. See *Sunday Times*, Jan. 16, 1876, and *Evening Bulletin*, Jan. 11, 1876.
126. "The Church and the Poor," *The Nation* 21 (Nov. 18, 1875): 321-22.
127. *Philadelphia Times*, Dec. 14, 1875.
128. This included 18 Sunday meetings, 40 weekly meetings, 56 noonday meetings, 14 Bible meetings, 48 young men's meetings, 36 women's meetings, and 36 women's and men's afternoon meetings, Report of the Committee,

Philadelphia Times, Jan. 19, 1876.

129. Cree, "Mr. Moody as Evangelist," p. 19.
130. Findlay, *Moody*, p. 269.
131. Loetscher, "Presbyterianism and Revivalism," pp. 65-66.
132. Methodist Episcopal Church, *Annual Minutes of the Philadelphia Conference*, 83rd Session, 1870 to 93rd Session, 1880.
133. Letter from John Wanamaker to Moody Bible Institute, Jan. 7, 1920, in the files of the Moody Bible Institute.

12. The Social Message

1. See chapter 1.
2. Moody, *Life of Moody*, p. 171.
3. Dwight L. Moody, *One Thousand and One Thoughts From My Library* (New York: Fleming H. Revell Co., 1898), p. 149.
4. Ibid., p. 150.
5. Ibid., p. 235.
6. Sermon, "The Rich Fool," in Moody, *New Sermons*, pp. 463-72.
7. Moody, *Life of Moody*, p. 263.
8. Transcript of radio broadcast of Nov. 27, 1936, at 11:10 A. M., on file at Moody Bible Institute.
9. Tribute from John Wanamaker, p. 2, in files of the Moddy Bible Institute.
10. Chartier, *Social Views of Moody*, pp. 31ff., deals with his relations with and attitudes to the working classes.
11. Quoted in Chartier, *Social Views of Moody*, p. 65.
12. See Josiah Strong, *Our Country* (Cambridge, Mass.: Belknap Press of Harvard University Press, 1963), pp. 55-58. Originally published in 1886.)
13. Carroll Smith Rosenberg, *Religion and the Rise of the American City: The New York City Mission Movement, 1812-1870* (Ithaca, N. Y.: Cornell University Press, 1971).
14. Josiah Strong was one of the exceptions. An ardent revivalist, he later moved into the Social Gospel movement. But this was not a characteristic response and Strong remains one of the few to make this transition.
15. Quoted in Chartier, *Social Views of Moody*, p. 31.
16. Ibid.
17. "A Newspaper Account of Mr. Moody in Chicago the Year of His Death," in William M. Smith, *Dwight L. Moody, an Annotated Bibliography* (Chicago: Moody Press, 1948), pp. 187-89.
18. Quoted in Moody, *Life of Moody*, p. 170.
19. "Finney's *Systematic Theology* is one of the most popular manuals of theology in the Pentecostal churches today," says *Present Truth* (1972), pp. 21-29, a magazine "devoted to undenominational Pentecostal truth."

Bibliographical Essay

This is not an exhaustive bibliography, nor does it list all the books used, but it represents the works most useful in preparing this study.

Charles G. Finney's Papers are in the Oberlin College Library in Oberlin, Ohio, but they are on microfilm and can be seen in Philadelphia at the Presbyterian Historical Society. Finney's *Memoirs* (New York, 1876), written when he was an old man and often inaccurate on details, is nevertheless an important source. His *Lectures on Revivals of Religion* (Cambridge, Mass., 1960) was first published in 1835, and was the most important handbook on revivals in the nineteenth century. Finney's *Lectures on Systematic Theology* (Grand Rapids, Mich., 1951) was originally published in 1851, and is useful, as are his *Reminiscences* (Oberlin, 1876) and *Sermons on Important Subjects* (New York, 1836). A recent, comprehensive biography on Finney is still needed; most important among the existing biographies, and the one most frequently used by scholars is George F. Wright, *Charles Grandison Finney* (New York, 1891). There are some uncritical works: Victor R. Edman, *Finney Lives On: The Man, His Revival* (New York, 1951); Frank G. Beardsley, *A Mighty Winner of Souls, Charles G. Finney* (Des Moines, Iowa, 1944). Biographical materials can also be found in some of the other works listed.

On Dwight L. Moody, the best single place to find material is in the Moodyana Collection at the Moody Bible Institute in Chicago.

281

There is in their files a wealth of information in the form of letters, clippings, sermons, and radio transcripts. A bibliography lists all material until 1948: Wilbur M. Smith, *Dwight L. Moody, An Annotated Bibliography* (Chicago, 1948). There are numerous collections of sermons: Wilbur M. Smith, ed., *The Best of D. L. Moody*, (Chicago, 1971); L. T. Palmer, ed., *The Gospel Awakening, Comprising the Sermons and Addresses, Prayer-Meeting Talks and Bible Readings at the Great Revival Meetings Conducted by Moody and Sankey* (Chicago, 1883); D. L. Moody, *One Thousand and One Thoughts from My Library* (New York, 1898); D. L. Moody, *New Sermons, Addresses, and Prayers* (Chicago, 1877); D. L. Moody, *Great Joy, Comprising Sermons and Prayer-Meeting Talks* (New York, 1877); D. L. Moody, *Fifty Sermons and Evangelical Talks* (New York, 1899); Simons M. Laird, *Evenings with Moody and Sankey: Comprising Sermons and Addresses at their Great Revival Meetings* (Philadelphia, 1877). There are numerous biographies of Dwight Moody, but the standard biography was written by his son, William R. Moody, one version done in 1900 just after his father's death and the newer edition in 1930: William R. Moody, *The Life of Dwight L. Moody* (New York, 1900 and 1930). Both editions, however, while detailed and accurate in most respects, are uncritical. A more recent biography is J. C. Pollock, *Moody: A Biographical Portrait of the Pacesetter in Modern Mass Evangelism* (New York, 1963), which is neither scholarly nor critical. Most of the works on Moody, whether done during his campaigns or after his death, are hagiographic in approach, as is: The Rev. Edgar Johnson Goodspeed, *A Full History of the Wonderful Career of Moody and Sankey in Great Britain and America* (New York, 1876). The best and most recent biographical work in the scholarly tradition is James F. Findlay, Jr., *Dwight L. Moody, American Evangelist, 1837-1899* (Chicago, 1969). A useful monograph is Myron Raymond Chartier, *The Social Views of Dwight L. Moody and Their Relation to the Workingman of 1860-1900* (Hays, Kansas, 1969), Fort Hays Studies N.S. History Series #6.

The numerous other revivalists whose work touched Philadelphia are accessible through their own autobiographies and memoirs: The Rev. James Caughey, *Helps to a Life of Holiness and Usefulness, or Revival Miscellanies* (Boston, 1856); The Rev. James Caughey, *Glimpses of Life in Soul-Saving, Selections from the Journal and Other Writings* (New York, 1868); Jacob Knapp, *Autobiography of Elder Jacob Knapp* (New York, 1868); Jarena Lee, *Religious Experience and Journal Giving Account of her Call to Preach the Gospel* (Philadelphia, 1849); Emma (Martin) Maffit, *Life and Services of John Newland Maffitt* (by his widow) (New York, 1906); Richard F. Mott, *Memoir and Correspondence of Eliza P. Gurney* (Philadelphia, 1844); Jabez Smith Swan, *The Evangelist, or, Life and Labors of Rev. Jabez S. Swan* (Waterford, Conn., 1873). "A Woman in the Pulpit," *Harpers Weekly* 16, no. 792 (March 2, 1872): 1-3, gives information on Sarah Smiley. Other material on these revivalists is fragmentary, but can be found through revival histories such as Noble, Conant, and Loud, listed in these notes.

Philadelphia ministers involved in revivals left records of varying degrees of completeness. Albert Barnes, pastor of the First Presbyterian Church of Philadelphia, delivered a sermon which was later published: *Life at Three-Score* (Philadelphia, 1859); Barnes's essay on revivals in cities received much attention: Albert Barnes, *Revivals of Religion in Cities and Large Towns* (New York, 1841). The Reverend James Patterson of the First Presbyterian Church of Northern Liberties, one of Philadelphia's most active revivalist ministers, left sermons, some of which are in manuscript form at the Presbyterian Historical Society of Philadelphia. Soon after his death, a committee of ministers was formed to use his diary and manuscripts to prepare a biography: Robert Adair, *Memoir of Rev. James Patterson* (Philadelphia, 1840). Letters of the Rev. Samuel Helffenstein of the German Reformed Church are in a collection at the Old First Reformed Church (United Church of Christ) in Philadelphia. For other figures in Philadelphia revivalism, see W. P. Strickland, *The Life of Jacob Gruber* (New York, 1860); Walter Herbert Stowe, ed., *Life and Letters of Bishop William White* (New York, 1937); Henry Bascom Ridgaway, *The Life of the Rev. Alfred Cookman, with some Account of his Father, the Rev. George Grimston Cookman* (New York, 1874); Alexander V. G. Allen, *Life and Letters of Phillips Brooks* (New York, 1900).

Handbooks of revivals represents a fine source of information on the mentality and methods of revivals. Finney's handbook has already been cited. Other important handbooks represent varying degrees of revival enthusiasm from the moderate pastor of the Second Presbyterian Church in Albany, William B. Sprague,

Lectures on Revivals of Religion (Albany, N.Y., 1832), to more ardent advocates: The Rev. James Porter, *Revivals of Religion: Their Theory Means, Obstructions, Uses and Importance* (Boston, 1849). Others are: E. Porter, *Lectures on Revivals* (Andover, Mass., 1832); Henry C. Fish, *Handbook of Revivals* (Boston, 1887). The Rev. Thomas H. Skinner, pastor of the Second Presbyterian Chruch in Philadelphia, wrote two books on the subject: *Thoughts on Evangelizing the World* (New York, 1836), and a later one that expressed diminished approval of revival measures; *Lay Evangelism* (Cincinnati, Ohio, 1875). In addition to these handbooks, advice on how to conduct a revival can be found in biographical works of the ministers and laymen involved.

Church records, in both manuscript and printed form, provide a rich source of data: The General Assembly of the Presbyterian Church, *Minutes* (Old and New School); Methodist Episcopal Church, *Annual Minutes of the Philadelphia Conferences*; German Reformed Church, *Minutes of the Synod of the German Reformed Church*, is in the Historical Society of the Reformed Church, Franklin and Marshall College, Lancaster, Pa.; German Reformed Church "Records of Communion Services and New Members Confirmed and Received into the German Reformed Church from 1832-1876" (in manuscript form), in Old First Reformed Church in Philadelphia. Organizational records and minutes were equally useful: Philadelphia, Young Men's Christian Association, Fourth Annual Report, 1858 (typewritten), also the published *Annual Report*, Jan. 20, 1876. The Philadelphia Tract Society, *Annual Report*, 1859, has lists of officers, constitution, and by-laws; Infidel Convention Held in the City of Philadelphia, Sept. 7 and 8, 1857, *Minutes*; American Society for Meliorating the Condition of the Jews, *Annual Reports*.

Church histories, both local and general, show the impact of revivalism upon each denomination. I have not listed general denominational histories, but they are available, and, with some exceptions, useful. Regarding Philadelphia, most useful works were: Alfred Nevin, *History of the Presbytery of Philadelphia* (Philadelphia, 1888); Thomas James Shepherd, *History of the First Presbyterian Church of Northern Liberties from its Organization to the Resignation of its Fourth Pastor* (Philadelphia, 1882); Henry C. Vedder, *A History of the Baptists in the Middle States* (Philadelphia,

1898); Robert Torbet, "A Social History of the Philadelphia Baptist Association, 1707-1940," Ph.D. dissertation, University of Pennsylvania, 1944,; William Williams Keen, *The Bi-Centennial Celebration of the Founding of the First Baptist Church of the City of Philadelphia* (Philadelphia, 1899); J. L. Rhees, *Error Refuted or, a Brief Exposition of the Leading Features of the Baptist Controversy in Philadelphia and its Vicinity* (Philadelphia, 1827); Francis H. Tees, *History of Old St. George's Methodist Episcopal Church* (Philadelphia, 1934); Elisha Bates, *The Doctrines of Friends: or Principles of the Christian Religion as Held by the Society of Friends* (Mountpleasant, Pa., 1825); Rufus M. Jones, *The Later Periods of Quakerism*, 2 vols. (London, 1921), 1: 435ff.; Joseph John Gurney, *Observations on the Distinguishing Views and Practices of the Society of Friends* (New York, 1840); Robert W. Doherty, *The Hicksite Separation* (New Brunswick, N.J., 1967).

For general information on Negro churches, see Franklin E. Frazier, *The Negro Church in America* (New York, 1963); Booker T. Washington, "The Religious Life of the Negro," *Black Church in America*, edited by Hart M. Nelson and Raytha L. Yokley (New York, 1971), and W. E. B. DuBois, "Of the Faith of the Fathers," in the came collection of essays. W. E. Burghardt DuBois, *The Philadelphia Negro* (New York, 1899) has a great deal of information on black religious practices and membership; see also Charles H. Wesley, *Richard Allen: Apostle of Freedom* (Washington, D.C., 1935); The Rev. William Douglas, *Annals of the First African Church in the United States, now styled the African Episcopal Church of St. Thomas* (Philadelphia, 1862).

William H. Furness and Philadelphia Unitarianism are the subjects of the work by Elizabeth May Geffen, *Philadelphia Unitarianism, 1796-1861* (Philadelphia, 1961). The German Reformed Church is the subject of several important works: David Van Horne, *A History of the Reformed Church in Philadelphia* (Philadelphia, 1876); John B. Frantz, "Revivalism in the German Reformed Church in America to 1850, with Emphasis on the Eastern Synod," Ph.D. dissertation, University of Pennsylvania, 1961. An early work, John W. Nevin, *The Anxious Bench: A Tract for the Times* (Chambersburg, Pa., 1843) was useful in understanding the struggle to defeat revivalism within the German Reformed Church. The Rev. H. Harbaugh, *Fathers of the German*

Reformed Church in Europe and America (Lancaster, Pa., 1872) is a useful source as well.

For information on missions to the Jews, the Presbyterian Historical Society has manuscript reports of missionaries engaged in these activities. See also: Albert Edward Thompson, *A Century of Jewish Missions* (Chicago, 1902) and Edward Dorr Griffin, *An Address Delivered at the Anniversary of the American Society for Meliorating the Condition of the Jews in New York, May 11, 1824* (New York, 1824). For the Jewish response to this missionary activity, see Joseph L. Blau and Salo W. Baron, eds., *The Jews of the United States, 1790-1840, a Documentary History*, 3 vols. (New York, 1963). There are included documents and letters relating to the ASMCJ. Lee M. Friedman, *The American Society for Meliorating the Condition of the Jews, and Joseph S. C. F. Frey, its Missionary* (Boston, 1925) is the only complete account of the activities of that organization, and is the work of an eminent Jewish historian. A recent article on this subject is: Lorman Ratner, "Conversion of the Jews and Pre-Civil War Reform," *American Quarterly* 13 (1961): 43-54. There is considerable material on Isaac Leeser, editor of *The Occident*, but an article by Bertram Wallace Korn, "Isaac Leeser: Centennial Reflections," in *American Jewish Archives* 19, no. 2 (November 1967): 127-41, is one of the best. Edwin Wolf, 2nd and Maxwell Whiteman, *The History of the Jews of Philadelphia from Colonial Times to the Age of Jackson* (Philadelphia, 1956) is extremely useful, but only for the early part of the century. A book by George Houston, *Israel Vindicated: Being a Refutation of the Calumnies Propagated Respecting the Jewish Nation* (New York, 1820) is useful on the response of the Jews to Christian missionizing, but the most valuable sources are Jewish periodicals, *The Occident*, edited by Isaac Leeser, and *The Jew*, edited by S. H. Jackson, listed among religious periodicals elsewhere in these notes. For the response of Philadelphia Catholics, periodicals provided the best source as well.

Contemporary accounts of revivals, while often colored by personal views, are a superb source of information. Secular newspapers of Finney's time took little interest in church affairs, except for a few brief lines announcing a meeting or a sermon. By the 1858 revivals, newspaper accounts grew fuller, and by Moody's two-month campaign, a daily account of proceedings, usually on page two, kept people informed of revival incidents and visiting, celebrities. The eyewitness descriptions of perceptive journalists add much to our information about the later revivals. *The Philadelphia Inquirer* and *The Philadelphia Evening Bulletin* are useful for both the 1858 and the 1875-76 revivals. Frequent reports were in the *Philadelphia Press* and the *Philadelphia Times*, as well. Secular periodicals such as *The Nation* and *Harpers New Monthly Magazine* were useful, but religious periodicals were most relevant, although one must read them with a sharp eye as to their orientation. Much of my data came from the pages of *The Protestant Episcopalian and Church Register, The Presbyterian Quarterly and Princeton Review, The Presbyterian, New York Evangelist, Oberlin Evangelist, Methodist Review, The Magazine of the Reformed German Church*, superseded by *The Reformed Church Messenger, The Mercersberg Review, Friends Intelligencer, The Friend*, Ashbell Green's *Christian Advocate, Catholic World, The Catholic Standard, Catholic Herald and Visitor. The Occident*, an important Jewish organ during the middle decades of the nineteenth century, provided a rich source of information, while *The Jew*, which defended Judaism from critics was short-lived, lasting only from 1823 to 1825.

Contemporary accounts of other kinds were valuable as well. Robert Baird's *Religion in America* (New York, 1856) presents the evangelical view of religion; Philip Schaff, *A Sketch of the Political, Social and Religious Character of the United States of North America* (New York, 1855) provides useful impressions of the American religious establishment through the eyes of a German churchman who spent ten years in America; the Rev. G. Lewis, *Impressions of America and the American Churches* (Edinburgh, 1845), presents the views of a minister in the Free Church of Scotland after a trip to America in 1844. The ascerbic pen of Mrs. Frances Trollope, *Domestic Manners of the Americans* (New York, 1832) described revivals, both rural and urban; Francis Lieber, *Stranger in America* ... (Philadelphia, 1835), provides another contemporary source of great value, as does Anne (Newport) Royall's *Sketches of History, Life and Manners in the United States* (New Haven, Conn., 1826). William B. Sprague's 9-volume *Annals of the American Pulpit* (New York, 1859) contains letters and testimonials regarding ministers, and are classified according to denomination. Many of the books on revivals were written to glorify the institution, yet are immensely useful: Edwin M. Long, *The Union-Tabernacle; or Movable Tent-Church* (Philadelphia, 1859), deals with the 1858 revivals, as does John Jenkins, *Plain Thoughts on the Present Great Awakening* (Philadelphia, 1858). Jenkins was minister of the Calvary Church on Locust Street in Philadelphia. William C. Conant, *Narratives of Remarkable Conversions and Revival Incidents* (New York, 1858) and the booklet issued by the Philadelphia YMCA, *Pentecost, or the Work of God in Philadelphia, A. D. 1858* (Philadelphia, 1858) are valuable sources for the 1858 revival in Philadelphia. W. F. Noble, *A Century of Gospel Work* (Philadelphia, 1876) gives a good account of the Philadelphia Moody meetings. Thomas K. Cree, "Mr. Moody as Evangelist" is a 34-page typescript in the YMCA Historical Library in New York that gives great detail about the Moody Philadelphia campaign.

A number of scholarly works dealing with revivalism are of great importance. William G. McLoughlin, Jr., *Modern Revivalism* (New York, 1959), is a comprehensive, analytical work on revivalism from Charles Finney through Billy Graham; Bernard Weisberger's *They Gathered at the River* (Boston, 1958) is an immensely readable, yet scholarly study of revivalism from the early nineteenth century through Billy Sunday. Whitney R. Cross, *The Burned-Over District, The Social and Intellectual History of Enthusiastic Religion in Western New York, 1800-1850* (Ithaca, N.Y., 1950), is a regional study that is excellent on Finney's early years. Alice Felt Tyler, *Freedom's Ferment; Phases of American Social History to 1860* (Minneapolis, Minn., 1944), explains humanitarian reform movements in terms of the new religious and social experiments of the period. Gilbert H. Barnes, *The Antislavery Impulse, 1830-1844* (New York, 1933), explores the relationship between revivalism and the anti-slavery movement; Timothy L. Smith, *Revivalism and Social Reform in Mid-Nineteenth-Century America* (New York, 1957), finds in mid-century revivalism the roots of the Social Gospel movement at the end of the century. Othniel A. Pendleton, "The Influence of the Evangelical Churches Upon Humanitarian Reform," Ph.D. dissertation, University of Pennsylvania, 1945, also explores reform aspects of the evangelical movement, as does Caroll Smith-Rosenberg, *Religion and the Rise of the American City: The New York City Mission Movement,*

1812-1870 (Ithaca, N.Y., 1971), who finds that what began with soul-saving turned to meliorative activity. Lois W. Banner, "Religion and Reform in the Early Republic: The Role of Youth," *American Quarterly* 23 (December 1971): 677-95 suggests the role of youthful converts in early reform movements.

Charles C. Cole, Jr., *The Social Ideas of the Northern Evangelists, 1826-1860* (New York, 1954), deals with the economic and social ideas of Finney along with other Northern evangelists, and finds them deeply conservative, while Clifford S. Griffin, "Religious Benevolence as Social Control, 1815-1860," *Mississippi Valley Historical Review*, 44 (1957-58): 423-44, suggests an alternative view to Barnes and Smith. Charles Howard Hopkins, history of the YMCA, has much data on the 1858 revivals, with which it was closely connected; Perry Miller's posthumous *The Life of the Mind in America, Revolution to Civil War* (New York, 1965) deals extensively with urban revivalism. William Warren Sweet, *Revivalism in America* (New York, 1944), is dated but still useful; Grover Cleveland Loud, *Evangelized America* (New York, 1928), while unfootnoted, has much information on nineteenth-century revivals. Of inestimable importance in understanding the structure of American religion, is H. Richard Niebuhr, *The Social Sources of Denominationalism* (New York, 1929). It is a major work on the characteristics and development of sectarian religion using classical sociological theory.

For an insightful analysis of the conversion phenomenon from the nontheological point of view, see William James, *The Varieties of Religious Experience: A Study in Human Nature* (New York, 1902). Edwin D. Starbuck, a student of James, in *The Psychology of Religion* (New York, 1904) finds the conversion experience uniquely an adolescent phenomenon, while George Godwin, *The Great Revivalists* (Boston, 1950), illuminates the sexual component in religion.

Two important studies of revivalism in Philadelphia are: Russell E. Francis, "Religious Revival in 1858 in Philadelphia," *Pennsylvania Magazine of History and Biography*, 70 no. 1 (January 1946): 52-77 from his "Pentecost, 1858; a Study in Religious Revivalism," Ph.D. dissertation, University of Pennsylvania, 1848, and Lefferts A. Loetscher, "Presbyterianism and Revivalism in Philadelphia Since 1875," *Pennsylvania Magazine of*

History and Biography, 68 (January, 1944): 55-72, which starts with the Moody revivals.

Nineteenth-century Philadelphia is described in various works: Robert DeSilver, *Philadelphia Directory and Strangers Guide for 1828, McElroy's Philadelphia Directory for 1857, Gopsill's Street Index and City Guide of the City of Philadelphia, 1875*. J. Thomas Scharf and Thompson Westcott, *History of Philadelphia, 1609-1884* (Philadelphia, 1884) is a 3-volume classic; Ellis Paxson Oberholtzer's 4-volume *Philadelphia: A History of the City and its People* (Philadelphia, 1911) is another important work, as are James Mease, *Picture of Philadelphia for 1824* ... (Phila., 1823); James Hosmer Penniman, *Philadelphia in the Early 1800s* (Philadelphia, 1923); *Philadelphia in 1824; or, a Brief Account of the Various Institutions and Public Objects in this Metropolis* (Philadelphia, 1824); R. A. Smith, *Philadelphia as it is in 1852* (Philadelphia, 1852); Ivan D. Steen, "Philadelphia in the 1850's as Described by British Travelers," *Pennsylvania History*, 33 (January, 1966): 30-49. The centennial city is described in Thompson Wescott, *Official Guidebook to Philadelphia* (Philadelphia, 1876) and Dorothy E. C. Ditter, "The Cultural Climate of the Centennial City: Philadelphia 1875-76," Ph.D. dissertation, University of Pennsylvania, 1947, which has descriptions of the Philadelphia Moody meetings. An important book on Philadelphia development is Sam Bass Warner, Jr., *The Private City* (Philadelphia, 1968), which traces the small, compact city to a sprawling, industrialized metropolis. Allen F. Davis and Mark H. Haller, eds., *The Peoples of Philadelphia* (Philadelphia, 1973), deals with the city in human terms, and treats the often unchronicled: the ethnic poor, the black, the ordinary people.

Philadelphia businessmen are accessible through various sources. The more prominent have left memoirs or have had biographers: John Wanamaker is the subject of three biographies, all unscholarly and uncritical, but useful: Herbert Adams Gibbons, 2-volume *John Wanamaker* (New York, 1926), Russell H. Conwell, *The Romantic Rise of a Great American* (New York, 1924), and Joseph H. Appel, *The Business Biography of John Wanamaker* (New York, 1930). A multi-dimensional biography of this important Philadelphian is still needed, but awaits the release of his papers for scholarly research. The activities of George H. Stuart can be found in *Life of George H. Stuart*, edited by Robert

Ellis Thompson (Philadelphia, 1890). Many of Stuart's letters to ministers and his handbills for the Moody meetings are available at the Presbyterian Historical Society in Philadelphia. Biographical information on less prominent businessmen can be found in: *Philadelphia, Pictorial and Biographical* (Philadelphia, 1911); Charles F. Warwick, *Warwick's Keystone Commonwealth* (Philadelphia, 1913); S. N. Winslow, *Biography of Successful Philadelphia Merchants* (Philadelphia, 1864); *Biographies of Philadelphians [Comprising Sketches of the Lives of Persons, 1861, Collected by Thompson Westcott]* scrapbook of clippings in Historical Society of Pennsylvania; Abraham Ritter, *Philadelphia and Her Merchants* (Philadelphia, 1860); E. C. Savidige, ed., *A Gallery of Eminent Men of Philadelphia* (Philadelphia, 1887); The North American, Philadelphia, *Philadelphia and Popular Philadelphians* (Philadelphia, 1891); Charles Morris, ed., *Makers of Philadelphia* (Philadelphia, 1894); *The Industries of Philadelphia* (Philadelphia, 1881).

Index